D0203452

Critical Essays in Modern Literature

Critical Essays in Modern Literature

The Fiction and Criticism of Katherine Anne Porter (revised)
Harry James Mooney, Jr.

The Fiction of J. D. Salinger (revised)
Frederick L. Gwynn and Joseph L. Blotner

Richard Wright: An Introduction to the Man and His Work
Russell Carl Brignano

The Hole in the Fabric: Science, Contemporary Literature, and Henry James
Strother B. Purdy

Reading the Thirties: Texts and Contexts
Bernard Bergonzi

The Romantic Genesis of the Modern Novel
Charles Schug

The Great Succession: Henry James and the Legacy of Hawthorne
Robert Emmet Long

The Plays and Novels of Peter Handke
June Schlueter

Yeats, Eliot, Pound and the Politics of Poetry: Richest to the Richest
Cairns Craig

After Innocence: Visions of the Fall in Modern Literature
Terry Otten

The Metafictional Muse: The Works of Robert Coover, Donald Barthelme, and William H. Gass
Larry McCaffery

The Grand Continuum: Reflections on Joyce and Metaphysics
David A. White

The Utopian Novel in America, 1886–1896: The Politics of Form
Jean Pfaelzer

A Varied Harvest: The Life and Works of Henry Blake Fuller
Kenneth Scambray

A
Varied
Harvest:

The Life and
Works of
Henry Blake Fuller

Kenneth Scambray

University of Pittsburgh Press

PS1728
S3
1987

Published by the University of Pittsburgh Press, Pittsburgh, Pa. 15260
Copyright © 1987, University of Pittsburgh Press
All rights reserved
Feffer and Simons, Inc., London
Manufactured in the United States of America

Library of Congress Cataloging-in-Publication Data

Scambray, Kenneth.
    A varied harvest.

    (Critical essays in modern literature)
    Bibliography: p. 179.
    Includes index.
    1. Fuller, Henry Blake, 1857–1929. 2. Novelists,
American–19th century–Biography. I. Title.
II. Series.
PS1728.S3 1987   813'.4 [B]   86-30827
ISBN 0-8229-3556-2

Portions of this book appeared in slightly different form in the following essays, and are reprinted with permission: "The Romance in Decline: Realism in Henry Blake Fuller's *The Cliff-Dwellers,*" *North Dakota Quarterly* 46 (Spring 1976), 19–28; "From Etruria to Naples: Italy in the Works of Henry Blake Fuller," *Italian Americana* 3 (December 1976), 56–71; "He Caught It for This: Four Letters by Henry Blake Fuller," *American Literary Realism* 13 (Autumn 1980), 266–69.

Contents

Illustrations   vii

Acknowledgments   ix

Introduction   3

1. The Marriage Question   11

2. Italy: From Etruria to Naples   31

3. Boston: Vulgar Dollars   44

4. The Chevalier of Vain Thoughts   61

5. Chicago: The Black City versus the White City   77

6. Art and Imperialism   98

7. A Decorous Realism   124

8. Delicate Affections and Dynamite   143

Notes   165

Bibliography   179

Index   193

MAR 1 8 1988

Illustrations

1. Henry Blake Fuller as a young man   45
2. Louise Washburn   47
3. The World's Columbian Exposition: Art Palace,
   Main Entrance   80
4. Chicago Day at the Columbian Exposition   80
5. Obelisk and Grand Vista North from Colonnade   81
6. Fuller and the Liver Pill (*Chicago Daily News,*
   18 April 1899, p. 4)   119
7. Caricature of Fuller (*Bookman,* 1890s)   145

Acknowledgments

This project was completed only with the generous support and cooperation of several institutions and people. I must extend a special thanks to the Newberry Library for a grant-in-aid that allowed me to begin my initial research into the Fuller Papers. My work there would not have been nearly as successful if it had not been for the tireless support and patience of Diana Haskell, Curator of Modern Manuscripts. I am grateful to the Newberry for permission to quote from the Fuller collection.

I owe thanks to Helen Ranney, niece to Henry Fuller, for the information and materials she gave me during our series of interviews. Mary Hastings Bradley, a friend of Fuller and a member of the Chicago art colony, was also kind enough to spend an afternoon with me reminiscing over her Chicago days and association with Fuller.

I would also like to acknowledge the following institutions for permission to quote from their collections of Fuller papers and manuscripts: American Academy and Institute of Arts and Letters; Robert Herrick Papers, Department of Special Collections, University of Chicago Library; Huntington Library; Rare Book and Manuscript Library, Columbia University: Hamlin Garland Collection, University of Southern California Library; Henry W. and Albert A. Berg Collection, New York Public Library, Astor, Lenox and Tilden Foundations; Special Collections, Morris Library, Southern Illinois University, Carbondale; Henry Blake Fuller Collection (#6332), Clifton Waller Barrett Library, University of Virginia Library.

Materials cited from the Boston Public Library are quoted by courtesy of the trustees of the Boston Public Library. Fuller letters to Charles Eliot Norton and William Dean Howells at Harvard are quoted by permission of the Houghton Library, Harvard University, and the quotations from the Fuller letters at Princeton are published with permission

ix

of Princeton University Library. I would like to extend a special acknowledgment to Professor W. W. Howells for permission to quote from the Fuller letters in the Houghton Library.

I owe a special thanks to Northwestern University for a Faculty Research Grant that allowed me to copy the extensive collection of Fuller letters at the New York Public Library and at the Huntington Library. These letters had not been known or used before in research on Fuller, and they provided me with valuable biographical information on Fuller's early and late years in Chicago.

Portions of my writing on *The Cliff-Dwellers,* Fuller's published letters, and his travel romances have appeared in *North Dakota Quarterly, American Literary Realism,* and *Italian Americana.* I wish to thank their editors for allowing me to reproduce sections of my work which have appeared in their journals.

I want to thank Professor George Knox, University of California, Riverside, for introducing me to Fuller. I am especially grateful to my colleague, Professor Katharine Hoskins, University of La Verne, for reading a draft of my manuscript and for making many helpful suggestions. I am especially indebted to Toks Oduwole at the University of La Verne Press for preparing reproductions of all of the photographs that appear in this text. I would like also to thank Professor Robert Gale, University of Pittsburgh, for his many helpful suggestions during the review process of my manuscript. A special acknowledgment must go to Jane Flanders, assistant editor at University of Pittsburgh Press, for her invaluable assistance in preparing my manuscript for publication.

I have dedicated this volume to Carole Scambray. Without her unwavering support and encouragement, I could not have finished this project.

A Varied Harvest

Introduction

In a New Yorker *article* on Henry Blake Fuller, Edmund Wilson wrote that in Fuller's European books "he is not very far from the tinted impressionism of Henry James, which seems to emanate from him like vapor."[1] Henry James was one of Fuller's earliest influences. He parodied James's fiction, along with Bret Harte's western stories, in a work published in *Life* in 1884. But at this early point in his career, Fuller was interested more in the romance of the transatlantic theme in James's fiction than he was in his craft as a novelist.

Provincial Chicago, Fuller's hometown, was an embarrassment to him. He looked east, to Europe and to Boston, for salvation from the city fate had allotted him. However, that midcentury Genteel Tradition centered in the East did manage to hold a small but very important place in Chicago after the Great Fire of 1871. Both of Fuller's parents claimed deep roots in the East, and Fuller imagined himself related to those eastern Brahmins who were directing postwar American culture through such periodicals as the *Century, Harper's Monthly, North American Review,* and *Atlantic Monthly.* In 1879, at the age of twenty-two, and again in 1883 Fuller did what was fashionable and expected of any young man of upper-class means: he went abroad.

He went also to cleanse the grit that he felt had begun to accumulate in his own soul from the few years he had already spent working in Chicago business and industry. He had little enthusiasm for that "stormy, husky, brawling" Chicago that Carl Sandburg would extol in his poetry after the turn of the century. In his temporary escapes to Europe, six in all, Fuller was motivated by the same concerns that would send the next generation of writers such as Ernest Hemingway, Ezra Pound, F. Scott Fitzgerald, and John Dos Passos to the cafes of London, Paris, and Rome.

3

After his second tour abroad and a brief stay in Boston, Fuller settled in Chicago, and by 1890 he completed and published his first European romance, *The Chevalier of Pensieri-Vani* (1890). Over his long life he wrote three more transatlantic romances: *The Chatelaine of La Trinité* (1892), *The Last Refuge* (1899), and *Gardens of This World* (1929). Edmund Wilson wrote of Fuller's travel romances, "In those of his books that take place in Europe, one is impressed by the thoroughness and exactitude of his knowledge of history, geography, literature, art, and architecture." However, none of his four romances would be as successful as his first, which catapulted him to local and national fame. To his genteel eastern critics Fuller was a refined voice in the wilderness; to his hometown critics Fuller was a hero, proof that culture was alive and well in their provincial city. The Harvard professor and Italianist Charles Eliot Norton received a copy of *The Chevalier,* and the high priest of eastern culture wrote a glowing letter to the young Fuller. Thus began a lifelong relationship between Fuller and Norton.

With his first romance, Fuller became a pillar of Chicago's art community during the period of his city's most significant cultural and economic growth. Throughout his life he was a regular visitor in the studios of artists such as Lorado Taft, Bessie Potter, and Ralph Clarkson. He became a member of the Little Room, an elite group of Chicago artists, architects, professors, and writers that was organized around the time of Chicago's Columbian Exposition of 1893. At midcentury he wrote about the Chicago art colony in one of his best works, *Under the Skylights* (1901), a collection of three long stories.

But Fuller's lasting contribution to American fiction must be based upon his realistic Chicago novels, *The Cliff-Dwellers* (1893) and *With the Procession* (1895). Again, in Edmund Wilson's words: "The objection sometimes made to Henry James that he knew nothing about American business is not at all in order in the case of part-time expatriate Fuller. He knew everything about the interest he administered—industry, real estate, finance, and the legal procedures entailed by these." In his first two Chicago novels, as Wilson notes, "the precision and elegance of Fuller's style—so unusual in the United States of the nineties—really makes a better showing" than in his European books.

The response to Fuller's realistic novels was not nearly as unanimous as was the reception of his first romance. Before his novels appeared, the war over literary realism had raged for nearly a decade in periodicals such as the *Forum, Critic, Bookman, Atlantic* (under William Dean Howells) and *Harper's,* in which by 1886 Howells had begun his column "The Editor's Study." Charles Eliot Norton, among those who favored "ideality" in fiction, wrote letters to Fuller in which he grumbled about what constituted the proper content for art. Fuller's other conservative critics likened his novels to what they derogatorily termed James's "scientific" realism and, what was even worse, to Emile Zola's cruel, naturalistic French stories.

The most lasting and important comments, however, came from the realists themselves. In his reviews and personal letters to Fuller, William Dean Howells wrote that Fuller's novels were the best he had seen yet, and he enlisted the young author in the ranks of the realists. He saw in Fuller's fiction another major step in the creation of the new, distinctly American novel that he had been promoting for nearly two decades from his posts at the *Atlantic* and *Harper's.* In an essay written at the end of the decade, Howells looked back at Fuller's contribution and linked his two Chicago novels with the works of William Payne, Stephen Crane, Harold Frederic, Mary Wilkins, James Branch Cabell, and Henry James.[2] Other realists such as H. H. Boyesen lauded Fuller's realistic stories, and Hamlin Garland was forced to admit that Fuller had beaten the realists at their own game. Indeed, as Larzer Ziff observes in *The American 1890s: Life and Times of a Lost Generation,* "In point of fact, Henry Blake Fuller was a man better qualified to express the social ferment of the nineties in fiction than Garland."[3]

But Fuller was uneasy with his success in the realistic form. He was not so eager to join the ranks of the realists, and he said so in letters to William Dean Howells and other friends. He cherished his friendship with Norton, yet he had now become a personal friend of Howells, the dean of American letters at the end of the century. Out of deference to Norton, he had toned down the realism in *With the Procession* and was gratified when Howells wrote to him in 1895, "Some days ago I was in Cambridge, and found Norton proud and glad of you in the midst of it."[4] Throughout his career Fuller divided his allegiance between the two camps, the Old-World romance and the new American novel.

With his first two realistic stories, Fuller attempted to censure the commercial and industrial orientation of his native Chicago. Kenny J. Williams writes in a cultural history of fin-de-siècle Chicago that traces the careers of Fuller and the architect Louis Sullivan, "Fuller had done all that he could to direct the establishment of 'culture' in Chicago: he had tried to make the city aware of true literary principles."[5] In his Chicago novels Fuller treated the same impersonal industrial and economic forces that Henry Adams would later identify in his *Education*. Fuller was a singular voice in Chicago fiction in the 1890s, but he was also in the vanguard of the national discontent over the impact of industrialism on American society. In *The Age of Reform* Richard Hofstadter turns to writers such as W. D. Howells, H. H. Boyesen, Robert Herrick (another Chicago writer), and Fuller to discover that "bitter caricature" of the fin-de-siècle businessman. As Hofstadter puts it, the realists' independent "Mugwump imagination" stamped an indelible image of the new captains of industry upon the national consciousness.[6]

Social reform, specifically Chicago's reform, was certainly on Fuller's mind when he wrote his first two Chicago stories. But Fuller had written a new type of novel as well. As Jay Martin comments in *Harvests of Change: American Literature 1865–1914*, "Fuller was clearly Howells's successor and Dreiser's ancestor, an intermediary between the two."[7] In the 1930s, after Fuller's death, Dreiser acknowledged Fuller as the father of the American novel.[8] Some twenty years later, Frederick Hoffman expressed his view in *The Modern Novel in America* that the novels of Fuller and Herrick "testify to the decline of the Jamesian moral perception."[9] Because of this shift in moral perception, Fuller has also been grouped with literary naturalists such as Frank Norris and Jack London.

For his contribution to American letters in the 1890s, romance writer Francis Marion Crawford and William Dean Howells sponsored Fuller's election into the prestigious National Institute of Arts and Letters. Though he was never elected into the elite inner sanctum of the institute, the American Academy of Arts and Letters, Fuller held rank at the turn of the century with the likes of Edmund Clarence Stedman, Mark Twain, Thomas Bailey Aldrich, Henry James, Henry Adams, Norton, and Howells.

But not even national honors would blunt Fuller's quarrelsome relationship with his hometown and his age. In 1899 he became one of over three hundred vice-presidents in the Chicago Anti-Imperialist League established to protest President William McKinley's war in the Philippines. Fuller made common cause with many prominent Chicago citizens such as Clarence Darrow and Jane Addams and with writers such as Howells, Norton, and Twain in the eastern anti-imperialist leagues.

Before the war was over Fuller published a satirical pamphlet of doggerel verse entitled *The New Flag: Satires*. With his privately printed book he joined William Vaughn Moody, poet and University of Chicago professor, in his protest against the war effort. In his poems Fuller pummeled McKinley and a whole host of national politicians and local Chicagoans who supported the war. The anti-imperialist league protests have been compared to the student protests over the Vietnam War in the 1960s and 1970s.[10] Fuller's poems have a familiar and contemporary ring in their accusations of racism and in their attacks on inept generals within the American military. Imperialism, Fuller lashed out on nearly every page, was inconsistent with the high ideals of a democratic society.

The war theme would erupt again in Fuller's fiction in his experimental novel *On the Stairs* (1918). Wilson reports that he would tell unsuspecting "foreign visitors that it was 'the great American novel.'" The novel does not live up to Wilson's claim, but it accurately portrays the moral climate and disillusionment in U.S. literature between the two world wars.

Fuller saw in the Lost Generation of the twenties the image of his own disaffection and alienation from his hometown and country. Since the beginning of the new century, Fuller had been a close observer of the new generation of writers that was changing the face of American fiction and poetry. Before World War I, Fuller had served on the Advisory Board for Harriet Monroe's *Poetry*. He promoted the works of young writers such as Ezra Pound. Yet he often disagreed with Monroe and cautioned her against turning her magazine over to literary special interests such as Pound's. Inspired by the experiments of the younger generation of writers, Fuller published a collection of his own free verse poems in *Lines Long and Short* (1917), influenced by Edgar Lee Masters's *Spoon River Anthology*.

In the twenties, however, Fuller was more the critic than the innovator that he had been in the 1890s. His countless reviews appeared in periodicals such as the *Freeman, Nation, New Republic, Commonweal, Dial, Harper's,* and the *Saturday Evening Post*. His motto in the 1920s was "Save the young." As Fuller wrote in a 1925 *New York Times Book Review* essay, he shared the younger Hemingway's dictum that "much of our fiction, in fact, derives from Twain" and that American poetry is equally indebted to Walt Whitman. In his reviews and essays he promoted the works of writers such as Thornton Wilder, Glenway Wescott, Theodore Dreiser, Willa Cather, Edith Wharton, and F. Scott Fitzgerald. In their letters to Fuller, Wilder and Wescott acknowledged him as the elder statesman in the development of the American novel.

Fuller liked to joke with his friends that one of his major vices was staying current with popular culture. From the very outset of their careers, D. W. Griffith and Charlie Chaplin had captured Fuller's interest, and he had become an avid moviegoer. In an essay in the *New York Times* entitled "The Melting Pot Begins to Smell" (1924), he complained bitterly about Hollywood's "ready-made orgies of the upper world and the under world." In *Not on the Screen* (1930), his last novel, he satirized cinematic form and attacked the decadence and compromise of artistic values in the films that Hollywood was churning out for mass consumption. Though flawed, *Not on the Screen* is a seminal and interesting work in a subgenre of novels about the cinema and Hollywood. This is a theme that has attracted writers as diverse as Luigi Pirandello, Vladimir Nabokov, Nathanael West, William Saroyan, F. Scott Fitzgerald, and Christopher Isherwood.

But Fuller's battle against commercial Chicago, imperialistic America, and decadent Hollywood does not tell his whole story. There is another side of Fuller's literary career and his life, perhaps the most important aspect of his life as a writer, that has gone virtually unexplored in all the previous biographies and essays about him. All accounts of his life and works depict Fuller as a writer who was frustrated solely by the commercial and industrial spirit that dominated his native Chicago. Actually, he led several lives: that of the writer, the sociable club man, and the private, isolated life of a homosexual in Victorian and early twentieth-century America.

If Henry Fuller failed to reform the overriding materialism of his hometown, he suffered an even greater personal failure in his inability as a homosexual to integrate his personal and artistic lives. The record of this struggle is revealed in a series of documents, published and unpublished, that span his entire life as a writer. The first is a revealing unpublished memoir begun when Fuller was eighteen years old, entitled "Allison Classical Academy." Allison was a boarding school in Wisconsin where Fuller spent his first year of high school. In his memoir of that year, Fuller's stratagem of never openly expressing his feelings toward the other boys and girls at the school has concealed his real concerns from all of Fuller's previous biographers and critics who consulted the text. Nevertheless, his selective memory of events, people, and relationships reveals a young Fuller who was trying to define his own special role among his personal relationships, male and female, at this point in his life.

In the course of his writing career, Fuller did write publicly about his homosexuality. One of the earliest, though indirect, discussions of the theme came in a series of anonymous letters published in the *Chicago Tribune,* letters unknown to all of Fuller's previous biographers. But his first overt public treatment of the homosexual theme came in "At Saint Judas's," a one-act play published among eleven others in *The Puppet Booth* (1896). Its publication came on the heels of the international publicity over Oscar Wilde's prosecution in England. The appearance of the play was a bold and daring gesture by Fuller. He realized that homosexuality was outlawed in his state and that, if Wilde's case was any indication, he could be prosecuted or at least ruined as a professional writer, in spite of his popularity at the time. In a quiet, circumspect way "At Saint Judas's" was Fuller's protest over the treatment of homosexuals in Victorian society, American and English. In their reviews of the volume, critics ignored the play.

Fuller did not write publicly on the theme again for nearly thirty years, until the publication of *Bertram Cope's Year* (1919). When Fuller finished the manuscript and circulated it in New York, none of his previous publishers would dare bring the novel out for him. Though he could ill afford it, he finally printed the novel at his own expense. If inattention to a novel because of its controversial content constitutes suppression, then *Bertram Cope's Year* was suppressed by the periodicals and most newspapers of the day.

Fuller sent a review copy to, among others, H. L. Mencken at *The Smart Set.*[11] But in his bloodless review of the novel, even Mencken, who scorned the hypocrisy of *boobus Americanus,* was afraid to discuss the homosexual theme.[12] Most of Fuller's personal friends remained silent, and those who dared to comment on the novel publicly were naive enough, or so they indicated, to question why he would even write such a work. As a result, *Bertram Cope's Year* was a failure. Discouraged, Fuller vowed never to write another novel.

It would be years before Fuller would receive any intelligent comment on the novel. Edmund Wilson wrote in 1970 that *Bertram Cope's Year* "has a kind of philosophic theme which seems to me to raise it well above the fiction of social surfaces of the school of William Dean Howells." The novel does appear to contrast with the realism of his earlier Chicago novels. But it was written in the same truth-telling spirit of Fuller's most realistic stories and of his most stridently critical essays on Chicago.

Fuller struggled his entire life as a writer to tell his whole story. Before and after the publication of his play and novel, in his diaries and letters Fuller left a wealth of material that reveals the marginal existence that he was forced to lead as a homosexual. Included in his papers is a collection of letters that he altered to obscure their homosexual content. These documents reveal the most important reason for his alienation and frustration as both a Chicago writer and a citizen during the American fin-de-siècle. In their memoirs written after his death, Fuller's many friends, one of whom was Hamlin Garland, depicted him as a writer who was embattled solely with Chicago's commercial and industrial identity. Fuller's later biographers have only repeated that same distorted and one-dimensional view of his life.

As a result of the silence over Fuller's homosexuality, his life and works have been largely misunderstood. It is impossible to separate Fuller's disenchantment with the materialistic values of his age from his equally important battle against the sexual mores of American society. He lost the battle on both fronts. Fuller's friend and University of Chicago professor, Robert Morss Lovett, wrote upon Fuller's death in 1929 that little was lost for literary America. But what he and virtually all of Fuller's critics since have failed to see was that much of what was truly valuable about Fuller's career as a fin-de-siècle writer was yet to be discovered. At the time of Lovett's remarks, *Bertram Cope's Year*, which appeared fewer than ten years before Fuller's death, had never been published by a commercial press and was out of print because of the truth it told about American society and its social values. The novel has remained out of print to this day.

Fuller made a seminal contribution to the development of the American novel in the 1890s. But his conflict with society is as contemporary as the struggle for acceptance waged by such writers as Truman Capote, Gore Vidal, Tennessee Williams, and Allen Ginsberg. His life is like the careers of so many twentieth-century writers and artists, homosexual or not, who have found themselves alienated from the prevailing values of mainstream American society. Because of the marginal life that Fuller was forced to live, his conflict is all the more revealing in what it says about the artist and society.

1
The Marriage Question

"Oh, this question that troubles me so much: What, after all, is civilization?" asked the twenty-two-year-old Henry Blake Fuller of Chicago.[1] His troubled query was written in 1879 just two days before he undertook his maiden voyage across the Atlantic to study civilization at first hand, with special emphasis upon Italy and its art treasures. Born January 9, 1857, Henry Fuller was the direct descendant of an old-line New England family that by the 1840s had settled in the midst of a bustling commercial center that was fast becoming the hub of the Midwest. Janus-like, Fuller's heritage pointed him in two directions, though he would not have admitted it. He was the scion of an older New England tradition. Yet he was also the legitimate offspring of the new commercial and industrial order that dominated his early family life and that directed the development of his native Chicago. However, his well-known dislike for commercial Chicago was only part of his conflict with his city. As a homosexual, he faced an even more profound alienation from his peers and society. The dilemma for Fuller between commerce and art and between his homosexuality and the mores of his society would remain forever irreconcilable.

On his father's side, he was the last male descendant of Dr. Samuel Fuller of the Mayflower.[2] Like many other men of his generation in the early 1830s, Judge Henry Fuller, Henry Fuller's grandfather, abandoned his New England moorings in search of opportunity and wealth, and he settled for the last time in Chicago in 1849. The horizons that Judge Fuller and his son George Fuller, Henry Fuller's father, established for themselves and for their families did not extend much beyond their business interests. The warp and woof of their world were limited to the industrial and commercial development of their adopted city. With business acumen and aggressiveness surpassed only by that

11

of the next generation of robber barons and empire builders, Judge Fuller built a sizable estate. Though no less committed to a career in Chicago's business community, George Fuller never equaled his father's more formidable accomplishments and never aspired much beyond middle-management positions in banking. After the Judge's death, George became curator of the family's estate but did not make any effort to expand the family's holdings in Chicago.

As one of the city's earliest entrepreneurs, real-estate owners, contractors, and railroad operators, Judge Fuller became a well-known and respected figure in the business life of his city. His requests for variances on city zoning regulations were regularly up before the Chicago City Council.[3] He laid the first forty miles of water pipe for his growing city. In 1853 he was appointed by President Pierce for a full term as Chicago's lighthouse keeper.[4] He laid the first section of tracks for the Illinois Central and Rock Island railroads in Chicago, and with the ex-mayor of Chicago, Frank Sherman, he laid the western section of tracks for the Michigan Southern.[5] In 1859 Judge Fuller and three of his Chicago associates incorporated the Chicago City Railway Company and were granted a twenty-five-year lease to operate the municipal street lines. He later appointed his son George treasurer of the company. In recognition of his contribution to the development of early Chicago, in 1871 he was asked to become a member of Chicago's Old Settlers' Society.[6] Before his death in 1879, Judge Fuller had become one of the largest real-estate owners in Chicago.

The few facts that are known about his life place Judge Fuller in that category of businessmen whose questionable practices Henry Fuller would expose in the 1890s in his first two Chicago novels. When Judge Fuller could not get what he wanted through legitimate channels, he found other means. It was reported at his death that Judge Fuller had earned the distinction in Chicago of originating the practice of laying track on Sunday. To beat a court injunction (probably in the 1850s) threatened by property owners along Halsted Street south of the Loop, Judge Fuller ordered his workers out on Sunday in a successful effort to outflank his opponents.[7] At other times when it became apparent that Judge Fuller and his associates could not outwit their adversaries, they resorted to payoffs. Peace, as one early historian of Chicago put it, could be "bought [only] on private terms."[8] It seemed to matter little whether a transaction were carried out under or over the table.

On the maternal side of the Fuller family, Mary Josephine Sanford
Fuller's heritage lay in that antebellum New England society characterized by the American fireside poets and the reassuring sermons of Uni-
tarian ministers. Henry's mother could trace her lineage back to Thomas
de Sanford, a Norman follower of William the Conqueror. The first San-
fords in this country came to Boston in 1631; the family later settled in
Connecticut before Mary's immediate family migrated to the Midwest.[9]

Mary Fuller was, of course, never expected to clutter her days with
the turmoil of Chicago's commercial and industrial development. Under
his mother's guidance, young Fuller received the benefits of a more refined tradition directed toward literature, music, and the arts. As with
most of the plutocrats of the era, things cultural and educational were
generally relegated to the maternal flank of the Fuller family. Although
she was arthritic and limited in her movements later in life, as a young
mother Mary Fuller was as prepared for her task as the Fuller men were
for theirs. The maids in her charge kept an orderly home for the Fuller
family and relieved Mary of the many time-consuming chores required
of a mother with three children. Left with time on her hands and ample
money, she saw to it that her son Henry had all the books he needed,
and she organized outings to concerts, plays, and the opera. During the
sultry Chicago summers, she took Henry and his two sisters to the family vacation home in Coonie, Oconomowoc, Wisconsin, often leaving
George in Chicago to carry on his business.[10] George Fuller had always
expected his son to pursue a career in business. But long before Henry's
graduation from high school, Mary Fuller, acting less by design than
on instinct, had turned her son's head toward other far more genteel
and aesthetic concerns.

Under Mary's guidance, the Fuller household never wanted for educational or cultural resources. In 1880, Fuller wrote to his friend Louise
Washburn that the most current art journals had "ornamented our par-
lor center-table nearly ever since I could walk alone."[11] Aside from this
one letter, there are no records covering Fuller's childhood much before
the age of nine. But judging from what has survived, we can conclude
that before beginning his formal education at Moseley School in 1868,
Fuller had already begun a course of informal home study directed by
his mother. She was largely responsible for introducing him to the works
of American and European writers and to drama, opera, and music. Beginning at age ten, Fuller was required by his mother to take private

cello and organ lessons, as well as training in harmony and orchestration.[12] With little support or encouragement from her husband, she was attempting to keep alive in her home a respect for the arts that had little place, at least for the time being, among the factories and shops of booming Chicago.

By the time Fuller was ten, the arts had become the center of his boyhood experiences, and they left an indelible mark upon his precocious mind. After seeing F. C. Burnand's *The White Fawn* at the theater one evening, Fuller discovered writing and wrote his first play, entitled "The White Swan."[13] One Christmas Fuller received as a gift a Swiss toy village, which he and a friend, Stella, converted to the mise-en-scène for many hours of imaginative play. This diminutive theatrical world later gave way to more elaborate productions, with Henry himself as actor and director and with paying audiences composed of the neighborhood children. In an unpublished essay entitled "Toy Village Theatricals," written in the late 1870s and intended for *St. Nicholas Magazine,* Fuller described some of these influences and activities as a youngster.[14]

During these years Henry Fuller was characterized variously by his many friends. Though not acquainted with Fuller as a young boy, Harriet Monroe, editor and founder of Chicago's *Poetry* magazine, heard of Fuller through her sister, who "used to tell her of this strange retiring boy who didn't fit in with the rather boisterous group that laughed and danced and rode horseback up and down Michigan Avenue in those days of wide lawns and gardens." A contrasting image of Fuller was given by one of his friends: when it came to running, "he could beat everyone of us, much to our chagrin."[15] As Fuller would write years later in a novel about this early period in his life, he even enjoyed playing football at the corner lot.[16]

But Fuller's real aspiration was to be seen by his peers as a reader and writer. From 1868 to 1872 Fuller attended Moseley School. According to the "Private Diary" and school notebooks he kept, he applied himself rigorously to his studies. His report cards show that he maintained a perfect attendance record, and his academic scores for the four years he spent at Moseley seldom fell below 95.[17] His commitment to his studies during this period did not go unrewarded. At the end of his last year at Moseley he won the first medal for his academic accomplishments. Upon taking the entrance exams for Chicago High School on

June 20, he scored 91, the highest in Chicago, a distinction he shared with only two other students in the entire city. The young Fuller based much of his identity on his scholastic success, and he was gratified to receive recognition.

During the time that Fuller spent at Chicago High School following his graduation from Moseley, he did not keep any record of his thoughts or activities. Judging from his report cards covering the year 1872–73, he devoted himself to his studies with as much determination and interest as he had at Moseley School. At the close of the fall semester, Fuller again ranked first in his class. At midyear, for reasons Fuller did not care to explain in his diary, he transferred to South Division High School, where he maintained equally high marks. During this time he continued reading. Sir Walter Scott, Wilkie Collins, and Bulwer-Lytton were among the writers who captured his interest. But most important, some time in 1872 Fuller discovered Charles Dickens, who would remain his favorite author for the next fifteen years. He read many of Dickens's novels, especially *Dombey and Son,* more than once before he became interested in the works of William Dean Howells and Henry James.[18]

Fuller spent the following summer reading and drifting between Chicago and Coonie, now his favorite retreat from the congestion of Chicago's bustling city streets. In the fall of 1873 Fuller changed high schools again and enrolled in Allison Classical Academy, a coeducational school established the year before by the Reverend and Mrs. J. Allison. Situated on the shores of Lake Oconomowoc, the academy consisted of a three-story school building with an adjoining cottage and a dormitory for boarding students. The Allisons patterned their academic program after that of the eastern private academy. As it turned out, their ambition and imagination far exceeded their capabilities and resources. Yet by the beginning of their second year of operation, when Fuller enrolled, they had managed to attract approximately thirty-five live-in and about fifty day students. With the aid of two other teachers, one of whom was their son, "Doc" Allison, the academy offered an ambitious curriculum of German, Latin, algebra, geometry, natural philosophy, and composition. On Saturdays the students went on hunting and hiking excursions into the countryside.[19] Though Fuller's second year in high school was one of the least eventful of his life, it was the most important of his teenage years.

However well-intentioned, the four members of the teaching staff at
the academy were unprepared to teach the broad curriculum they offered.
They were even less prepared to supervise the more than eighty students that Allison had enrolled in its second year. "The academic machine," Fuller wrote many years later, "was laughably, if not perilously,
loose-geared."[20] As Fuller explained, the academy suffered generally
from a "laxity of discipline."

At Allison Fuller studied only as much as the distracting circumstances in his room would allow. After moving from the Drake Hotel
in Oconomowoc where they were initially lodged, Fuller and his roommate Charlie Norris shared a well-furnished carpeted room on the top
floor of the cottage. Also lodged in their "queer little brick house," as
Fuller described it, were four other boys who shared the other two bed-
rooms on the upper floor. As he explained in "Allison Classical Academy," Fuller's unpublished account of his year, his room became the
regular meeting place of what he termed the Jolly Quartette, composed
of four other boys, including Charlie and one day student, Ernest Thompson. Fuller did not number himself among the four. Because the win-
dows of Fuller's and Norris's room did not face the Allison's living quarters, their room among the three others on the top floor became the logical
site for the Quartette's late-night visitations, which nearly always lasted
long after the 10 P.M. curfew. Often, Fuller and his cottage mates would
launch elaborate plots to frighten the unsuspecting "Doc" Allison and
his roommate, who lived below and who were ostensibly charged with
the boys' supervision.

In spite of the distracting influences of cottage life, Fuller studied
hard, became the chief debater on the school's debating team, and was
chosen editor of the school newspaper, *Ours*. He shared part of the responsibility for the copying and proofreading of the paper with a female
student, Carrie Streeter. Under Fuller's editorship, the paper published
poems, essays, columns, letters to the editor, and satirical notes on Allisonian fashions. Fuller worked hard on the only two editions of the paper
before a lack of funds and resources shut the paper down by the end
of March. Combined with his high marks in class and his success in
the debating society, Fuller's work on the newspaper earned him the
respect of his classmates. But all was not work for Fuller. At Christmas
he, with the rest of the student body, joined in a Christmas play based

upon N. T. Bayly's ballad, "The Mistletoe Bough." The production became "one of the pleasantest episodes" of the school year for the Allison students.

The year passed all too quickly for young Fuller. With the debating society on the wane and *Ours* defunct by the end of March, the late-night activities in the cottage occupied much of Fuller's time and attention. As summer break approached, he was sorry to see one of the happiest and most successful years of his life pass.

II

The end of Fuller's year at Allison Classical Academy marked the beginning of the most important period in his life. In little more than six months he would return to his experiences at Allison in a short history, recounting a well-selected group of activities that he shared in during his year at the academy. In the meantime, to fill the leisure hours of his summer, he began a new diary entitled "A Legacy to Posterity." As his entries reveal, Fuller devoted much of his time during the summer of 1874 to the study of German and to Dickens's novels.

By the end of August, Fuller's parents—mainly his father—had decided not to send him back to Allison. Their decision denied him the only acceptable avenue he had for making friends and pursuing his interests. On September 21 Fuller tersely noted in his diary, "The 'business of life' formally inaugurated. Ovington's Crockery 122 State Street." With little concern for his son's desire to return to school, George Fuller felt that it was time for Henry to begin work. The bitterness Fuller felt over his forced labor would never allow him to forgive his father.

But his work at Ovington's was only half of the problem that Fuller had to face in Chicago. School or no school, his associations with young people were becoming more problematic all the time. He reported in his diary that in the middle of August he had spent three weeks in Coonie and had "found a large number of boys and girls of and about [his] own age at the Draper," though he left "without forming any eternal friendships." His reluctance to become too involved with his peers was beginning to take on a new dimension. For during his year at Allison, if not before, it had become clear to the adolescent Fuller that his friends' interest in the opposite sex had changed radically. He realized that his homosexual preference would not allow him to participate openly and uninhibitedly in the society of his peers. This, more than anything else, began to separate him from others.

Fuller's conscious withdrawal from society, which would characterize his adult life in the minds of so many of his Chicago friends, begins in this period. At seventeen he had already begun to avoid parties and other activities because in most cases these social affairs included young women. He admitted to himself in "A Legacy" that he was not capable of conforming to the necessary forms of "masculine polite society" that such occasions required. Whenever young men and women gathered at parties, club meetings, or dances, Fuller confessed that these functions were the cause of an "embarrassment most perplexing and disagreeable." When in the presence of young ladies, Fuller lost all sense of ease and social grace. He wrote in "A Legacy," "I have mingled very little in society – the society of young people. I have little desire for it; often a dislike – more, a positive aversion." But as Fuller went on to confess, there is no mystery why he had cultivated a distaste for these mixed social gatherings: "In my associations – particularly with ladies – I am controlled by a great unwillingness to conform to many forms of etiquette, and to many set formulas of speech." When he heard "meaningless words in an endless repetition from the lips of tender young goslings," the young Fuller became ill at ease. Moreover, he became impatient with his male friends when he was forced "to witness an unvarying officious adoration of and the same deferential attendance on ladies from buds blossoming into manhood!" At the end of his long self-analytical passage, Fuller concluded, "I, refusing to go duly through these forms, and driven to expressions less felicitous, to deportment less orthodox – and by means of this, my embarrassment is increased more than any would imagine possible."

Fuller wrote in his diary that he felt unable to make conversation freely in the presence of young women. At the most crucial moments while making small talk, his verbal ability would fail him: "I begin a sentence with great velocity – stumble – repeat, make, and this is the unkindest cut of all, a grammatical error – an error in pronunciation – and finish in utter confusion." Fuller mistakenly believed that his linguistic failures were the result of his reading too much and too rapidly. As Fuller himself reported in his letters and diaries during this period, his success as a debater hinged upon his always eloquent and witty performance. However, in the wrong social gathering, language threatened to expose his true feelings. Halting and stuttering were the outward expression of his ambivalence. Even the tortuous syntax of his diary entry reflects his confusion. While he wanted to make friends his own age, he was at the same time repelled by the sexual interest that young men and women had in one another. He thought the polite forms of masculine and feminine behavior unnecessary and irrelevant. The form had no content for young Fuller.

As an adolescent he was never free from the pressure to conform. Consequently, at times he would assume a conventional posture toward young women for the benefit of his friends, and even perhaps to amuse himself. One such instance was a letter he wrote to Louise just after beginning his year at Allison. In describing his new friends, he wrote, "While most of them are 'horrid boys,' there are yet a number of 'the dear creatures,' four or five of them in the vicinity (so they say!) of sweet sixteen. Ask me how I divide my heart piecemeal among so many, for besides these, there is the 'Norwegian Blonde,' the 'Irish Blonde,' and others of the domestics with whom I am desperately in love. As you see, I am very susceptible!"[21] But soon a more mature Fuller would come forward in another letter to Louise and use conventional language on a somewhat less conventional subject in Victorian America—homosexual love.

For the time being, the young Fuller would not dare broach the subject of homosexuality with his friends. As a description of his relationships with the girls at Allison, the above letter to Louise was not accurate, but it was consistent with the public posture he assumed at times to mask his true feelings. While still attending Allison, Fuller found himself the nearly suffocated *objet d'amour* of several female admirers. As the editor of *Ours,* he used the impersonal form of the "Post Office" (the letters-to-the-editor column) to discourage their persistent overtures. Fuller wrote, "The Editor takes advantage of the P.O. to inform the young lady readers of 'Ours' that the marked attentions of two or three of their number are exceedingly disagreeable to him; that his heart has long been bestowed upon another whose position they cannot hope to usurp." There was another person, but it was not a girl. When a relationship with a girl threatened to become intimate, Fuller made a very hasty and decisive retreat. He had already begun to make those strategic withdrawals from his friends that would characterize his relationship with society for the remainder of his life.

III

In spite of Ovington's consuming the lion's share of his time, Fuller still kept up, albeit in a more limited manner, his literary and theatrical interests. Early in October 1874 he heard Clara Louise Kellogg sing in Mozart's *Marriage of Figaro*. By the end of the month he had reread *Dombey and Son*, had seen *The School for Scandal* at the McVicker's Theater, and had finished reading *Bleak House*. He was frustrated by the contradiction between the life that he wished to lead and the one that he was now forced to endure at the crockery. To compound the problem for him, on November 10 an astonished Fuller reported in his diary that Allison had gone into foreclosure and had been closed. This dashed any hopes of his ever being reunited with friends at the academy.

After the Christmas holiday and now without even the faintest chance of returning to Allison, Fuller found himself at the beginning of January at the age of eighteen a very disconsolate and melancholy young man. In spite of the crockery's drain upon his time and energy, he did manage to keep up his reading. He finished Gibbon's *Decline and Fall of the Roman Empire* in late January. But without school his reading no longer had any context.

At the beginning of March 1875, Fuller inexplicably took a year's leave from the crockery. He never explained in his diary why he was allowed to quit his job. Freed from the drudgery and the restrictions of his work, he immediately made plans for a visit to Coonie. While still in Chicago, on March 4 he recorded in his diary, "In order to keep alive the memory of happy Allisonian days, I have begun for myself alone a series." He entitled his new diary "Allison Classical Academy."

He explained in "A Legacy" and in the new diary that he intended to capture some of the camaraderie and "good old times" he had shared with the other boys in the cottage and to recall some of the outstanding events of the year. However, in spite of Fuller's stated purpose in writing "Allison Classical Academy," the diary soon became something more than a mere series of recollections of the good times he had spent with his friends at the academy. Its significance lies less in what it recalls from Fuller's year at the academy than in what it reveals about the eighteen-year-old who wrote the diary. Through his memory fragments, Fuller focused upon only selected events and people for that year.

But just as important as the events he describes is when and at what distance Fuller began his work. He started it more than a year and a half after the first incidents he describes in the opening section, and he did not complete it until July 21, 1876, more than two years after he had left Allison. The writing also spanned the entire school year of 1875, when Fuller reentered South Division High School to finish his last year of formal education. There was considerably more to sustain his interest in his diary keeping than the mere recording of the events of a single school year, especially one so far removed from his current interests and activities. In "Allison Classical Academy" Fuller attempted to define, more clearly than he had ever dared before, his homosexual feelings for the other boys of his age group. The historical accuracy of the diary is less significant than Fuller's perceptions of the events he describes.

The most revealing parts of the diary are those sections devoted to cottage life and to his two personality profiles: one of Frank Donaldson, among Fuller's closest friends during that year, and the other of Flora Van Nostrom, who became infamous for her amorous relationships at Allison. In the sections on cottage life and on Frank Donaldson, he romanticized his relationship with his male friends. By contrast, with the girls at Allison, he was more prosaic. It is very clear in "Allison Classical Academy" that he viewed the girls only from a distance, avoiding their manifold plots to win the attention of the boys, himself included. He described, but always in matter-of-fact terms, many of the activities he shared with them, such as his association with Carrie Streeter on the academy newspaper. He bore the girls no malice. Actually, he reported that he was pleased that Carrie had been elected associate editor of *Ours*, and not someone of lesser ability. He was simply not attracted to girls.

The role that the eighteen-year-old Fuller assigns himself in his diary is as important as what he says about the other boys and girls. On the surface Fuller characterizes himself, when in the society of his friends, as a somewhat withdrawn, reserved person. Though always present during the nocturnal parties in his room, he went out of his way to point out that he did not number himself among the Jolly Quartette. He explained, one evening, rather than participate in the Quartette's activi-

ties, he declined the usual cigar and was content to sit on the end of
the bed and make "saucy remarks" about the card game in progress, to
his roommate's annoyance. Because of the aloof posture that he assumed
at times, he was occasionally excluded from the boys' other activities.
But Fuller was selective about when and under what circumstances
he chose to depict himself as an outsider. He was not always excluded
from the boys' schemes and games. He enjoyed the long evenings spent
in Charlie's and his room. He never failed to join in the fun when the
boys chose up teams and had pillow fights, which at times "were produc-
tive of enough noise to raise the dead" and often sent their bedsteads
crashing to the floor. In one such battle, Fuller writes, they "stood a
siege of half an hour" in his room. Added to these rollicking and "rough
and tumble" late-night battles, Charlie, as Fuller described him, could
often be seen "coolly attired promenading the hall." Encouraged by the
other boys, Frank Donaldson would perform "capers" in Fuller's room,
dressed only "in a short and airy gauze undershirt." It was lucky, Fuller
adds, that Mrs. Allison and her daughters never dared to visit the "upper reaches" of their cottage after 10 P.M. After exhausting themselves,
the boys would often snuggle together two at a time in bed until awak-
ened and called down for breakfast and classes by "Doc" Allison. The
camaraderie that developed out of sharing such close quarters with the
other boys remained for Fuller the most important aspect of the year
he spent at the academy.

Even so, there was a legitimate reason for Fuller's occasional withdrawal from his friends. If his complaints about the form of masculine
society in "A Legacy" are any clue, Fuller's unwillingness to participate
is understandable. What he failed to realize while at Allison, but had
begun to comprehend during the months he was writing his account
of his year there, was that the adolescent interests of his friends were
undergoing a fundamental change. Fuller's friends, with characteristic
impatience, anticipated their manhood, and however prematurely, they
were eager to enter that new, mysterious, adult society that awaited them.
They aped their elders by playing cards, smoking, and drinking. They
pursued, sometimes without restraint, the girls at Allison, some of whom
lived in the girls' dorm near the lake. No prude, Fuller was not shocked
by such activities, as he would never be in his adult life. Rather he simply was not interested in that particular form of masculine society his
friends were so impatient to enter.

The problem of Fuller's withdrawal and growing isolation was compounded by his affection for Charlie and Frank. Since he could not express his feelings, they remained bottled up at the time. Later, when he began writing "Allison Classical Academy," those feelings overflowed in the exaggerated romantic style he adopted for those sections involving the other boys, especially Charlie and Frank. He described his relationship with Frank as "intimate," but intimacy was something Frank no doubt cared to share only with girls. Charlie Norris had won the distinction of being the "young despoiler of female virtue" at Allison and had become notorious for his daring, midnight escapades in the girls' sleeping quarters. Yet Fuller referred to Charlie as "my darling" and as "my loving mate." He also endearingly named Charlie his Telemachus. Though Charlie did not return his affection, Fuller wrote that Charlie and he "dovetailed very well, and until my dear child was led astray, bid fair to rival Damon and Pythias." Later when Charlie became partial to Paul Weiss, Frank's roommate, a jealous Fuller complained that from "rosy morn till dewy eve" Paul and Charlie whispered "sweet little chatterings" that Fuller found intolerable. Once when he found himself neglected by the other boys, Fuller announced falsely that he was leaving Allison. When this brought only a part of the response Fuller hoped for, he affectionately chided his "poor darling's foolishness" for his neglect of his admirer and "mentor."

This oblique form of self-definition extends into other parts of the diary. Writing the chapters on Flora Van Norstrand and Frank Donaldson offered Fuller further insight into the relationship that he shared with his peers at Allison. To Fuller they became the symbols of an alien heterosexual society. In winning her notoriety as Allison's "dark lady," Flora the Fair may even have made an amorous gesture in Fuller's direction before he took decisive action in the newspaper's "P.O." In the chapter on Flora, Fuller confesses that if he could not recall her success in the classroom or in the Debating Society, he could certainly "give an account of her innumerable 'affaires d'amour' which shook the very foundation of Allisonian discipline, and cast numberless wrecks in the desolate shores of unrequited affection." Fuller makes it clear that he kept more than just an arm's length from such philandering, whatever Flora's charms or successes with the other boys.

In "Edmund Dalrymple," written many years later, the adult Fuller was able to define more clearly than he had in "Allison Classical Academy" what real interest for him lay behind Flora's character. In spite of all the other boys' rush for her attention, "Dalrymple [Fuller] seemed to regard her as a mere person, a generalized human creature with no definite place on either side of that incisive line which divides the race into two elemental parts." He understood, as his letters to Louise demonstrated, the pedestal on which women were supposed to be placed. But for him personally they held no romance.[22] Regardless of what Flora had come to represent for the other boys, for Fuller she represented one more aspect of his experiences at Allison that separated him from his male friends. Fuller was the onlooker in her affairs, never the participant. Yet he could not afford to be indifferent to what she had come to represent for him in the years that followed his residence at the academy.

Frank Donaldson was far more interesting to Fuller. He wrote that Frank was the most deserving of all the students at Allison "of a chapter all to himself." This was not due, however, to qualities in Frank's character that Fuller might have chosen to emulate. On the contrary, Fuller called him "the most harum-scarum, mischievous, careless, good-natured and erratic youth that I have ever met." One side of Frank's character was the opposite of all that Fuller hoped and believed he stood for in the eyes of his peers: Frank was incapable of ever applying himself to his studies. He would sometimes announce with enthusiasm an interest in a new area of study, like a new language, only to abandon the project within a matter of weeks. He was an instigator and the central figure in the midnight forest parties that scandalized the citizens of Oconomowoc and earned the academy a bad name. At times he brazenly defied academy rules, and for his misbehavior Reverend Allison applied the rod. But Frank bore the welts indifferently. Yet, as Fuller explained, "however lax were his ideas of morality and however minute his conscious scruples," there was another, more cultured side to Frank's character. Like Fuller he appreciated fine music. Together at the piano they enjoyed their favorites—the "Carnival of Venice," the "Blue Danube," and other Johann Strauss waltzes. They danced together and sang their favorite aria, "Ah, che la morte," from Verdi's *Il Trovatore*. Bright and cultured, yet erratic and undisciplined, Frank always remained an enigma to Fuller. If there was any potential for a romance among his peers, Fuller found it in Frank's personality, even if Frank could not share the same feelings.

For Fuller, "Allison Classical Academy" was less a sentimental journey than a thinly disguised personal history. But it is by no means unified in its intent. As the uneven text illustrates, at nineteen, when he finished the diary, Fuller's view of those past experiences still remained unclear. Yet "Allison Classical Academy" is a seminal work among the documents Fuller wrote during the two years after he left Allison. In it he attempted for the first time to clarify the major problems that he was now beginning to face as a homosexual in commercial Chicago and Victorian American society. In the diaries that followed, Fuller would be far more open in his attempts to define his relationships with young men and women of his age.

IV

Though Fuller finished "Allison Classical Academy" in midsummer 1876, he did not relegate his friendships made at the academy to the past. He corresponded with Frank, Charlie, and others over the next few years. He followed their careers and lives with interest, yet he was disappointed over the conventional course that they all began to follow. Not long after leaving Allison, Paul Neil and Charlie Norris both married. By 1879 Frank Donaldson, who was living in the East, also married. Fuller was especially disappointed at the news of Frank's marriage, and in February 1879 he returned to his "Allison Classical Academy" manuscript to make a special entry: "Alas my child you are following in the fatal footsteps of Paul and Charles. After so long and stout a resistance against the wiles of the fair, fickle, and false, you have at last succumbed!" The levity with which he treats Frank's marriage in his entry belies his real concern. Long before Frank and others began taking that decisive step, while writing "Allison Classical Academy" and working at Ovington's, Fuller became embroiled in a public debate over what he termed the "Marriage Question."

In October 1875 Fuller wrote in "A Legacy," "I awoke one morning and found myself famous. Last Sunday, as well as the Sunday before, I had an article in the Tribune on the 'Marriage Question.'" The editors of the *Chicago Tribune* had made available a young people's column that was, over a period of several weeks, devoted to the marriage question and to the general issue of male-female relationships. That Fuller wrote to the paper underscores the significance of the subject in his thoughts.

If he was not especially attracted to young women, then what of marriage? The letters illustrate a certain ambivalence toward women and his future. In them Fuller is bellicose, satirical, and generally unkind to women. In one letter he outlined what he considered to be the perfect wife and even suggested the possibility of marriage for himself. Until he made up his mind and informed Louise Washburn in his letters to her in the early 1880s that he would never marry, marriage would remain one problem that he could not ignore. At age eighteen the issue was still a complex if not confusing one for Fuller. Just what lay ahead for him as a homosexual he could not say.

In his letters to the *Tribune* he bore the sole responsibility for turning the otherwise polite discussion in the column to personal invective and attack, most of it directed at him. His entry in "A Legacy" was not accurate.[23] He had not published two articles, but instead, by October 12 when he made his entry, four letters. Nor had he actually become "famous"; his true identity remained hidden behind the pseudonym "Harry B. Free," with which he signed all of his letters. The pun was not lost upon his adversaries, since he revealed in one letter that he was a bachelor.

In his first letter of September 4, which the editors of the *Tribune* entitled "You'll Catch It For This," Fuller outlined four reasons why any right-thinking young bachelor should never marry. He wrote, "Girls are well enough to talk to for a moment, but not to marry. They require too much capital for a good investment, and a young man is not going to drop three or four pegs in society because he can't support his wife." Furthermore, he complained, young women were social butterflies and fickle, and because of their uninhibited social dissipation, "they were all in bad health." He concluded his letter by complaining that eligible women had no "ability to keep house" and knew "absolutely nothing about economy." He then followed his first letter with another on September 11, which the editor of the *Tribune* entitled "Not a Bit Scared." In this letter Fuller reiterated his complaints against what he termed the "city belles," those same young wives who would unashamedly spend all of their young husbands' money. His last two letters, entitled again by the *Tribune* editors, "This Young Man Needs Taking Down" (September 19) and "Compliments of H.B.F. and Some More Allusions" (October 30), were basically restatements of his previous two letters.

Fuller's letters were a futile if not a pathetic plea to reverse the direction of social intercourse among his peers. He called for more intellectual and impersonal relationships so that he could be more comfortable with the women of his age group. While he objected to the form of heterosexual social intercourse that he was forced into at times, he still subscribed to the conventional view, as he admitted in his last letter, that "it is the law of Nature for men and women to marry, and every young man feels this." There was no satire or humor intended here. At the core of his anonymous letters is the ambivalence that was already beginning to divide his life and thoughts between his own sexual proclivities and the values of his society. As a young man Fuller had absorbed and accepted the general wisdom of his day, but he could not conform ultimately to the standards set by Victorian America. He found the form of heterosexual American culture single-minded and unbending in the face of his own sexual preferences and social needs. Similarly, he had already discovered that the commercial society around him in Chicago, manifest in the values of his own father, was equally indifferent if not hostile to his interests in literature, music, and the arts. A profile of the mature Fuller was beginning to emerge. His conflict with both the commercialism of his hometown and the sexual mores of his society would plague his consciousness and uneven career as a writer for the next half-century.

While Fuller wrestled privately with this new set of problems, he did not allow his disagreement with his society to interfere with his relationship with classmates and close friends. During his last year at South Division High, begun in the fall of 1875, he remained popular and in the thick of school activities. As one acquaintance described him during this time, "He was full of boyish pranks, fond of writing notes and verse and was much given to drawing caricatures of some of the boys and girls who interested and amused him." When he was asked to perform before his classmates, he exhibited "a fine command of English and expressed himself with clearness and charm" and was at times even asked by the school principal to read his papers aloud before the class.[24] Away from school, Fuller spent many hours reading romance writers such as Ann Radcliffe. At this time, for his own amusement he wrote an essay, based upon his wide reading, entitled "A Feast for the Gods," in which he self-confidently proposed to fill the "deficiency" he found in Samuel Taylor Coleridge's criticism of the romance form.

In June 1876 Fuller graduated from South Division High, and in his entry in "A Legacy" on the twenty-third of June following the commencement exercises, Fuller noted glumly that his school days were no doubt over. In October he would again be forced by his father to return to the drudgery of Ovington's Crockery. But the eighteen-year-old Fuller took some solace in the fact that for the summer at least he would be free.

In late August he spent several days in Coonie, and on August 25, apparently while there, he started a new diary dedicated to personal thoughts and concerns.[25] On his way north, Fuller stopped in Milwaukee to visit friends from Allison. When he arrived in Coonie, he made several sentimental visits, some with Ernest Thompson, who still lived there, to the cottage and old schoolhouse now occupied by new tenants. While staying at the Draper Hotel, the family resort, he participated in evening charades and sang in a choral group with the other hotel guests. After an unexpected success in the second charade of the week, Fuller wrote in his new diary, "I orated on platonic love, all with bursts of eloquence."

In spite of the cheerful tone of his diary entry, Fuller did not enjoy his visit to Coonie that summer. The Draper was not as Fuller remembered it. Even the people, Fuller complained, were new and unfamiliar. But the apparent change that had occurred in Coonie since Fuller's stay there nearly two years before was not the real issue for him. Rather, it was his growing sense of the past and its irretrievability. His friends and the good times they shared were gone. His visit to the old school served only to intensify his feelings of isolation from other people his age.

His efforts to romanticize Coonie and his past were understandable. In the summer of 1876 Fuller stood between the two worlds of his fading youth and his future as a businessman in Chicago's commercial center. But the young Fuller would never outgrow the conflict that he faced that summer; it would only broaden and intensify. In just a few years it would develop into a conflict between the industrialism of nineteenth-century American society and his romanticized view of the Italian past. Indeed, his new journal contains a fragment of Fuller's first effort in imaginative travel fiction that suggests in tone and subject the opening paragraph of his first romance, *The Chevalier of Pensieri-Vani.*

The last months of Fuller's teenage years were among the most crucial of his life. In one sense, it was a period in which he was forced to come to terms with himself, as a future businessman, a genteel man of letters, and, most important, a social person. For more than two years he had avoided in "A Legacy," in his letters to the *Tribune,* and in "Allison Classical Academy" the issue that he finally was able to define clearly for himself in his new journal. In his opening remarks he had dedicated his journal to more introspective and personal thoughts, and in fulfillment of that end Fuller wrote the most personal and candid passage that he had ever written in any of his notebooks. On September 15, 1876, he wrote that he was "meditating an advertisement for a bosom friend" to be placed in the Sunday *Tribune.*

It seems incredible that I have paddled so far out into the sea of life without hailing a bosom friend. Such is the melancholy fact. I have never yet found a thoroughly congenial person whom I could make friend and confidante; never yet found one to be my Pylades, my alter ego. Perhaps I am to blame; I never make advances. I don't encourage advances in others; perhaps I am too fastidious.

But my advertisement:

First the qualifications. The youth must be—I am conscious that I expose myself in a most vulnerable point, and am certain that I shall receive a thrust from some moralizer—the youth must be handsome. I would pass by twenty beautiful women to look upon a handsome man. A man with a fine form, a beautiful head, and a handsome face is a feast for my eyes. Why could I not have lived with Sophocles? Why could I not have caught a glimpse of Byron's glorious head?

Again my youth must be of aesthetic tastes. He shall love literature, art and music. Oh, to find a few in this rough and tumble squabble for dollars and cents, dollars and cents, who can find in books something better than bullion, and in culture something higher than cash.

Third, my youth must be moral; I don't ask for religion, but for morality. He will be honest, conscientious. In our days, when the Almighty Dollar is the highest goal of man's ambition, it is a grand, a proud thing to be a man of truth and honor. Who can read unmoved Macaulay's tribute to the whole-souled integrity of Addison?[26]

The advertisement, of course, was never placed. But the mere gesture toward some form of public utterance struck a chord that would reverberate throughout Fuller's career as a Chicago writer. He would never resolve his ambivalence between, as one friend said of him, his penchant to be a "closed mouth custodian of his own affairs" and his desire to tell it all. The young Fuller who penned the confessional passage in his journal saw the humor in the suggestion to publish such an advertisement in Victorian America. In "Edmund Dalrymple," however, the older and much more seasoned Fuller at mid-career recognized the essential tragedy at the core of his life: "How, he [Dalrymple] asked himself on each occasion, shall one contrive to be at the same time an artist and gentleman? How at once give himself out and hold himself in? How deliver one's message to the general public and yet maintain the well bred reticence of the private person?" Throughout his career as a writer Fuller would grapple with the propriety of treating the homosexual theme in his fiction. In 1919 he would finally elect to develop it openly in his full-length novel, *Bertram Cope's Year*. But the novel's reception would only confirm in him his lifelong suspicion that he could never be open with the American public.

In his proposed advertisement for a companion, Fuller had brought together what would soon become the two most important and perplexing elements of his life: the catchpenny values of commercial Chicago and his homosexuality. At nineteen he had come forward to face squarely the two issues that now served and would always serve to distinguish his thoughts and behavior from the dominant values of his native city. Together, his homosexuality and his scorn for the havoc created by industrial capitalism in Chicago would soon separate him socially and intellectually, personally and professionally, from his native town. His forced labor at the crockery, begun again in October 1876, would also begin that alienation from his family, including his mother, that would result in the unsympathetic portrayal of his family life in *On the Stairs*. As a result, Fuller for the next ten years and slightly more would begin a quest that would direct him away from Chicago and the influence of his family — to Europe and to Boston — in search of more acceptable soil. He would attempt to strike a balance between his genteel tastes in the arts and letters and his desire to find a society that did not impose upon him the requirements of a more conventional social behavior.

2

Italy: From Etruria to Naples

At age nineteen in the summer of 1876, having finished his last year of formal schooling, Henry Fuller faced a long and unwanted career in banking. In his partially autobiographical novel, *On the Stairs,* Fuller implies that, without consulting him on the matter, his father had already plotted his career for him. Like his fictional counterpart Raymond Prince, he would not be given the option to attend college. Instead, George Fuller put his son to work in the lower ranks of a local bank, with the understanding that in time Henry would work his way up to a more responsible position. But George Fuller's plans for his firstborn were inconsistent with Henry's tastes. Not an unkind father, George Fuller nevertheless had become estranged from his son over the years. Later in *On the Stairs* Fuller dramatized the tension that at times prevailed in the Fuller household in the late 1870s. Fuller wrote that when James Prince found his son reading, he told Raymond that "he was working too hard and too late — that it would hurt his health and probably injure his eyes." As a man who had spent all of his adult years in some form of commercial enterprise, George Fuller could never approve of the hours that Henry spent studying under the dim lamps in the Fuller home.[1] For the businessman in this era of America's development, a young man could do better than spend his time reading and writing.

Dating as far back as his first job at Ovington's in 1874, Fuller had become painfully aware of the growing division between him and his parents. Even if George Fuller did not understand the more genteel, literary side of his son, then Mary Fuller certainly did. But she failed to intercede on his behalf. For this Fuller judged her harshly, at the time as well as later in life. In a letter written to Louise in 1879 while he was abroad on his first tour of the Continent, Fuller wrote, "I'm firmly convinced that a mother with a presence of mind is just about the best thing a family can possess."[2] He could remember a time when his mother was far more sensitive to his needs. It seems that during this period Mary Fuller had become distracted from her maternal duties by an aggravated arthritic condition.[3] Years later Fuller wrote somewhat unsympathetically that his "mother might have been kindly, . . . if she had not had herself." When she could not find medicinal relief, she would escape from Chicago's cold, damp climate. From Fuller's standpoint, she had become far too self-centered. With the added responsibility of looking after Fuller's two younger sisters, Harriet and Mary, she had little time left for her older son, who had now graduated into the arena of his father's influence anyway. However, there was little companionship in his relationship with his banker father, and Fuller found himself at this time "an independent, detached, isolated individual."[4] His lot was not a happy one.

In one sense, Fuller's conflict with his parents was typical of the struggle for independence that nearly all adolescents face when they approach their majority. He rebelled against both his father and the city his father represented. As he wrote of Raymond Prince in *On the Stairs*, "It might be said that he had simply reached the 'critical' age, when Idealism calls the Daily practicalities to its bar and delivers its harsh imperious judgments; when it puts the world, if but for a few brief months, 'where it belongs.' . . . He passed judgment not only on his parents, whom he had been finding unsatisfactory, and on most of his associates, . . . but on the community as such." Armed with the confidence that characterized his student years, the nineteen-year-old Fuller had already begun to turn a critical eye both upon his parents and upon the values of his own society. Fuller found too "that the town allotted to him by destiny was crude." From this time forward, Fuller could never remain indifferent toward Chicago's evolution as a city, and he would never tire of attempting to amend its shortcomings.

During this period Chicago was undergoing its greatest development, commercially, culturally, and demographically.[5] Its population soared as a great influx of European immigrants filled Chicago's shops and neighborhoods. To Fuller's great chagrin, the control of the city's municipal government fell into the hands of men like the Irish "lords of the levee," King Mike McDonald, Bathhouse John Coughlin, and Hinky Dink Kenna.[6]

In stark contrast to this low life, as Fuller saw it, was the other Chicago, financed and directed by such men as Gustavus Swift, Philip Danforth Armour, Marshall Field, Charles Yerkes, Cyrus H. McCormick, Walter Loomis Newberry, Potter Palmer, and George Pullman. Shortly after the fire, the Chicago Academy of Design was established, the precursor of the Chicago Art Institute. Instrumental in Chicago's cultural uplift were the many social, musical, and literary clubs established in the seventies. Out of this movement came Theodore Thomas's Chicago Orchestra, established in 1891. And in the spring of 1893 the Columbian Exposition would serve as Chicago's magnum opus; it was to be the crowning glory of the city's cultural efforts begun in the 1870s.

These were some of the aspects of his city that were beginning to influence Fuller's life. But whatever the contradictions he saw in Chicago's development, the growth of the arts would provide him with a small group of friends that would share his interests throughout his life. Chief among his friends at this time, and for many years to come, were Louise Washburn and their mutual friend Clara Ray. Louise would always remain Fuller's favorite. Their friendship was different from that typical adolescent relationship between boys and girls that he had complained about in his diary. Actually, they developed a relationship much like the one that he had called for in his letters to the *Tribune* on the marriage question. For Fuller, Louise was a close friend with similar intellectual interests, not a sexual partner or potential wife. She shared all of his musical and literary interests. Together they traded books, discussed art, literature, and history, attended concerts and plays, and participated in informal choral groups. Over the years Louise would become his confidante and would be privy to some of his most intimate thoughts.

Anticipating his return to Ovington's in the fall, Fuller became despondent. In early August 1876 he did not feel well, and he recorded in his diary, "in the dumps, physical and mental."[7] But his depression was relieved, at least temporarily. For in early October Fuller's roommate from his year at Allison Classical Academy, Charlie Norris, was going to pass through Chicago on a trip to the East.[8] He invited Fuller to join him on a visit to the Centennial Exposition in Philadelphia, including side trips to New York and Washington, D.C. For the nearly twenty-year-old Fuller, who had never traveled without his parents beyond his short jaunts to Coonie in southwest Wisconsin, his wish to undertake the trip with his friend was no small matter. "After numerous confabs and consultations both here and at headquarters," he wrote in his diary, "I decided to go." His parents apparently allowed him to make his own decision. The trip was an important break for him. He discovered that it was possible to be independent and out from under his father's heavy-handed influence. It was a prelude to a much more ambitious journey yet to come. On the evening of October 5, Fuller and Norris boarded a train in Chicago and headed east, where they spent more than three weeks visiting the sites and the international exhibits at the fair.[9]

Whatever freedom Fuller won for himself at the time, he still had to face the scenario his father had written for him. Less than a week after his return, he began work at Ovington's. The daily routine and the long hours at the crockery over the next eight months – again Fuller failed to list his responsibilities – were reminiscent of his first job at Ovington's two years before. However, by September Fuller found some respite from his work. George Fuller had arranged a new job for him in a local bank, and on September 29 Fuller wrote in his diary, "Set free from the daily contact with the things I loathe. Ovington's adieu, I pray, forever."

But even as he made his diary entry, he realized that his father had still more definite plans for his future. In George Fuller's mind, Henry's first banking job was to be a brief apprenticeship for bigger things to come in Chicago's Loop district. On June 1, 1878, Fuller moved to Home National Bank, where his father was an officer and where Fuller assumed the more responsible task of bookkeeping.

Throughout this period Fuller's routine away from work changed little from what it had been before. In his spare time, encouraged no doubt by Clara and Louise, he joined a "singing school" composed of several other young people. He found time to keep up his reading, and at some point in 1877 or 1878 he began a study of architecture. Among the books he read was John Ruskin's *Seven Lamps of Architecture*, which was to influence his views for many years to come.

Fuller discovered an ally in Ruskin, who sought to amend both the form of modern architecture and the industrial age's neglect of public monuments. Fuller began to view architecture as a form through which a nation was able to maintain a sense of continuity with its past, as well as beautify its cities. As a result, he would never accept the architectural innovations in the works of the great Chicago architects such as William Le Baron Jenny and Louis Sullivan, who would form the basis of the Chicago School of architecture in the 1890s.[10]

Though he began to spend much time studying architecture, Fuller did not neglect entirely his writing or his music. Early in 1879, he wrote a five-part doggerel poem entitled "We Girls," in which he satirized the misadventures of thirty-one females. The *Chicago Tribune* published the poem, signed "X," in five installments between February 23 and March 23, 1879. Otherwise, music remained an important if not dominant daily pastime, as it would remain for many years to come. He was an active participant in many formal and informal choral gatherings. On the first of April Fuller attended a production of Gilbert and Sullivan's *H. M. S. Pinafore* in Chicago. As a diversion from the Italian opera that Fuller enjoyed, he found light comic operas entertaining. He was so impressed with the work that he returned in June and July to see the Chicago Church Choir Company's performances of *Pinafore* at Haverly's Theater.[11] His interest in Gilbert and Sullivan began a study that would culminate in the two operas Fuller completed and attempted to stage in the late 1880s, both closely patterned after Gilbert and Sullivan's work.

For nearly five months *Pinafore* was the rage among Fuller's small group of friends, who were caught up in the Gilbert and Sullivan craze that consumed both England and America at the time.[12] In mid-April Fuller, Clara, Louise, and other members of their singing group met after work and on weekends at a member's house to play cards and to perform selections from *Pinafore*. But the group's amateurishness and merriment did not prevent it from undertaking the project with some seriousness. As Fuller noted, in an echo of *Pinafore*, the performances were "greatly to our credit." In mid-August Fuller wrote in his final entry in "A Legacy" that the group met at Louise's house for "one grand final jumble of bezique and Pinafore." Fuller's usual reserve was nowhere in evidence during these rollicking sessions.

During the evenings that he did not spend out with his friends, Fuller started planning for his first European trip. The death of his grandfather at the end of June did not change his plans for a late-summer departure. On the blank pages of an old diary, he began in early 1879 to plan the itinerary that would take him through at least seven European countries. His tour would culminate in what had already become for Fuller the highlight of his pilgrimage, Italy.[13] The diary contains a sketched map of the British Isles, the Netherlands, Western Europe, and the northern tip of Africa. With a colored pencil he traced a rough line of the path that he planned to follow during his year abroad.

Whatever Fuller's educational goals, the practical considerations that led him to take his first tour were far more important. Though he left no record of how he financed the trip, it seems that he had managed to save enough money to make the tour feasible, with or without aid from his father. But much more important for Fuller, he left an unmistakable record in his diaries of his contempt for the jobs he had held. Fuller felt it was high time to break the relentless logic of the "family tradition" that had placed him in line to succeed his father as a chief functionary in the Chicago business combine. He was well aware that his trip abroad would signal his independence in a way that his Philadelphia trip only vaguely suggested. No longer dependent upon his father for financial support, the twenty-two-year-old Fuller saw himself less as a son than as a bachelor with a life of his own. There was much that Fuller's parents approved of in their son's interests, but there were other issues, such as Henry's study habits, on which he and his father could never agree. Other matters, such as Fuller's homosexuality and his struggle with society, his parents would never know about. By the summer of 1879 he had already freed himself from his father's influence, though George Fuller was not aware of this. All that was left for Fuller was the symbolic flight to drive the point home.

II

On August 17, Fuller left Chicago aboard a train bound for New York City. Upon his arrival, he called his one-time close friend and former Allisonian, Frank Donaldson. After dining with Frank that evening and no doubt reminiscing over their academy days, Fuller bid his friend a final goodbye and boarded the *S.S. Sythia* bound for Liverpool. Frank would never appear again in any of Fuller's journals. Fuller no doubt realized at the time that he had little in common with his friend, who was now married and pursuing a career in business. Fuller's voyage abroad helped him to define more clearly than ever before his own values as a Chicago-bred, genteel man of means. His New England Anglo-Protestant heritage would pose no small problem for him as he confronted the social and religious customs of central and southern European Catholic culture. He was relieved to find himself lodged aboard the *Sythia* with an Englishman and a Canadian. "To think," Fuller wrote shortly after the liner headed for the high seas, "I might have been put with some of the Cubans or Mexicans."[14]

From the beginning of his voyage, Fuller began writing what would develop into a three-volume travel diary, entitled "A Year in Europe." Having read widely before his trip abroad, Fuller was prepared to write his own critique of European culture, or so he believed. While traveling, he would read Mark Twain's *The Innocents Abroad* and William Dean Howells's *Venetian Life*. For his own diary Fuller assumed a style more like Howells's sober approach to his subject than Twain's satirical attack upon European decadence. In one sense he was still the passionate pilgrim worshiping at the shrine of western culture. But he would not idealize his European experiences in "A Year in Europe." That had to wait for the proper distance and a more appropriate form. In addition to his almost daily entries in his diary, he maintained a regular correspondence with Louise. He often developed impressions of his travels more thoroughly in his letters than in his diary. With his letters home, his diary, and his three lengthy articles for the *Chicago Tribune,* signed "H. F.," Fuller would write more during his year abroad than he had at any previous time.[15]

After his arrival in Liverpool, he set out on a tour of several small English towns, including Oxford and Stratford-on-Avon, where he did the obligatory "Shakespeare localities." On September 7 he arrived in London. Like Oxford, London did not live up to his expectations. He had little to say about the city in "A Year in Europe." He found it far too commercial in spirit and felt that he would have to return to the country and small villages to find the England he preferred.

He arrived in Paris during the first week of October and was as disappointed as he had been in England. Ever since his arrival in London, he had noticed the contrast between the photographs and sketches of the monuments he had studied before his trip and their actual appearance. He complained in a letter to Louise that in Augustus Hare's *Walks in London* "a lot of scraggly carelessness produces a picturesqueness and ideality quite surprising."[16] In fact, Fuller continued, "When I compared some of his sketches in his 'Walks in London,' with the actual realities, I had to rub my eyes in astonishment." Likewise, while in Paris, Fuller complained to Louise that he carried with him a sketch of Notre Dame that was "so highly poeticized that even its own mother wouldn't have known it." For the untraveled Fuller, such picturesque renderings of the Old World served only to raise "expectations" that were never realized. "Let me earnestly caution you," he continued, "to read every book of travel 'with calm judicial frame of mind,' to take photographs with a grain of salt, to view sketches with invariable suspicion, and to take every water-color drawing as an up and down lie."

For the first time in his life Fuller was forced to deal with that conflict which would remain at the very center of his own concerns as a writer and critic. "Tell me as an artist," he asked Louise, "is the mission of art to glorify common things?" In partial answer to his own question he admitted, "I am becoming more and more convinced that the enjoyment is in the anticipation or in the retrospection, seldom in the actual seeing itself." While in Paris he visited with Bishop and Mrs. Cheney from Chicago, and he complained to Louise that in their discussion of Westminster Abbey he enjoyed the monument far more than he had while studying it firsthand in London.[17] The discussion nearly made him "want to take the first train north." The irony of Fuller's complaint was that if this had been another time, the late 1880s for example, he would have been far more willing to concede that Europe is best suited for the imagination, regardless of whether or not the subjects have even been visited. Without realizing it at the time, he was already beginning to define for himself the very role that Europe, and especially Italy, would play in his travel romances, beginning with *The Chevalier of Pensieri-Vani*.

Yet he was not totally immune to those picturesque versions of the Old World in his travel books. It would be far from the truth to imply that at twenty-two Fuller had made up his mind on the subject. Italy was the focus of his pilgrimage, and he went on in the same letter to Louise to develop his own picturesque view of what he expected to find across the Alps: "The place would be some romantic balcony overlooking the Grand Canal in Venice; the time, a summer moonlit night; from the distance there would be wafted to us the gentle strains of 'Farewell, My Own,' in which the sweet voice of the gondolier and the dulcet strums of the . . . lute would be harmoniously mingled. . . . That would indeed be 'ethereal.'" Fuller was aware of the contradiction in his letter. For him, as for so many English and American writers in the nineteenth century, Italy was appropriately observed only under the soft glow of a full summer moon. But he would soon find that for his own Anglo

Saxon, Protestant American values Italy would need considerably more at times than the cosmetic touch of a summer moon.

Upon his arrival at Fontainebleau, Fuller was excited over the start of his first tour through Italy. Yet he was confused over which image of Europe to accept, the artist's conception or his own observations. On November 6 Fuller wrote in his journal, "Oh this question that troubles me so much: What, after all, is civilization?" With his first close study of Italian culture he expected to answer his question definitively.

For Boston Brahmin society and for scores of American artists living in Rome and Florence at the time, Italy was the source of high culture. It stood in stark contrast to American provincialism and to the overriding materialism of post–Civil War industrialism in America. Fuller's goal was the same as that of his compatriots in the East and abroad. His tour, he believed, would put him in touch once and for all with the experiences he felt a man of his class and sensibilities deserved. Yet much of what he found in Italian life would pose more than a few problems for him and his genteel Protestant-American values. The real, too often, would riot in the face of the ideal.

Though Fuller had carefully educated himself to appreciate the monuments that represented Italy's rich past, he was not prepared to deal with contemporary Italian society. Nearly all American travelers in the nineteenth century carried with them stereotypes of European manners and morals.[18] While Fuller idealized Italian high culture of the past, he condemned what he perceived to be the decadence and disorder of contemporary Italy.

After stops in Dijon and Lyons, Fuller entered Italy through Turin, before traveling to Genoa. In the North he did not find the Italy he had imagined. He found Genoa immaculate and well deserving of its title as the "city of palaces." He took special note of the abundance of sculpted nymphs and satyrs "in all the various degrees of un-dressiness." But a surprised Fuller complained, "Must I confess that I am a little disappointed in Italy? – it is so much cleaner and honest than I had expected." He wrote that in all of his travels throughout England and France his hotel in Genoa was "one of the neatest places [he had] struck yet."

Fuller's expectations of the Italian character were no less frustrated. He began by "assuming as a matter of course that all Italians were, and of necessity must be, thieves and rascals." While in Genoa, Fuller recounts a story of how he expected to be cheated by an Italian boatman and how he expected to "hurl torrents of bad Italian at him" over the price of his services. Instead, the humbled Fuller writes that they came to a quick agreement. But Fuller's well-schooled image of Italy would not be overthrown by the exemplary behavior of one Italian boatman and the cleanliness of one Italian city. He knew that he would yet find the less immaculate Italy and the swarthy Italian of romance fiction. Before heading south Fuller wrote, "But I mustn't judge Italy altogether from Genoa; wait till I get to Naples."

He traveled south to Pisa, and at the end of November he reached Florence, where in the statuary that adorns the streets he was offended by the "evil of such pernicious nudity that meets the eye at every turn." But overall, his visit to the city was made comfortable by the Americans he met and the evening he spent at a friend's apartment. During his first two days, he visited the Monastery of Saint Mark and wrote a detailed description of it to Louise, accompanied by meticulous sketches of the monastery, a segment of the city, and one of Florence's antique bridges over the Arno.[19] The following week he traveled on to Siena and to Orvieto, which would play an important role in *The Chevalier*.

Rome was the focus of his journey. After having some difficulty finding a room, Fuller purchased a copy of Hare's *Walks in Rome* to complement his Baedeker. Together, he believed, they made "a very strong team."[20] Fuller arranged to take Italian and French lessons from a private tutor, and found that he could practice his Italian with the family in whose home he had found lodging. He spent the following day resting and reading at the Pincio overlooking the city.[21] On his third day, Fuller ranged "over the whole city—ancient, medieval, and modern." He covered the Corso, the Capitoline Hill, the Forum, the Colosseum, the Lateran Palace, Santa Maria Maggiore, the Pantheon, the Piazza Navona, the Pincio, Trastevere, Saint Peter's, Castello St. Angelo, Santa Maria del Popolo, and San Trinità dei Monti. As he phrased it, it was "an eventful day."

Though inspired by what he had seen, he found the seventeenth- and eighteenth-century baroque facades of the Corso overwrought and untidy. In spite of the influence of European architecture on the homes along Chicago's Prairie Avenue, the city's Gold Coast of the 1880s and 1890s, Fuller still demanded greater simplicity. "Italy has been telling architectural lies for three centuries or more," he complained, "so that even now when she don't [sic] achieve the false, she cloaks the true."[22]

The structures along the Corso were not actual buildings, in his view: "Almost every constructional feature in their fronts is so covered over and smoothed down by an omnipresence of plaster, that I seem to be looking at the masks of buildings, or the embalmed mummies of buildings, or at a set of dirty architectural drawings."

The Protestant in Fuller nearly always influenced his judgment. He was not at all sympathetic to Italian Catholicism and to the baroque center of Catholic worship: "The Papacy had made Rome a boneyard and a dung-hill." And after nearly six days in Rome and a thorough study of the basilica, Fuller concluded, "St. Peters is wholly pagan. Morally, St. Peters is a glorification of a dis-christianized papacy. As a building St. Peters is rather grandiose than grand; to call it a 'beautiful Christian temple of worship' is inadmissible, for it is neither beautiful nor Christian, to pronounce it a 'temple of Catholic faith' is rankly absurd." He was offended by icons and by the elaborate religious ritual. "It is only in a few of the great basilicas," Fuller wrote, "that the Protestant idea of the pomp and circumstance attending the rites of Rome can be at all realized. Few things are more slovenly and shabby than an ordinary Italian church festival. . . . It is only Northern Protestants whose bump of order is fully developed."

What disturbed Fuller, like so many American Protestants, was not only the "pagan" elements of Catholicism but also what he perceived to be the egregious disrespect and indifference with which the Italians treated sacred rites. While still in Genoa, Fuller complained, "From my present slight acquaintance with the country and its inhabitants, I should say that the average Italian comes to Mass for one of four purposes—to pray, to beg, to spit, or to blow his nose. It is quite thrilling to see an old fellow stand just outside the chancel-rail, and spit, spit, spit, right along steady on the marble pavement through the very adoration of the sacrament. And it is a trifle more thrilling to see the kneeling bishop stop short in his chanting, pull out a big red bandanna, and give forth a blast loud enough to raise the dead." In spite of his indignation, Fuller no doubt saw the humor in his own fastidiousness.

As his published travel romances would demonstrate, Fuller's anti-Catholicism influenced only a small part of his approach to Italian culture. For he was very much the passionate pilgrim, far more than "A Year in Europe" indicates. In December he wrote to Louise that Rome above all other cities he had visited was the most enjoyable. "If you have been disposed to envy me any part of my trip," he wrote, "envy me Rome."[23] Fuller's favorite spot in the entire city was the view from the Villa Medici on the Pincian Hill. To judge from his testy opinion of Saint Peters's, it would be impossible to guess why. From his perch in front of the villa he could see "that wonderful dome." For hours on end his antipathy toward baroque architecture was set aside. Ideality, not critical or scholarly analysis, ruled. His favorite time was "twilight," under the soft glow of a "half-moon." At other times he would return to the Pincio and search for an even more striking view from which to study the Basilica. He would "retire back two, or three or four hundred feet, and squat down on the walks and stand up on the marble seats and trespass on the grass, and group the dome with obelisk and fountains and clumps of foliage." All of these maneuvers Fuller executed, as he said, "after the manner of the most crazy enthusiast." Even his Protestant scorn for Catholic ritual was compromised in the face of his idealized view of Catholicism's central role in Italy's history. He celebrated Christmas by attending mass at Santa Maria Maggiore, and he admitted to Louise that he preferred "the great ecclesiastical display of the good old Papal days" above Rome's modern improvements.

With Rome still fresh in his imagination, Fuller had only one city left to visit before he turned north to begin the final leg of his journey. In Naples Fuller found that one side of Italian life that he had expected to see all along, but which had hitherto eluded him. More than in any other Italian city, in Naples Fuller became the innocent, vulnerable American traveler. He was appalled by the Neapolitans' treatment of him.

After little more than a week, Fuller concluded, "Well, the Neapolitans are intensely offensive and utterly despicable. . . . For there is much to be observed in Naples that I should expect to see, with but trifling changes and variations, in Smyrna or Alexandria: Physically the same slothful, slatternly filthy habits and startling disregard of the common decencies; mentally, the same greedy sharpness, nimble impertinence, unscrupulous cunning, and a total lack of honor and veracity; morally the same shameful rottenness and corruption with the same dark surroundings of *prostitute, mezzani,* and *bagasione* multitudinous." During his evening walks he was accosted by troups of *mezzani* (pimps) on the streets who attempted to distract him from his more cerebral concerns. Bootblacks and carriage drivers taunted him whenever he refused to purchase their services. Even the gamins in the streets mocked his French and Italian and mimicked his English. The Neapolitans made Fuller feel more like a *straniero* than he had felt anywhere else in Europe. Neapolitan street life dramatized more clearly for him than any other aspect of Italian society the wide difference between his American values and Old World culture. He felt little inclination to idealize Neapolitan life or the city's lower classes.

After a short visit to Pompeii, Fuller headed north to Venice and stopped briefly in many of the cities he had earlier visited. While in Venice, he read Howells's *Venetian Life*. After three unsuccessful weeks in Venice and some additional traveling in the Italian lake country, he headed toward Germany through Switzerland.[24] By now Howells's fiction had begun to interest him even more, and he read *Lady of Aroostook* on the train between Geneva and Lausanne. Switzerland he found dull, and Munich, "the capital of beer and art," as he described it, impressed him even less. He made brief stops at several other German cities before traveling to Paris, Belgium, and Holland. He reached Canterbury at the end of July and breathed a sigh of relief upon finding himself "once again among an English speaking people." After a tour of the cathedral, he returned to London and immediately embarked upon a cathedral tour that took him to Cambridge, Ely, Peterborough, Lincoln, York, and Durham. From Durham he traveled to Edinburgh, and from there to Liverpool, where on August 19 he caught the *S.S. City of Richmond* outward bound.

By August 29 Fuller was in New York, and by September 1 he was home in Chicago. Having been gone for slightly more than a year, Fuller returned from the most important and far-reaching experience of his young life. He must have rejoiced at finding himself at home in the comfort and security of the large Fuller house on Michigan Avenue. But he could never again allow his father's money or influence in Chicago to overshadow the independence he had won during his year abroad.

3

Boston: Vulgar Dollars

Upon returning from his year abroad in the summer of 1880, Fuller re-entered the life of his city as a young man of some distinction. Though Fuller's grandfather had died two months before his departure, there is no record of whether he directly received any part of the estate. Rather, it appears that the property in the estate fell under the management of George Fuller. Henry began to feel some of the weight that his family carried in Chicago, even with the patriarch now gone. As he says of Raymond Prince in *On the Stairs,* he returned from his first tour abroad to discover that he had "come back with money, position and a certain aureole of personal distinction." Though Fuller would have been loath to admit it, the history of Chicago's commercial growth was as much a part of his own personal family heritage as the distinction he preferred to claim for himself as a genteel, well-read young bachelor.

Now sporting a full, well-trimmed beard, the stylishly dressed young Fuller was the life of any party that gathered around a keyboard, whether piano or organ. When confronted with the southern European Catholic culture he had studied abroad, his consciousness of his own New England heritage had come to the fore; he now referred to himself as a "staunch Protestant," if not theologically, then at least temperamentally. While abroad he had been able to exercise an independence of thought that he had never quite experienced before. As a result, Fuller was no longer too reserved or timorous to make an oblique reference now and then to his own sexual preference. In a letter to Louise while he was still abroad, he had referred to the "gloriously handsome" Italian boys he observed on his tour.[1]

But the twenty-three-year-old Fuller had yet another problem to overcome. As a bachelor of some means and position in Chicago society, he was a prime target for Chicago's young women. Chief among them

Henry Blake Fuller as a young man

in Fuller's circle of friends was Louise Washburn, one of the most eligible of his companions. From time to time she would report in her letters the unsuccessful attempts made by certain of her admirers to win her affections. Yet she remained aloof and always discouraged her more amorous suitors. In a fatherly manner Fuller would chide her for mistreating them. He told her in jest – a prophecy that turned out to be all too true – that she was sure to become an "old maid" if she did not stop turning young men away from her doorstep.[2]

It appears that Fuller's advice to Louise was a thinly veiled warning that she should not discourage any of her suitors on his account. Less certain, however, is the connection between Louise's spinsterhood and her long relationship with Fuller. If she was quietly waiting Fuller out, it would be more than a decade before he would give her a more solid indication of his own sexual preference. Some time in the 1880s Louise apparently had begun to cultivate feelings for Fuller that went beyond the friendship that Fuller was striving to maintain in their relationship. Years later, Louise confessed to a relative that Henry Fuller remained a part of her past that she was never quite able to forget. Her friendship with young Fuller was only a half-fulfilled relationship that never developed to her satisfaction. If she was in love with Fuller, and it does appear likely, Fuller neither encouraged nor returned her feelings.[3]

Fortunately, by twenty-three Fuller had made up his mind to avoid the duplicity and charade that marriage would have meant for him. While abroad he wrote to Louise, "It makes me feel just awful to have everybody go and get married."[4] In one sense Fuller viewed the marriage of his friends as a "personal deprivation," an adumbration of the possible isolation that awaited him as an unmarried homosexual male in a monogamous, heterosexual society.[5] Between Louise and Fuller, the "marriage question" would remain alive for several more years. For Louise it appears that whenever enough distance separated them to merit a letter, the marriage issue was opened, and this in turn only gave Fuller occasion for more disclaimers. Fuller was seldom evasive: he would never marry.

The marriage question would gradually fade as an issue in Fuller's life. His aversion for the life of his city was far more problematic. Upon his return, he found the commercial spirit of the city as oppressive as ever.

Some time shortly after his return home, Fuller wrote a long, prosaic poem entitled "Pensieri Privati."[6] Written on the blank pages of one

Louise Washburn

of his diaries that he had abandoned several years before, "Pensieri Privati" was Fuller's personal manifesto against the materialism of, as he described Chicago, "this ganglion of trade." Though amateurish, "Pensieri Privati" was Fuller's most complete expression of both his opinion of his native town and of its commercialism.

> You think me then dissatisfied? and so
> I am, I am. Pray where should discontent
> Grow ranker than just here, 'mongst men intent
> on non-essentials, empty, earth-bound, low.

Most striking in his attack was Fuller's insight that the men and women who were caught up in the capitalist system were controlled, mind and body, by the forces and laws of the marketplace. "They make it," Fuller wrote, "and they are by it made." Fuller's insight as well as despair over the individual's loss of will within the modern economic system would form the major theme of all his realistic Chicago novels, from *The Cliff-Dwellers* in 1893 to *Not on the Screen* in 1929, the year of his death.

By the end of 1880, Fuller had delineated the major social and personal issues that would affect his life, from the materialism of his town to his own homosexuality. To understand these issues more thoroughly, the young Fuller would need more time and experience. Otherwise, by the end of 1880 he had all the advantages his class had to offer him: he was well traveled; he could read four foreign languages and was passably conversant in at least two; he played two and possibly three instruments; he was widely read; and he was economically secure. Although disconsolate over the city that life had allotted him, he had few doubts about his ability to avoid the lure of the less refined side of Chicago.

Fuller pursued his interest in the arts and never gave up hope that he would soon return to Europe. Where Fuller worked and when during the next decade is uncertain. He would never again keep a personal record of his thoughts and activities. If he returned to work at Home National Bank, it was not for long. However, Fuller did work during these years to cover living expenses. Whatever the windfall from his grandfather's estate, it was either not sufficient or not bequeathed in a manner that would allow Fuller to draw upon it.

During this time he worked at odd jobs. At some point in the early

1880s he worked for the widely known social gospeler, the Reverend Lyman Abbott, at Chicago's Christian Union, where Fuller prepared manuscripts "through the medium of shorthand." He also worked for a time filling library mail orders at Jansen, McClurg, and Company. There Fuller must have had his first glimpse of Chicago's literary community. Columnist Eugene Field, the Reverend Frank Gunsaulus, and other Chicago writers used to meet in what Field named the Saints and Sinners Corner, where the men would gather to talk literature and politics.[7]

In the summer of 1881 writing was still important enough to Fuller for him to make another successful attempt at publishing. In July and September he published two anonymous poems, "The Ballade of the Tourists" and "The Ballade of the Bank-Teller," in *Puck*. In the latter work Fuller satirized the impersonal economic forces that he saw shaping the lives of Chicagoans. "The Ballade of the Tourists," the first to appear, was a realistic corrective to the wrongheaded, idealized notions about travel that the average tourist, himself included, lugged abroad. Alluding to his own experiences in Naples, he complained that all too often the individual American abroad became the "scapegoat" for all Anglo-Saxon tourists.[8]

In spite of such complaints, in April 1883 Fuller planned another escape from Chicago, apparently having saved some of his earnings to pay for another tour of the Continent. This time, with less preparation than before, Fuller confessed to a friend that his trip was for the "fun" of it.[9]

Yet behind this frivolous mask, Fuller intended to use this trip to sever once and for all the family ties that conspired to relegate him to a life in commercial Chicago. He informed his parents that after his tour abroad, he planned to live in Boston. This time his separation would be complete; he would establish himself in faraway Boston to begin a wholly new life. As the center of American culture, Boston could provide him with the resources nearer to his tastes and habits.

In April 1883, Fuller sailed for London aboard the *S.S. Scythia*. He decided against keeping a record of his sightseeing. The diary that he did write is slim compared with the descriptions that crowd the pages of "A Year in Europe" (1879–1880). Drawing upon his experiences from his first tour, Fuller would avoid, where he could, what he felt were the modern encroachments upon European culture. With this in mind, on April 14 he embarked upon a four-day cathedral tour that took him through the English countryside to Winchester, Salisbury, and Wells. On the first evening of his return to London, he attended a play at the Savoy Theater.[10] Fuller still remained displeased with the city's pervasive "commercial spirit." Just before leaving on April 24, Fuller wrote "Nobody but an American, I suppose, would ever think of idealizing London; and only the most rampageously enthusiastic of Americans." With much of the novelty already worn thin by his first tour, Fuller went on in his diary to give the city, including its climate, a verbal sacking, while damning a selected handful of sights with minimal praise.

After six days in London, Fuller joined three friends from Chicago and traveled with them to Paris, where he spent two days visiting Notre Dame, the Louvre, the Musée Grevin, and the Eden Theater. From there Fuller beat a hurried path to Switzerland. He made short stops in Basel and Lucerne and traveled over the Saint Gotthard Range to Italy, stopping briefly in Milan, Genoa, and Pisa. Fuller explained why he gave these cities such a cursory review: "Genoa, Pisa, Milan—the St. Gotthard and the Lake of Lucerne—even Paris and London, are all merely incidental and introductory to one chief theme," Rome.

He did not record his impressions of his second visit to Rome, which he had covered thoroughly in "A Year in Europe." He wrote to Louise that he was hoping to revisit many of his favorite sights. He took side trips into the Roman campagna and to Ostia, where he spent the afternoon sightseeing with a young Russian.[11]

Fuller made stops at the Villa Mondragone and the Villa Falconieri. The first he mentioned in a letter to Louise "for the sake of 'Roderick Hudson,'" which Fuller had read in Pisa and Rome. The second he mentioned "for the sake of 'Signor Monaldini's Niece.'"[12] Referring to the luncheon scene on the terrace of the Villa Mondragone in chapter 12 of *Roderick Hudson*, Fuller wrote, "You may say whatever you please about Henry James, but (with all Europe at his command) he does know how to arrange his scenery." In the same letter Fuller went on to relate a discussion he had had in Siena earlier with Mrs. Frank Lee Benedict, wife of the American novelist: "We both agreed that James's nature and genius were on a higher plane from Howells'; that the 'Lady of the Aroostook' was the best and most delightful and altogether creditable thing (both to himself and to his country) that Mr. Howells had yet done."[13]

Fuller had recently begun to discover Howells's and James's fiction. On his second tour abroad, while riding the trains and relaxing at his destinations, he read more of their novels than at home. For the time being, Fuller would still emphasize what he saw as the picturesque settings of their transatlantic stories more than he would the emerging realistic elements of their fiction. But an unmistakable and profound change had occurred in Fuller's reading and literary tastes. While on his first tour abroad he had searched old London for Dickens memorabilia and the locales of his novels, he now explored other cities and the countryside for the sake of identifying settings from James's and Howells's novels.

Leaving the settings of James's fiction and Rome behind on May 31, Fuller traveled north, stopping at Siena, Pisa, Florence, and Venice. At the beginning of his week in Florence, Fuller joined a group of American tourists that numbered at its smallest, nine, and at its largest, thirteen. Never before had he enjoyed himself so much as he did in the company of these young people. They found themselves so compatible that at the end of the week Fuller and his companions traveled together to Venice.

For the first time Fuller realized why Venice was always held in such high regard by visitors. That "Byronic Venice" that had eluded him three years before became the only Venice Fuller saw during his second tour. To Louise he confessed that he could not help himself; he had to "indulge in a little idealizing." After all, he wrote, "'They all do it'—H[owell]s, J[ame]s and the rest; so why shouldn't I?" By the time he and his friends reached Venice, their number had shrunk conveniently to nine—five men and four women, all between twenty-five and thirty, except for one, a pleasant middle-aged gentleman, who went along, as Fuller put it, "to keep us straight." "All real Americans too," Fuller wrote, "and all bent upon having a real good, jolly, up and down American time. And we had it."[14]

After six days in Venice, Fuller traveled with his companions to Lucerne and Interlaken, and from there he traveled alone to Vevey. He visited the garden of Trois Couronnes, the hotel where, as he reported to Louise, "Miss Daisy Miller first made Mr. Frederick Winterbourne's acquaintance."[15] He reached Germany by the end of August, but he spent very little time sightseeing.

Beginning in Basel, Fuller's travels became more of a chore. With his friends gone, he became "riled and cross" at the slightest irritation. By the beginning of September he was forced to admit that he was "sick and tired of the whole business." He made a hurried retreat through Paris, stopping briefly to visit the American church and a few other sights before traveling to London and Liverpool. His last three weeks in Germany, France, and England were so unpleasant that he felt he had "had quite enough of Europe." He vowed that he would not return for at least another five years and would never again travel as a tourist.[16] But Fuller would honor his vow only in the breach. Over the next four decades he would make four more tours and would plan a fifth in the final months of his life.

II

Boarding the *S.S. Cephalonia* on September 16, Fuller began his journey to Boston, where he would live for the next nine months. For the first time in his adult life he was without a specific direction and totally free to follow his own interests, regardless of his parents' wishes. He described his condition to Louise as an "'I don't care'" state. But he also felt that since he had now won his total freedom, it was time to "'try'" something. "As long as I don't know just what particular the 'try' is going to take," he wrote in mid-ocean, "I think it rather better for several reasons, to make it out of Chi[cago] rather than in." The "several reasons" Fuller alluded to were obvious enough. Chicago, in spite of its upward movement, hardly represented the city with which a fledgling young artist or writer would wish to identify himself. In Boston Fuller expected to find a city that was far more dedicated to the arts.

While still aboard the *Cephalonia*, Fuller had a preview of what he had expected to find in Boston. He was impressed with the quality of passengers on his New England–bound liner, and he reported to Louise, "A hundred and fifty-nine of them are Bostonians in good standing, and the ship has a tone rather different from any other I have ever sailed in. There is less smoking, drinking, card-playing and 'pooling' than I ever saw before, and no gambling whatever." This was owing, Fuller went on, to the large number of "Rev.'s, Dr.'s and Prof.'s" on board ship who spent their time perusing Latin grammars and "profound works on history and political economy." Never before had Fuller found himself in the company of so many people with whom he felt he had so much in common. He wrote to Louise, "Our chief 'divertissement' – we have no amusements – is chess, – varied by diary-keeping (which seems compulsory) and by the sketching-out of essays and lectures. Everybody on board seems to have dabbled in foreign tongues. The talk at our table is largely of Italian, Spanish and German." He was as impressed with the eastern dialect he heard – "it's all 'cahn't' and 'shahn't'" – as he was with the Harvard men who lounged about the deck and the smoking rooms reading French novels to each other. "Boston," Fuller concluded, "of course, leads to literature and Boston literature leads at once to the 'Atlantic.'"[17]

In what specific way Fuller planned to apply himself when he arrived in Boston remained his own well-kept secret, which he did not divulge even to Louise. It was no secret, however, at least for Louise and his other friends, that he wished to settle in Boston to live without "help or favor" from anyone, especially his parents. While there, he expected to indulge his tastes and interests in a way he believed he never could in Chicago. He planned to have "a real 'intellectual'" time attending concerts, lectures, and readings, as well as becoming acquainted with what Fuller termed the "night people." At first he was evasive and noncommittal in his letters from Boston, even with Louise, but he was only attempting to avoid the pressure and expectations that would be raised if he made his intentions known. He was, after all, trying to escape from such pressures by moving to Boston. Only later would he explain to Louise that all along he had expected to make his way "into literature through shorthand."[18] He intended to begin his writing career in the shadow of what he believed to be the standard-bearer of American letters, Boston's *Atlantic Monthly,* edited at the time by William Dean Howells.

Upon arriving in Boston on September 23, Fuller found lodging in a boardinghouse that would be his home until the following June. After taking a general tour of the city, he continued the church tour that he had begun in Lucerne two months before. Every Sunday for six weeks Fuller chose a different Protestant church and attended the service.[19] But his walks around the city were not limited to the study of churches. Shortly after his arrival, Fuller made a special effort to learn the address of William Dean Howells on Louisburg Square, and he made a pilgrimage to the great man's house to draw a sketch of his residence. One afternoon Fuller loitered in the vicinity of the house waiting for Howells to return home just to catch a brief glimpse of the famous writer and editor. Recalling that day in Boston when he was still unknown and unpublished, Fuller wrote in 1903, "No. 4 Louisburg Square still sticks strongly in my memory. It was there that I first saw the distinguished occupant — a curbstone view. He came along the sidewalk, in the winter twilight, feeling for his latchkey, and favored the young pilgrim loitering there with a bleak and forbidding frown that made something of an impression."[20] Fuller could not have realized at the time that Howells was soon to become the single most important influence in his life.

While keeping up with current fiction, he came upon the debate in the *Atlantic* and elsewhere between Howells and his critics over literary realism. In the beginning Fuller was not impressed with Howells's defense of the novel and the need for a national literature independent of Old World forms and content. He was still too much of a devotee of romance fiction, even though his tastes had begun to shift perceptibly. In April Fuller wrote to Louise, "I'm quite taken with G. W. — he seems to be walking all around Howells."[21] But the soundness of Howells's argument would eventually begin to sway Fuller. In Boston Fuller began to reflect seriously upon all that he had been reading, from his childhood passion for Dickens to his more recent discovery of Howells's and James's fiction. After Fuller began following the periodical war over realism and Howells's defense of the new novel, Dickens's and James's fiction would begin to slip from their hitherto favored status. Nevertheless, over the years he would remain divided, as his own works reveal, in his allegiance between Howells and his enemies, between the novel and the romance.

Following his plan, shortly after his arrival he took a job "shorthanding" for the Boston office of the New York Christian Union. Even though his work demanded most of his time, he managed to visit regularly the periodical room at the Boston Public Library. Some time in late January or early February Fuller attended George Washington Cable's reading of a chapter from his as yet unpublished work, *Dr. Sevier*. Later he followed the installments of *Dr. Sevier* published in the *Century*. Added to his periodical reading were serializations of Francis Marion Crawford's *Roman Singer* in the *Atlantic* and Henry James's "Lady Barbarina" in the *Century*. Because of Crawford's Italian settings, Fuller preferred his romances over Cable's southern stories. But compared with both writers, James still impressed him more. After finishing the first installment of "Lady Barbarina," Fuller wrote to Louise, "There's no use in trying to anticipate Henry James."[22]

In addition to evenings and weekends spent haunting the periodical room at the public library, Fuller set out to do what he had all along expected to accomplish while in the East. The short prose works that Fuller published while in Boston show the influences of the American writers that he had been reading over the last several years. These short pieces, published between January and June 1884, including one poem in which he satirized marriage, are amateurish and immature and have little intrinsic value as works of art. However, all of them, including the poem, develop themes that would appear time and time again in his novels and stories in the years ahead.

The first story Fuller published appeared in the January *Life* with the imposing title, "A Transcontinental Episode, Or, Metamorphoses at Muggins' Misery: A Co-Operative Novel by Bret James and Henry Harte." It was a heavy-handed parody of both Bret Harte's sentimental western stories and Henry James's more refined transatlantic novels. Years later, after Fuller had published his first Chicago novel, he regretted that he had treated James so roughly and hoped that the story would remain forgotten.[23] Following his first story, Fuller published a short poem entitled "Some Day" in the March *Life*. Consistent with his attack upon romance themes in his prose pieces, Fuller's poem was a satire on the divorce-plagued status of contemporary marriage. His third piece, published in *Life* in April, was entitled "The Story of Naphtha: A Tale of Culture, Fashion and Duplicity, by Elizabeth Hodgson Phelps and Frances Stuart Burnett." Here Fuller satirized the sentimental tales of Elizabeth Stuart Phelps and Frances Hodgson Burnett. Fuller explained in a letter to Louise, "'Naphtha . . . is a poetical compromise between 'Avis' and 'Bertha,'" the heroines from Phelps's *The Story of Avis* and Burnett's *Through One Administration*.[24] In "The Long and the Short of It: A New England Idyl," which appeared in the June *Life*, Fuller merely aimed a more generalized satirical punch in the direction of the romance fiction of the day.

As Fuller's stories began to appear in *Life*, he became less reticent to speak about his writing. "Don't go to encouraging a career for me on the strength of those few things in 'Life,'" he wrote to Louise in April; "they were only designed to amuse me—and to help pay my bills."[25] In spite of his warning to Louise, he was hopeful, perhaps more than he should have been, that his writing would soon begin to pay his bills. He intended to free himself from the drudgery and distraction of other types of work. He revealed to Louise that for his first three pieces he published in *Life* he had earned, in Oscar Wilde's words, sixty "vulgar dollars," and he expected more from *Life* in the near future. He confessed, "Perhaps I shall have a career after all." While Fuller's optimism was premature, during his months in Boston he had produced more fiction than he had at any other time in his life. Admittedly, it was not much in volume or in quality, but the pieces he wrote and the payment he received for them gave him a sense of what was possible financially and literarily if he could only dedicate himself to writing fiction.

Unfortunately, these auspicious beginnings were accompanied by several disabling physical ailments that ultimately drove him back to Chicago. Within a month of his arrival, probably at the beginning of November, Fuller began having eye trouble. His affliction worsened over the nine months he was in the East. By the end of winter he was forced to retire early nearly every evening for more than a month. Fuller tried a number of eyewashes and lotions, and finally resorted to eyeglasses. To add to his discomfort, just before Christmas he was bedridden "with a remittent fever," together with what was apparently diagnosed as a blood disorder, contracted, so he believed, in a barber shop. Fuller was forced to resign his post with the Christian Union, sell his typewriter, and return to the crockery trade in Boston. His illnesses stood in the way of many of the activities he had planned for himself, and he was forced to conclude that his time in Boston was "the most doleful and wretched six months I ever had."[26]

With his ill health plaguing him and his debt at his boardinghouse growing faster than his ability to pay it, by June he was forced to return to Chicago and to the financial security of his parents. He had been gone for more than a year, yet his mother and father apparently held no animosity toward him. From Henry's standpoint they had always been too concerned over his health, especially his mother. Consequently, Fuller did not inform them of his illness and asked Louise not to tell them.

Arriving in Chicago, the twenty-seven-year-old Fuller moved into his parents' home on Michigan Avenue. As always, he looked to the family resort in Oconomowoc as his refuge. Fuller no doubt had more reservations about his return than he cared to admit to himself or to his friends.

Never again would he be free enough to consider a permanent move away from his hometown.

Fuller must have reasoned that if he could not make Boston the base from which he would launch his literary career, then Chicago would have to do. While dividing his summer between Oconomowoc and visits with Louise and other friends, Fuller began writing short fiction for the local press. In response to one contest for "a realistic story with a local flavor," Fuller wrote a short story entitled "Between the Millstones," which became the basis of his first Chicago novel. Although the manuscript was rejected and then lost by the editors, Fuller was not discouraged. He followed that piece with a light satirical story entitled "The Romance of a Middle-Aged Merchant and His Female Private Secretary," which won the *Chicago Tribune*'s ten-dollar prize for the story of the week. In the fall of 1884, while on a trip to Philadelphia with his father, who was seeking medical treatment, Fuller wrote another story, "Pasquale's Picture." After a rejection by the *Atlantic,* the story was finally accepted by the *Current.*[27] As Fuller explained in a letter to Louise, the story was based upon a gondolier he had met in Moreno on his previous tour abroad. None of the stories brought Fuller any closer to the career he was seeking. But the stories did have at least one element in common that would contribute to his success: a greater fidelity to experience than he had exhibited in any of his previous poems or stories.

In December 1884 George and Henry returned from Philadelphia. George's condition continued to deteriorate, and in 1885 he died. His city eulogized him with a brief obituary; the new generation of Chicagoans were informed, "His death is regarded as a personal bereavement by many of the makers of the city, among whom he was held in the highest esteem."[28]

If Fuller spoke of his father at all in later years, it was only as the breadwinner in the family. Rarely did Fuller discuss his family with anyone at any point in his life.[29] But while in Boston the year before, Fuller was moved in a letter to compare the influences of his newly adopted city with those he had left behind. "Well, I like [Boston] very much," he wrote. "About George Fuller I am not so sure."[30]

With the passing of his father, Fuller was relieved of one pressure, but as the only surviving male heir, he was forced to assume responsibility for the general maintenance of the estate and family property.[31] He would now be burdened with providing for the welfare of his mother, two sisters, and later his nieces. Fuller's fate was sealed: he would never again be free to move away. Oconomowoc, for the next decade at least, would remain his chief escape whenever he began to feel he had had enough of Chicago's crowded streets and air pollution. Fuller began to feel more than ever the city's limitations.

But less obvious at the time was his growing interest in contemporary literature, especially the war over literary realism. There is some irony in Fuller's attempted self-exile to Boston, where he went in search of culture and to escape commercial Chicago. When he arrived, among the very first people he encountered was William Dean Howells, who at the time was encouraging American writers to write honestly and directly about their own experience. With the rise of the power and prestige of the new middle class, literary America was developing new ways of depicting the lives of the new class of businessmen and workers. Residence abroad or in Boston would not have solved Fuller's problem. In fact, according to his own view, exile abroad may well have only amplified his dilemma as a writer. No matter where he chose to reside — New York, Paris, Rome, or Boston — he would have been forced to reconcile himself to Howells and to take a position in the controversy over literary realism.

By 1885 Fuller understood the nationalistic implications of Howells's point of view. Integral to Howells's support of literary realism was his conviction that the United States, as much as any European nation, deserved a national literature, one created from the specifics of the American experience and not from outmoded European forms such as the romance. In a sudden reversal of his opinion, betraying nearly all that he had previously written in his personal letters, in 1885 Fuller wrote an essay entitled "Howells or James?" In it Fuller unequivocally chose Howells's fiction over James's, and he sided with Howells in the war over literary realism.

The cutting edge in Fuller's unpublished paper was his disagreement with Howells over his essay "Henry James Jr.," published three years before in the *Century*.[32] Whereas Howells had argued that James was the new leader in American fiction, Fuller held that Howells, not James, was the only logical candidate for the leader of the new realism. Fuller attacked the same issue between the Old World and the New, between democratic and aristocratic society, that would soon preoccupy Howells in his essays in the "Editor's Study." Fuller's point was not that American democracy was superior to European culture or that European society was decadent and corrupt; rather, he argued that James could not be the leader of American fiction as long as he chose to remain abroad and deal with transatlantic themes. Fuller argued that James was far too divorced from American life to portray the American character as honestly or as realistically as Howells had in his novels.

In Fuller's eyes, James had abandoned the American experience and the middle-class social fabric for an aristocratic, Old-World setting. In the simplest terms, Fuller believed that "Howells [was] a realist, and James an idealist." He described James's concerns as "exclusive" and of a "circumscribed character," which ultimately led him away from the specifics of the American experience. "Mr. Howells," Fuller wrote, "in 'The Rise of Silas Lapham' will still farther extend the field of sympathetic realism which he first entered in the 'Modern Instance.' Mr. James, in the 'Princess Casamassima' . . . will bring to still a higher degree of perfection his own particular little garden of exotic culture which has already blossomed with 'Roderick Hudson' and the 'Portrait of a Lady.'" Noting that there was a new class making a strong bid for power in American cities, Fuller asked which writer is equipped to deal with the new American middle class — "he who deals with the normal earning of money at home, or he who prefers to deal with the exceptional and privileged spending of money abroad?" Overlooking the psychological dimension that James had brought to literary realism, Fuller chose Howells largely because he represented the new class more thoroughly in his novels.

Fuller would never again be so certain about his unequivocal choice of realism over idealism in the American novel. He admired James's fiction more than his essay indicated. As he once admitted to a friend, he enjoyed *The Portrait of a Lady* "'more than any novel [he] ever read.'" Yet he also regarded *The Rise of Silas Lapham* "'as the great representative novel of American manners.'"[33] Years later in a letter to Howells, Fuller wrote, "When I came back from my first trip abroad, in 1880, I turned a sudden corner and came upon you and Mr. James. You were leading Lydia Blood by the hand, and he was leading Isabel Archer.[34] These two 'ladies' united to 'form' me and to wean me away from 'Dombey and Son' and 'Bleak House,' which had sufficed me for years. Then followed the decisive grip of 'Silas Lapham.'"[35] But Fuller's opinion of Howells's brand of literary realism would always remain a complex issue. Fuller would never make a total commitment to realism, not even after the success of his first realistic Chicago novel. For Fuller the romance simply offered too many imaginative possibilities that delivered the reader, as well as the writer, from the commercial ugliness of American society and from the crass materialism that he saw dominating middle-class values.

The nationalistic theme aside, the realism debate would ultimately come down to an ill-defined question of aesthetics for Fuller. At no point in his career could he escape the nagging and difficult question of what was the most "artistic" form for prose fiction. In spite of his disapproval of James's self-exile, Fuller was more than slightly sympathetic to the reasons that led James to set his novels in Europe. Fuller realized that Europe was simply the most logical place for an American writer to turn when he needed resources that the rather sparse American social and cultural fabric did not contain. Adding to Fuller's dilemma was his weakness for that idealized view of Old World culture that he had defined for himself on his first tour abroad. Ultimately, as he would phrase it several years later, he did "not care to have the king show himself in his shirtsleeves."[36] If the first half of the 1880s brought Fuller a step closer to his career, it did so only by exposing his divided allegiance. Though he did not realize it at the time, he had already laid the groundwork for his literary career as both romancer and novelist.

4

The Chevalier of Vain Thoughts

In January 1886, when Fuller turned twenty-nine, he had not yet taken any definite steps toward establishing himself in a secure job. What the future held for him he could not say, nor did he appear to be too concerned about it. Though both "The Romance of a Middle-Aged Merchant" and "Pasquale's Picture" anticipated his later prose works, Fuller did not capitalize on his brief apprenticeship. While he realized that an occasional short story would never provide enough income to make a living, he had not yet abandoned the notion of becoming a writer. He continued to write, but he did not publish any of the stories he completed during this time.

To pay what few expenses he had, he worked in a small downtown business office in the old Tremont House on Lake Street. This portion of Lake Street, Fuller explained years later in his unpublished reminiscence, "My Early Books," "was given over to commerce in its heavier and more serious aspects."[1] Outside his window streetcars rumbled by and trucks overloaded with sheet iron and other hardware goods bumped over the rutted street.[2]

The only bright spot in this commercial scene was the occasional omnibus that would deposit "important theatrical people from the East" in front of the Tremont House. But aside from the distraction of an occasional star, his work was routine and generally boring. Fuller was apparently able to tolerate his work there—probably filling orders and invoices—only because it made few demands upon him. The office was seldom busy, and more often than not he worked alone at his large desk, situated next to the office manager's. It was here, in the midst of Chicago's financial and commercial district, that one day in 1886 Fuller began the opening lines of *The Chevalier of Pensieri-Vani,* his first travel romance. In "My Early Books," Fuller wrote, "I reached down into the waste-basket, fished up a discarded envelope, and began. . . . The Chevalier advanced toward me out of the supersaturated atmosphere; confident, but a stranger. I had yet to learn how far he would go, what he would do."

But Fuller was not yet committed to finishing his picturesque tale. He would work on it occasionally, nearly forgetting about it for a time, over the next several years. Otherwise, he fell into a routine of work and socializing. He saw Louise regularly, and together they visited their ailing friend Clara Ray, who remained bedridden. When he could afford the time, he took his usual brief trips to Oconomowoc. Since the publication of his stories and return from Europe, Fuller had become even more popular with his south Chicago acquaintances. They looked upon him as a cultured and worldly young man and praised his stories when they appeared in the local press and elsewhere. Among those who complimented Fuller on his stories were Bishop and Mrs. Cheney of Chicago's Reformed Episcopal Church.[3] With a little coaxing, Mrs. Cheney successfully enlisted the dapper young Fuller into the literary society that she had organized.

Since his return from Boston, Fuller had shifted his interests almost entirely from English and continental writers to American authors. His reading during this period took in the full range of American writers, from Helen Hunt Jackson, Sarah Orne Jewett, Francis Marion Crawford, George Washington Cable, and Mary N. Murfree to William Dean Howells and Henry James. His unfinished essay of 1886, "The American School of Fiction," indicates that Fuller had not solved to his satisfaction the issue of James's expatriation and the predominant influence of European writers and settings upon American fiction. Nor would "The American School of Fiction" prove to be his last word. Rather, written as it was on the heels of the "Howells or James?" essay, it exposed his divided allegiance between Europe and America. He contradicted much of what he had previously said in "Howells or James?"

Fuller opened his newest remarks with the suggestion, "It behooves us to pause for a moment in our complacent progress, and acknowledge our sense of obligation to the Old World" for the positive influence it has had upon American prose fiction, both the romance and the novel. Not once throughout the essay did Fuller raise the far more relevant and controversial issue of literary realism. With this very serious omission Fuller was able to link Howells's novels with Francis Marion Crawford's romances through the European element in both writers' fiction. Fuller now looked more favorably upon that ideality he had always identified with James's "garden of exotic culture."[4] America has "plenty in the way of footlights, it is true," Fuller wrote, "but not much in the way of background." He was gratified that James had not forsaken the Colosseum in Rome for "the Grand Central Depot of his native city" or for Niagara Falls. "I should have been very sorry," he wrote, "to lose . . . the portrait of a Lady for any such reason as that."[5] Clearly, Fuller was giving ground here where he had once taken a firm stand in "Howells or James?" against the "European motive" in American fiction.

About the same time that Fuller penned "The American School of Fiction," he became deeply involved with his musical society. This probably explains why he never finished the rough draft of his essay. Beginning in 1887, the group became more active, and its members competed to produce original songs and even operas. He reported to Louise that he had "as good as given up literature. In fact," Fuller added, "I have given the old girl (this is Literature personified) the g[ood] b[ye] in favor of music."[6] His involvement in the musical society was all too reminiscent of his high school days when he could not rest until he was first in his class. Fuller prided himself on his musical ability and knowledge, and he could not accept being outdone by any member of the group. During this period he wrote more than a half dozen short songs and, most impressive of all, the scores and libretti for two complete comic operas. For the time being he also apparently set aside the unfinished manuscript of *The Chevalier*.

In December he wrote to Louise, referring here to another member's just-completed opera, "Our block is cutting a pretty wide swath in the musical field. In fact," he went on, "Music's heavenly maid has been advertising for room with board at Mich. Avenue 24th St."[7] He was also making a veiled reference here to the one opera he had already completed and to the new one he had begun only three weeks before. "Pipistrello," his first operetta, was completed sometime in 1887. This was followed by "Mariquita," begun the first week in December 1887 and completed by the end of September 1888.[8] Both full-length comic operas were the products of Fuller's earlier enthusiasm for Gilbert and Sullivan, and both bear the distinct influence of their work. No less important, his talented young friends in the musical society provided him with the confidence and the audience to follow through with such a prodigious undertaking.

Fuller's claim that he had given up literature is understandable, considering the great amount of time that he must have put into composing his two operettas. For his model he made a thorough analysis of the structure of *H.M.S. Pinafore.* He counted the number of lines in the longer airs of the opera and then applied the formula to his own libretti.[9] He followed no specific Sullivan piece in composing the score, but the fragments of his notes indicate that he relied heavily upon the Englishman's style and form.[10] Otherwise, in both works he followed the conventional plot devices of disguise and counterdisguise that were the main stuff of romantic comic opera of the period. While the pieces appear dated by contemporary standards, the music is light and without pretense. It is well unified with the dialogue, lyrics, and general comic atmosphere of the operas. His rhymes are more often than not amusing and clever. Overall, considering Fuller's limited musical training, the two works are well crafted musically and ingeniously plotted, if derivative. "Pipistrello," set in seventeenth-century Italy just south of Rome, is perhaps the less impressive of the two. With "Mariquita," set in seventeenth-century Spain, Fuller seems to have taken more care, and he also had the experience and benefit of already having written one complete operetta.[11]

Fuller began a third operetta, and possibly a fourth, neither of which he finished.[12] Between 1887 and 1890, Fuller thought enough of his two operettas to make unsuccessful efforts to publish at least one of them and to have both produced by a professional company.

II

If Fuller was disappointed that his operettas were never produced, he hardly had time to brood over it. He devoted many hours a week in 1887 to musical composition, but not wholly at the expense of his literary interests. It appears that some time shortly before or after the completion of his last operetta Fuller finished the romance he had begun in his Lake Street business office.

Apparently, he had worked infrequently and without much dedication on the romance over the previous two to three years. Not until he had nearly completed the last chapter did he consider the possibility of publishing the slim volume. Still, he remained unsure which activity, his music or his fiction, would in the long run provide him with the career he imagined for himself in Chicago. When he finally completed his romance in the winter of 1888–89, he sent the manuscript to several New York, Boston, and Philadelphia publishing houses. One well-established New York firm was interested enough to quote Fuller publication costs, but finally rejected his offer to publish it at his expense.[13] Disappointed, Fuller relegated the manuscript to the bottom of a trunk for approximately another year while he returned to his music.

In January or February 1890, Fuller made a second effort to have his romance published at his own expense. He sent his manuscript to J. G. Cupples of Boston, who agreed to publish the book on Fuller's terms and under the pseudonym Stanton Page. Cupples's acceptance of *The Chevalier of Pensieri-Vani* effectively overshadowed any future plans Fuller may have had for his musical compositions. Enthusiastic over the appearance of his first published volume, he dedicated his summer and early fall at Oconomowoc to reading the proofs. But when the volume did appear in November, to Fuller's great disappointment the book was "a rather imperfect volume." Because of his inexperience with preparing a manuscript for publication and proofreading, the first edition was filled with many misprints.[14]

In spite of the textual errors that marred the first edition, *The Chevalier* won Fuller immediate fame in Boston and New York, as well as Chicago. Somehow, Charles Eliot Norton received a copy of the romance, possibly upon Fuller's initiative, and in December 1890 the Harvard professor and well-known Italianist wrote a quick reply. "Every lover of Italy should like your book," Norton wrote, "for you have won from her her charm for your pages."[15] He went on in his letter to offer his help to Fuller in preparing his text for a second edition. He felt that the romance was "worth more trouble" than Fuller had taken with it. Still somewhat unsure of his accomplishment, Fuller misunderstood Norton's criticism and wrote a lengthy, self-effacing reply, apologizing for some of the more "affected" and far "too involved" passages in the romance.[16] But this posture would be very short-lived. Norton wrote to Fuller the day after Christmas that he had misunderstood his criticism. As a token of his good faith, Norton enclosed a short note he had received that same day from James Russell Lowell, to whom he had mailed a copy of *The Chevalier* as a Christmas gift. In Lowell's words, "It tastes of genius."[17] Such unqualified praise from both Norton and Lowell was all that Fuller needed to hear. He had succeeded beyond his wildest expectations.

Fuller's exchange with Norton, all of it private and preceding the newspaper reviews of the romance, marked the auspicious beginnings of Fuller's literary reception in both the East and the Midwest. His disappointment over the rejection of his operettas and the initial rejections of *The Chevalier* evaporated in the face of the book's acceptance, even if he was financing its publication. Encouraged by the response from Boston and Cambridge, Fuller apparently informed his publisher of Lowell's glowing remarks, and Cupples solicited their use to promote the book.[18] Fuller followed Cupples's request with a letter to Lowell asking for his support, while making it very clear he had no desire "to coin [his] words of praise into dollars, present or prospective." In a bold and forthright letter to one of America's most distinguished writers and scholars, the unknown Fuller explained, "I only want to secure such recognition from the best people as I have come to believe myself entitled to. And such recognition, in these clamorous days, is slow in coming, unless brought on by a word from some influential quarter."[19] There was no reticence here. Fuller wanted his work to be promoted, and he was not too reserved to solicit support on his own behalf—a pattern he would follow with the publication of nearly all of his succeeding works.

Fuller did not have to wait long for more widespread recognition. Coincidentally, on February 12, the day Fuller had written to Lowell seeking his support, the *Boston Evening Transcript* published a review of *The Chevalier* in which it revealed Norton's enthusiastic endorsement of the romance and the special delight he took in Fuller's protagonist, the Cavaliere. "This delightful Florentine Cavaliere is introduced," the anonymous reviewer reported, "by Charles Eliot Norton. . . . It has been said that Professor Norton introduced this delightful Italian to his friends; they, of course, to other friends, and so he goes from house to house with his wit and his charm and his elegance." The reviewer noted that the romance was having a "reception a true gentleman and charming dilettante should have in Boston high circles." Pointing to Fuller's year in Boston and to his New England roots, the reviewer went on to claim Fuller for the East. But a condescending tone was unmistakable, especially when the reviewer described Chicago as that "proud commercial city of the West."[20] He seemed to imply that the rude commercial boom town on the fringe of American culture could not have produced a book of such grace and refinement.

Boston's condescending remarks started a journalism war that for a short time caused the reviewers of *The Chevalier* to lose sight of the romance in their reviews. The Boston *Saturday Evening Gazette* joined the *Transcript* and questioned Chicago's ability to appreciate such a refined work. Louisville sounded a similar note in the *Courier-Journal*. Not to be outdone by Boston, New York was quick to point out that it too had high praise for *The Chevalier*. In reply, Chicago made a hasty but futile response in the local press.[21] Even if his native city had taken a lambasting from the standard-bearers of American culture in the East, Fuller must have been gratified to find himself so quickly enlisted into the ranks of eastern Brahmin society.

Having pummeled each other sufficiently, reviewers finally began to focus upon the merits of Fuller's romance. However self-righteous or avenged the factions may have felt themselves to be after the dust settled, Fuller and his publishers were the only real winners. In the wake of the publicity generated by the partisan exchange, J. G. Cupples issued a second and third edition of *The Chevalier*. By November 1891, Fuller made arrangements with the Century Company to bring out a revised fourth edition, with an additional chapter. Out of gratitude for Norton's initial support, Fuller offered to dedicate the latest edition to him.[22] With the fourth edition carrying a dedication to Norton, Fuller took extra care to correct the textual errors that marred the first edition.

Though not justified in his belief, Fuller was satisfied that in *The Chevalier* he had evaded all the conventional categories of prose fiction, and his reviewers only seemed to reinforce that opinion. While his critics found the work charming and delightful, they often admitted that it defied classification as a travel book, romance, or novel. One reviewer wrote, "it is certainly not a novel, and yet it has characters and incidents. It is not an essay on painting, music and bric-a-brac in Italy, and yet that is what its pages are full of. It is not a simple tour through the 'back woods' of Italy, and yet that is the name which comes nearest of all to the description of the thing."[23]

The work, however, was far from the new thing that Fuller and his supporters believed it was. At best, *The Chevalier* is broadly eclectic, drawing upon many long-established conventional forms. In bringing them together, Fuller did not contribute anything new to the form of prose fiction. The popularity of *The Chevalier* at the time only underscores the idea that Fuller merely charmed his nineteenth-century readers with many familiar elements that they had long admired and had expected to find in fiction. It should be added that William Dean Howells, who in 1890 was still writing his column for *Harper's Monthly,* never joined the chorus of supporters that promoted *The Chevalier* in the eastern and western press. That Norton and Lowell were the book's chief supporters from America's literary Pantheon and that Howells was conspicuously absent from among the reviewers suggests the nature of the romance's appeal at the time.

The characters in *The Chevalier* are universal types who in most cases fail to achieve more than the status of caricature. Although Fuller made every effort to draft a plot that would allow him to eschew the stock figures of the sentimental romance—the innocent, the femme fatale, the chivalric knight-errant—his characters follow the same general formulas. Actually, they conform to the theory that Fuller had developed in "The American School of Fiction," completed just about the time he was beginning to write his first romance. He explained that in the international novel of the future characters would become generalized types representing certain values. Following his own theory, Fuller created a cross-section of international characters, each representing the general, stereotypic temperaments of their respective countries.

The Cavaliere is Fuller's idealized conception of the Italian temperament, learned and sophisticated, yet dynamic and imaginative. As for the Italians he encountered in Naples, they have no place in Fuller's idealized romance, at least not in the same form he characterized them in "A Year in Europe." The Cavaliere is joined by many other idealized types, from the English aristocrat, the duke of Avon and Severn, and the German margravine of Schwahlbach-Schreckenstein, to the French aristocrat, Seigneur Hors-Concours, who tends a "small patrimony in the Alps of Savoy" and calls "himself a Frenchman or an Italian as the exigencies of the case require." This group of distinguished Old-World types is joined by "the venerable Gregorianius," Fuller's archetypal German scholar. His character is based on the famous German nineteenth-century historian, Ferdinand Gregorovius, author of *History of the City of Rome in the Middle Ages.*[24] Completing Fuller's collection of Old-World types is the Prorege, the beneficent monarch of the fictitious isle of Arcopia, Fuller's utopian state. In contrast to such sophistication and title among Fuller's select group of Europeans is the archetypal American midwesterner, George Occident, Fuller's representative of the unsophisticated, growing middle class in the United States.

Occident is a type who would appear time and again in Fuller's fiction. At one point he debates the Prorege over the virtues of American democracy, a debate Occident loses to his eloquent opponent. But Fuller's skeptical view was no shrill protest against democracy and the middle class. Central to the rise of democracy and the power and influence of that great middle stratum of society, or so Fuller believed, was the growth of industrial capitalism. Fuller looked with the same distrustful eye as Henry Adams did in the *Education* upon the growth and development of this force in Western culture. The Prorege's utopian monarchy is hardly Fuller's total answer to the complex problems posed by industrialism. But Fuller understood as well as any of his contemporaries and successors the effects of the machine age upon that great middle class. It would be wrong to say that he was totally without sympathy for those who, like his own father, were cogs in the industrial system. It had become clear to Fuller that men and women had become enslaved to the machine and that all too often they were expected to perform like one. Even the rich man, the Prorege says, becomes "a slave to his chronometer."

Of all the characters in the story, Gregorianius provided Fuller with one of the most important themes in his otherwise shallow plot. Whatever the shortcomings of American society, Fuller would always, throughout his writing career, deem it fatal for any of his American characters to escape to Europe. The answer to their European dilemma would always be clear: his characters would either return to the States or remain abroad and suffer the consequences of alienation from their homeland. In "Howells or James?" Fuller attacked James's self-exile as a reckless denial of all that was vital, or at least potentially vital, in his heritage.

In *The Chevalier* Fuller dramatizes this same point with the death of the venerable Gregorianius. The episode is among the most significant parts of the romance. In his single-minded dedication to his scholarship, Gregorianius is "living through other lives, and making but a thin blood by dieting on the unnutritious husks of a dead-and-gone past." Lost in the shadowy byways of ancient history, his spirit has been sapped by his own parasitic clinging to the unknowable and far away.

In the end, the Cavaliere can only make him comfortable in a remote chamber where he dies. Alienated from his own German ancestry and languishing in the obscurity of the past, he is little more than an "abstract alien." In various ways Fuller would return again and again in his fiction to the theme and lesson in the German scholar's death.

If the European risks becoming an alien even on his own soil, Fuller understood first-hand that the risks were even greater for the Anglo-American abroad. In the end of the romance, Occident decides to return home with his new bride, the American-born Signorina. They are both natives of Shelby County, U.S.A., and they believe they can be happier there among "old scenes and old friends."

Occident is the first of that group of Fuller's American characters who would always make the wise decision, in Fuller's judgment, to return to their homeland. Gregorianius, on the other hand, is the first of a long line of characters who make the foolish decision to separate themselves from their own heritage. There is in Occident's return and Gregorianius's death that conventional American suspicion of what the burden of antiquity meant to the youthful American. While residing in Rome, Hilda in Hawthorne's *The Marble Faun* turns from her original art work to become a mere copyist. Similarly, in James's *Daisy Miller,* Winterbourne is trapped between Geneva and New York; his instincts have been blunted by his loitering in Old World society for too long. It is Winterbourne's fate that Occident successfully eludes in his decision to return home.

Fuller would always have an inflated opinion of *The Chevalier*'s place among his works. But that stemmed more from his own sentimental view of his beginnings as a writer than the quality of the romance. His characters are mere stereotypes of the ethnic temperaments they were designed to typify. And like many of the romance writers of the period, Fuller attempted to yoke together art and morality. "The line between art and morals," Fuller tells his reader early in *The Chevalier,* "as the most advanced of us know, cannot be too rigorously maintained." That line is too often violated in favor of the didactic.

However, by firing off at so many targets—industrial capitalism, democracy, materialism, the middle class, the American abroad—Fuller did lay out many of the themes that would preoccupy his writing and thinking for the next forty years. *The Chevalier* was less a convincing dramatization of the many complex and legitimate issues raised than it was an incubation or testing of them for more auspicious times to come. The subject of literary realism, the most significant theme that had preoccupied his mind in the months before he wrote *The Chevalier,* was not treated. However, Fuller had not forgotten about it. Realism would play a central role in his next romance, before he would write two of the hardest-hitting novels Chicago had ever produced.

III

The months following the appearance of *The Chevalier* were busy and exciting for Fuller. Some time after the romance was published, Fuller, his mother, and two sisters moved from Michigan Avenue to 3343 South Park Avenue, where Fuller took a third-story bedroom.[25] Even further removed from the usual household distractions and family visitors, he could continue his reading and writing without interruption. In the months that followed the publication of his romance, Fuller collected more than forty reviews of *The Chevalier* from around the country, and he read them all carefully. To his friends he would often appear uninterested in his reviews, but privately he was never indifferent to what his critics had to say. As he wrote to Norton, whom Fuller now considered among his closest friends, "The question of royalties is not the first question with me. I got most of my satisfaction from the comments on my work which reached me—partly from the better class of press notices."[26]

Equally important to Fuller as press notices from the East was his recognition by literary Chicago's growing elite group of poets, novelists, and journalists. In December 1891 satirist Eugene Field, then writing his column "Sharps and Flats" for the *Chicago Daily News,* invited Fuller to a "very literary luncheon" at the Union League Club in Chicago.[27] Field admitted that he "did not know what a literary luncheon" was, but assured Fuller that there would be "no snobbery" displayed by those invited.[28] The group included Franklin Head, Harriet Monroe, the well-known minister Frank Gunsaulus, and William F. Poole, whom Fuller had written to a few years before asking for a job at the Newberry Library. Head and Monroe would remain among Fuller's closest friends throughout his life. Together, with several other Chicago artists and writers, they would establish the Little Room in 1893.[29] Because of his prominence in Chicago, the Reverend Gunsaulus would play a central role in one of Fuller's Chicago stories written at the turn of the century.

Besides Fuller's popularity in Chicago, he had also won something of a more personal victory, one that would remain private and less obvious to his family and close friends. He had now in his early thirties found a place in society and a form of social intercourse that was suited to his own preferences. Interestingly, the kind of luncheon that Field had invited Fuller to was like the type of social engagement he had outlined in his letters on the marriage question published fifteen years earlier in the *Tribune*: males and females socializing more as intellectual equals than as sexual opposites seeking partners. His ascent as an important Chicago writer gave him a new status and threw him into another group of people altogether. With this "better class" of Chicagoans, as Fuller would have described them, the evenings and afternoons that he enjoyed with his friends could be spent on more cerebral concerns.

He was eager to exploit the popularity he had won. Even before the Century Company had published the new edition of *The Chevalier,* Fuller began in the summer of 1891 what he termed his "companion to *The Chevalier*."[30] By the first week in August he had completed the final pages of his latest romance, entitled *The Chatelaine of La Trinité,* and had already been approached by at least one major New York monthly to serialize it. He explained years later that it "was meant to do for the Alps — French, German, Swiss and Italian — what its predecessor had done for Italy itself."[31] Fuller wrote to Minna Smith, literary editor for the *Boston Transcript,* to tell her that he hoped he had done himself "more complete justice" with his new romance than he had in *The Chevalier.*[32]

In another effort to promote his new work, Fuller prematurely offered to dedicate *The Chatelaine* to Charles Eliot Norton, before it was decided that Century's fourth edition of *The Chevalier* would carry Fuller's inscription to him.[33] Curiously, even though Norton lent his unqualified support to *The Chevalier,* he was more cautious with Fuller's second romance. He had not read *The Chatelaine,* and he was not at all certain that he wished his name to be associated with it. To reassure Norton, Fuller informed him that R. W. Gilder, editor of *Century Magazine,* and Horace Scudder, editor of *Atlantic Monthly,* had given his manuscript a favorable appraisal. Fuller did not want Norton to think that he was "simply a man of one book." In the process of attempting to prove otherwise to Norton, as well as to his other readers, Fuller had given his friend the impression that he was moving too quickly for his own good. Norton cautioned him "about the embracing of a completely – and merely – literary career." But Fuller hardly considered his friend's advice at all; as a young man in Boston, he had dreamed of a "completely literary career." Now that he had it within his grasp, he was not going to allow the opportunity to slip by him. Hereafter, Fuller would write only for publication and profit. He vowed that he would no longer waste his time and talents in the dreary basement of commercial Chicago. His main desire was to make work outside his writing unnecessary. With his mind set firmly on that objective, he took the *Century*'s offer to serialize his new romance beginning in the following June 1892.

With the royalties from *The Chevalier* and two publication contracts for his second romance, Fuller hastily planned a third European trip, focusing upon Spain. Even before he had any idea of how *The Chatelaine* would be received by his critics, he planned to use his tour of Spain to gather material for yet a third European romance. That fall he began a study of Spanish and made a cursory review of Spain's leading contemporary writers.[34] He planned to return to Chicago in June, the month *The Chatelaine* was scheduled to begin its first installment in the *Century*.

On December 31, Fuller headed north through Canada, then east to New York on the first leg of his trip. While in New York he visited his publisher, the Century Company, and worked on the final drafts of *The Chatelaine* before its serialization in the June *Century Magazine*. On January 5, after three days of work in New York, Fuller sailed for Southampton, England. He carried with him commissions for two articles, one from the *Century* and the other from Chicago's prestigious *Contributor's Magazine*. Both articles would appear the year following his return home and would be little more than descriptive travel sketches.[35] This time around, Fuller made another effort to maintain a journal, with the intent of drawing upon it for his articles and his proposed new romance. But he apparently had little enthusiasm for the project. He recorded little more than the names of towns, accompanied by short descriptive passages.

As his sparse journal entries imply, Fuller's third European trip was not a great success. London and Paris he had visited before, and the time he spent in the two capitals on this tour was uneventful. He traveled to southern France and spent a month in Nice before moving on to Rome, still his favorite European city. There he spent another lei-surely month visiting his old haunts and taking side trips to Sorrento, Capri, and Amalfi. Otherwise, Fuller had committed himself to a thor-ough tour of Spain. Beginning on April 10 from Gibraltar, Fuller spent six weeks traveling through more than twenty Spanish towns. He never stopped for more than six days and often not more than one in each of the towns he visited. Granada, Madrid, Segovia, and Barcelona re-ceived the closest scrutiny. In Seville Fuller attended a bullfight in which six bulls were killed, but the genteel Fuller saw no romance in the after-noon ritual. "I had no fun," he reported home to Louise, "but knew when to turn away; so I was not quite so much disgusted as bored, es-pecially at the second one."[36]

Upon his return to the United States in late June, Fuller headed for Boston to complete his business with G. J. Cupples, who had published the first edition of *The Chevalier*. Boston still held "a great glamour" for Fuller.[37] He was in Boston for little more than a day and made a short trip to Cambridge, where he attempted but failed to find Norton at his home, Shady Hill.[38] On the afternoon of the twenty-ninth, Fuller ar-rived in Chicago, nearly six months to the day after he had left for Europe.

Shortly after his return and while *The Chatelaine* was still being se-rialized in the *Century* (May–October 1892), Fuller began to draft the outline for his Spanish romance. Complicating his plans was the time Fuller had yet to devote to reading the proofs for *The Chatelaine,* sched-uled to appear in book form in October. He also accepted a commission to write a series of articles to be published in the *Morning News Record* in September on the Columbian Exposition, which would open in May 1893. For his research Fuller visited the uncompleted fairgrounds sev-eral times. After finishing the articles, he then moved to the family re-sort in Oconomowoc, where he hoped to work on his new romance for the remainder of the summer and fall. It was not long before Fuller dis-covered that he was not nearly as interested in Spanish culture as he thought he would be. He even feared that the proposed Spanish romance might somehow compromise his first two works in the eyes of his read-ers.[39] In spite of his misgivings, by the end of October and the last in-stallment of *The Chatelaine* in the *Century,* Fuller had managed to com-plete the first chapter and had written a general outline of the rest.[40]

But Fuller's hard work and plans for his new romance were to no avail. When the Century Company published *The Chatelaine* at the end of October, Fuller learned first-hand about the capriciousness that can attend a professional writer's career. His critics quickly confirmed the misgivings he had had about his newest romance.

Never again would Fuller have the unanimity of opinion among his readers that *The Chevalier* had generated. In the East the *Boston Transcript* and the *Critic* were generally positive in their reviews of *The Chatelaine,* but they were far more restrained in their praise than in their reviews of Fuller's first romance.[41] The most acerbic of all came from the *Harvard Monthly,* the one place where Fuller no doubt had hoped for a more positive appraisal. Perhaps the cruelest blow of all was the accusation that Fuller wrote his latest romance only because his other was successful.[42] Fuller was cut to the quick by the suggestion that he had succumbed to his popular success and had attempted to capitalize upon it with a second, hastily written product. This attack he would not easily forget.

At home, the *Chicago Tribune* review was enthusiastic.[43] But Chicago's prestigious *Dial* could not bring itself to give *The Chatelaine* a positive reception. For the *Dial,* the romance had "little charm" and "appeal[ed] to artificial tastes," with characters that were "little more than personified abstractions."[44] Fuller was so shaken that he immediately shelved all plans to finish his Spanish romance.

Fuller wrote to Norton that he found many of the reviews "surpassingly brainless."[45] But whatever Fuller's disappointment over *The Chatelaine*'s reception, he realized that there was much truth in the criticism, both of his motivation for writing it and of its form. As in *The Chevalier,* each chapter title bore the name of a town or location in Switzerland and Italy. To match the European types he had earlier created, he created another group of broadly representative characters with allegorical names. These caused the *Dial* to complain that the characters were mere abstractions, without any life or depth as individuals.

While his critics' opinions were well founded, they could not see that the work was an important step in Fuller's development as a realistic writer. *The Chevalier* is at least unified in its characterization and picturesque treatment of the Italian landscape. *The Chatelaine,* on the other hand, is a badly divided book. Aurelia West, the protagonist, is a realistically drawn character based upon the many upwardly mobile young women Fuller knew in Chicago. She does not fit well into the company of the generalized European types. In her social aspirations she typifies the characters in Fuller's realistic novels. The main action of the story focuses upon Aurelia's efforts to return the Chatelaine to the position of social respectability her family once enjoyed. This quest for social status contrasts with the esoteric, scholarly pursuits of the Chevalier and Gregorianius in his previous romance. There is even a Parisian fictionist in the story named Fin-de-Siècle. The approach of his school of fiction "was simple enough—close observation, accurate transcription, nothing more. . . . No passion, monsieur, no preferences; above all, no fancy." He has a debate with another character over the merits of literary realism. His opponent, the governor, espouses the cause of ideality in fiction, which Fin-de-Siècle condescendingly calls "false romanticism."

Fuller was aware of the change that was beginning to take place in his fiction. Like Aurelia West, the male characters in his aborted Spanish romance had also begun to develop in the "wrong" direction. This was part of the problem that he was having with the book before he put the manuscript aside in frustration. "The real trouble," Fuller explained in a letter to Norton, "comes from the young men who (even after being pieced out with a young hidalgo endowed with a Moorish ancestry and possibly a Madrilese viciousness) are probably making themselves a little too realistic for my theme or for my taste or even for my abilities."[46] Fuller "confessed" in his letter to Norton that he had created an American newspaperwoman, whom he intended to put "on the track of Columbus." Even the influence of the Columbian Exposition had managed to intrude here upon his story. The final step that would bring him to the realistic form of his Chicago novels was nearly complete. As the next few months would illustrate to Fuller, there would be no antidote to the realistic impulse that had long been a part of his literary tastes.

5

Chicago: The Black City versus the White City

By the beginning of January 1893, the thirty-six-year-old Fuller had become something of a luminary in Chicago society, in spite of generally bad reviews of *The Chatelaine.* His observations on current events and his books were sought by the most prestigious magazines and publishing houses in the East and Midwest. He was invited into the society of Chicago's literati, and he began to hobnob with the city's leading citizens, especially now that preparations for the opening of the fair in May were in full swing. Fuller was gratified to number Charles Eliot Norton among his friends. In the fall of 1892 Norton sent Fuller gift copies of his translations of Dante's *Vita Nuova* and the first volume of the *Commedia.*[1] Fuller's income also took a radical turn for the better at this time. He described himself in a letter to Louise as "a person of means," able to "gad about" as he chose.[2] It is unlikely that his royalties from his first romance provided all the capital he needed to make him totally independent. He did receive something for the serialization of *The Chatelaine,* but it did not sell and did not survive a second printing. More than likely, his father's estate, including the real estate Fuller now managed for his mother, was beginning to pay larger dividends. In any case, he was able to quit his job at the Lake Street office.

This was an active and stimulating time for Fuller. In March 1893, the *Century* published his travel sketch "Westminster Abbey," and in April the *Contributor's Magazine* published "Holy Week in Seville," another essay from his previous tour. With the commission to write his article for the *Contributor's Magazine,* the official organ of the Contributor's Club, he found himself associating with some of Chicago's most prominent and wealthy citizens. The club's roster included such influential Chicagoans as Mrs. William Armour, Mr. and Mrs. Eugene Field, General and Mrs. A. C. McClurg, and Mr. and Mrs. Potter

Palmer. The intent of the club was to bring together writers and publishers with Chicago's business community in a common effort to promote the arts. As a neophyte in Chicago literary circles, Fuller was impressed with his new friends.

There was, nevertheless, another part of Fuller that would always
remain ambivalent about his place in society. He had opened the subject of his homosexual feelings in "Allison Classical Academy" and in
"A Legacy," but his private expression of these feelings would never
suffice for Fuller. Implicit in his early journals was that urge to tell his
complete story. Yet before him, as he realized, stood an obtuse if not
out-and-out hostile society, which had earlier led Fuller to feelings of
culpability over his homosexuality. Some of that same guilt would persist, but the adult Fuller developed a hostility toward the general censorship that the Judeo-Christian tradition leveled against the homosexual in society. There were times when he was outraged over the narrow
values of his contemporaries. Oscar Wilde's persecution in England in
1895 filled Fuller with as much contempt and scorn for his society as
did Chicago's rampant commercialism.

As an articulate social critic, Fuller found both precedent and company for his views against the ravages of modern industrial capitalism.
John Ruskin was among the first of those dissenting voices that Fuller
read and with which he identified. Nearly every way he turned in the
1890s and after, he found his opinion shared by a wide variety of distinguished thinkers, from Brahmins like Charles Eliot Norton in the
East to the enigmatic University of Chicago professor, Thorstein Veblen. But where could Fuller turn in Victorian America for some precedent that would aid him in his battle against the darkness that shrouded
the subject of homosexuality? Though he had read Greek and Roman
literature on this theme, it did not enable him to deal with his own culture. His literary success only intensified his dilemma. Even though he
had a well-established audience willing to listen, he could not tell his
whole story as he wished. But he would never shrink from trying.

Fuller's need to test this issue outside the privacy of his journals came
forward in a curious letter to Louise. Clearly, he no longer felt guilty
over his sexual predilection. Interrupting a stylistic parody on another
subject with which he began his letter, Fuller continued in the same
tone and explained to Louise,

I must interrupt my melancholy word picture long enough to confirm you in your wondrous picture of the delectable youth whom I honor by sharing his bed and board.

Far from being a "brunette," he is a brilliant strawberry blonde of the deepest dye. His "lashing jet black eyes" are represented as nearly as possible by two—really two—angelic orbs of azure blue. His age, ah! his age! Fifteen last July; but he appears much older. His name?—that you may never know. His initials are C.N.; but whether it is Cecil Northampton or Cal Nipper—will forever remain a mystery.[3]

It is not certain that any such person did in fact exist. It was, however, possible, since Fuller wrote the letter in October 1891 at the family resort in Oconomowoc and away from his mother's house.

Louise may have goaded Fuller into confessing his sexual preference. Judging from the context of Fuller's answer, in her last letter she must have informed him that a mutual friend had married. This was her way of opening the subject up for their discussion, since Fuller would never take the initiative. But he only good-naturedly mocked the newlyweds and marriage in general. He wrote, "And m-a-r-r-i-e-d!!! Let me pause, and give way to my emotions in four stars." He then drew four starlike images. These exaggerated comments follow on the heels of his confession about his anonymous lover. This may also have been Fuller's indirect way of informing her about the status of their own relationship. To discourage her attentions he certainly would not have wanted to imply that he was interested in another female. He did not wish to alienate her, nor would he have wanted to spark her competition for his affections. She had brought up the subject before in their correspondence, and Fuller had discouraged her from thinking that one day he might consider marrying. Here Fuller took what must be considered the final step, and a hazardous one at that, in his efforts to convince his friend that he would never marry. This more confident and self-assertive posture would pay some small but important dividends in his writing over the next several years.

While Fuller would never totally withdraw from participation in his city's cultural or social life, discretion and a certain defensiveness would always characterize his social posture. His many close friends would be

The World's Columbian Exposition: Art Palace, Main Entrance

Chicago Day at the Columbian Exposition

Obelisk and Grand Vista North from Colonnade

puzzled by his often elusive nature. Nevertheless, with his overnight rise to fame, he willingly took his place on the rolls of Chicago's most prominent writers and artists. The activities surrounding the fair gave Fuller even greater opportunity to meet and mingle with Chicago's elite, and the fair forced Fuller to look even more closely at the contradiction between his city's commercial identity and its efforts at cultural uplift.

The impact of the fair upon Fuller cannot be overestimated: it formed the basis of his next two novels. Over the last several years, Europe had been the predominant influence in his life, but he could not ignore any longer his own hometown, especially now that the entire nation's attention was riveted upon the grandiose classical buildings rising out of the lakeshore mudflats and dunes in Jackson Park. He hoped that the Fair would do for his city what its overconfident supporters promised it would, but Fuller's optimism would be short-lived.

As Fuller wrote later, the fair was Chicago's postgraduate course in the arts. It was his city's boast to the rest of the world that the midwestern burg on the shores of Lake Michigan had finally come of age. In honor of Chicago's new wealth, little was spared in the construction and operation of the fair, which cost nearly thirty million dollars to construct. Chicago's share alone was ten million. Central to the fair's fundraising and organization were Chicago businessmen like Marshall Field, George Pullman, Philip Armour, Potter Palmer and his wife Bertha, who was president of the Board of Lady Managers, Charles Yerkes, and E. T. Jeffrey, president of the Illinois Central. The list reads like a Who's Who of Chicago business.[4]

Fuller could not agree, finally, with his friends and the fair's wealthy patrons that they had in fact changed their city. As soon as he put aside his Spanish romance in December, he began on January 11, 1893, his first Chicago novel. All along, while the fair's promoters were playing host to European nobility and trying to entice sophisticated easterners to visit, Fuller was quietly writing his own story of his city. It was out of his disagreement with what he termed the "local idealists" that he was moved to write *The Cliff-Dwellers,* the most devastating attack that any Chicagoan had yet written about the city's commercialism. Like Henry Adams, Fuller too must have sat upon the steps of one of the monumental yet temporary buildings and pondered what the fair meant for his city. Left untouched by the idealism that built the fair was the commercial and industrial order that dominated the lives of the vast majority of Chicago's citizens. It was this side of his city that Fuller wished to expose in his new novel.

Within six weeks, Fuller completed what he referred to as his "opus magnum," *The Cliff-Dwellers.*[5] Between June and August, the novel was serialized in *Harper's* and appeared in the late fall of 1893. Why Fuller had made a radical shift from the picturesque settings of his romances to the realism of his first Chicago novel perplexed many readers, especially those who had supported his previous two books. But having been stung by the negative reviews of *The Chatelaine,* Fuller confessed in a letter to Minna Smith that he was "tired of having *The Chatelaine* reviewers tell [him he] couldn't write a novel." In a rather shrill defense of *The Chatelaine,* Fuller proclaimed, "[It is] the best thing I have done and the only thing I truly care for." This was an opinion formed in the heat of battle; he would never again be so generous. Still smarting from the reviews, Fuller even went to the extreme of telling Minna Smith, referring to *The Chevalier,* "It seems impossible at the present writing, that I should have gone mooning about Tuscany."[6] Given his long and intimate courtship with Italian culture, Fuller could not have meant his disclaimer to be taken seriously.

Having undergone his initiation by fire with the publication of *The Chatelaine,* Fuller was no longer a literary tyro. As a student of the periodical war over literary realism of the 1880s and early 1890s, he no doubt fully expected the critical storm that his realistic novel would cause in the East and Midwest. *The Cliff-Dwellers* caused a sharp ideological division between the proponents of the romance and those in Howells's camp. Nearly all on both sides acknowledged the originality of Fuller's novel. Even his detractors recognized the essential truth of his portrayal of life in Chicago. The complaints against it were the usual ones leveled against the realists of the period: the sordid, base details of divorce courts, business scandals, and financial failure, personal and corporate, had no place in art. Lucy Monroe, herself a Chicagoan and writer for the *Critic,* complained that the novel was without "idealization" and that Fuller's "effort to be realistic is too apparent."[7] Abroad, the London *Times* went to the extreme of likening Fuller's brand of realism to what the reviewer described as Zola's "delight in what is loathsome and cruel."[8] At home Chicago was wounded that its native son would capitalize upon his fame and expose family secrets, especially at a time when the midland city was making such a formidable claim for empire with the Columbian Exposition.

Fuller would never be indifferent to any of his critics, yet the newspaper and magazine reviews still counted much less than the opinion of his friend Charles Eliot Norton, with whom he had not corresponded for more than a year. Norton was very much on his mind during the writing of *The Cliff-Dwellers,* but he was hesitant to send Norton a copy of his starkly realistic tale. When he finally did so, he assured his friend that he had reserved a copy for him, but that he had been holding it in his room for more than a month. "The truth is," Fuller wrote in a letter to Norton, "I have always felt intuitively that you had a real distaste for Chicago, if not a positive disgust. I learned from Mr. Burnham (and was glad to hear it) that you accepted the White City; but the Black City – the horrible, grimy mine from which the local fictionist must dig his material – seemed too far from Shady Hill to make any bridge between them possible."[9] Norton's response only confirmed the author's anxiety. While praising Fuller as a "man of imagination," he finally concluded, "Your disgust seems to me to have carried you too far in your book for its artistic perfection, and for its moral lesson."[10] Fuller did not expect anything different from Norton, and he answered by vowing to write another novel that would present "our city's better side – if only for the sake of sending a few presentation copies to the academic East."

While genteel readers like Norton recoiled before Fuller's latest, the realists in American letters were quick to enlist yet another writer into their burgeoning ranks. H. H. Boyesen wrote to Fuller to congratulate him on his "achievement." Two months before in his review of the novel, he wrote that Fuller's style was "mature, vigorous and at times brilliant."[11] Upon reading *The Cliff-Dwellers,* Hamlin Garland recognized at once that Fuller "had beaten the realists at their own game."[12] Above all the laurels cast in Fuller's direction, William Dean Howells's review in *Harper's Bazar* carried the greatest weight for Fuller. This was the famous writer on whose curbstone Fuller had patiently waited to glimpse in Boston in the early 1880s. Howells was delighted that Chicago had found its oracle. He placed Fuller among the growing number of realistic regional writers, from Bret Harte in California to Sarah Orne Jewett in Maine. Howells praised *The Cliff-Dwellers* as "a work of very great power" that had "reproduced with unerring distinctness the life it had dealt with." He also praised the "rich poetry of the imagination" that shaped the book and its "equally truthful" characters. He was moved to compare Fuller favorably to Henry James and even Zola. Above all, Howells was more than a little gratified that Fuller had left behind what he termed the "nebulous romanticism of *The Chevalier of Pensieri-Vani*" for the "electric glare of the realism" in his latest.[13] Howells could hardly find room and words enough in his review to list all of the aspects of the novel that impressed him.

The acknowledgments Fuller received from both Garland and Howells began friendships that would endure for the remainder of his life. He explained to Howells that the novel "merely represents the wrist-and-elbow exercise of a new man who hopes to 'get his hand in' for better things."[14] To Garland, however, Fuller made it more obvious that it would be premature to enlist him in the veritists' club on the strength of just one novel. "There are a good many ways to skin a cat," he wrote to Garland, "and the realistic way, I dare say, is as good a way as any."[15]

Before the more famous Howells, Fuller was not so forthright. Actually, his response to Howells could be interpreted to mean that he had already laid plans for another realistic novel, written perhaps with more care. In any case, Fuller did not make it entirely clear to Howells that he was not fully committed to the new novel. He was awed by Howells's response, and was reluctant to say all that was on his mind for fear of offending America's most influential writer and critic.

Thus Fuller's dilemma began to deepen. Counted among his friends and supporters now were Howells and Garland, midwesterners and realists, who beat the bushes regularly for recruits into the realist school of fiction. On the other side, equally if not more important to Fuller at this time was Charles Eliot Norton, Brahmin and easterner, who remained a staunch advocate of a sentimental, disembodied romanticism in literature. To Louise, away on her second tour abroad, Fuller revealed far more of his feelings than he dared to in his letter to Howells. He made it clear to her the obligation he felt toward Norton and his other eastern supporters: "I was glad to please him [Howells], but was no more glad than to have pleased some other people." He explained that he had "intimated" to Howells that he was "not to be counted upon as a realist fixed and sure."[16] But he was not nearly so clear in his letter to Howells. The record of his thoughts at this time is muddled, revealing the depths of the dilemma he now faced.

At this point in his career, Fuller still leaned toward the more conservative values, literarily and socially, of genteel Brahmin culture. Furthermore, he felt a deep commitment, which he would never betray,
to that group of writers and scholars that had initially supported him.
Offended by Howells's derogatory reference to his first romance, Fuller
pointed out to Louise that a writer for the *Florence Gazette* "didn't seem
to think the Chevalier . . .'nebulous,' and I don't believe that many Italian travelers do. Yet I can understand how it would seem so to an American realist."[17] To eastern critics like Agnes Repplier, who had written
a long, complimentary review of *The Chevalier* for *Lippincott's Monthly,*
Fuller remained grateful. For Howells, in spite of his unqualified support for *The Cliff-Dwellers,* Fuller still reserved a little hostility for his
silence on the publication of his first romance. Repplier, Fuller wrote
to Louise, "was on 'my side' long before W.D.H. was ever aware of my
existence." But time would soften Fuller's attitude. Over the years he
would cultivate a deep respect for Howells's accomplishment, a respect
that would more accurately reflect the opinion expressed in "Howells
or James?" Only then would he look back with gratitude upon Howells's review of *The Cliff-Dwellers.*

Owing to his defensiveness, Fuller did not explain to Howells the
care that had gone into his new novel. What he failed to reveal either
to him or to Garland was that *The Cliff-Dwellers* was a carefully designed
attack upon the false ideality and sentimentality of the popular romance
of the 1880s and 1890s. True, he wrote the novel quickly, but behind
it were years of reading and study of the realistic novel, mainly Howells's works. He did not merely set out to level a broadside against corrupt Chicago businessmen, though many of his contemporaries wished
to read the novel that way. Certainly, Chicago had his undivided attention at this time. But as with *The Chevalier,* Fuller attempted in *The
Cliff-Dwellers* to write a book that was new and different in its approach.

Fuller's critics did not realize the influence of the war over literary
realism upon the writing of *The Cliff-Dwellers.* Just as "The American
School of Fiction" served as the theory behind Fuller's first two romances,
"Howells or James?" expressed the theory behind *The Cliff-Dwellers.* As
Fuller explained in "My Early Books," for his plot he went back to the
few scattered notes he had managed to preserve from his lost manuscript
"Between the Millstones." Fuller noted in his essay that "the Colum-
bian Exposition helped along a hearing for Chicago in fiction" and had

given him the confidence to use his city in his novel. But Howells gave Fuller the method he needed to capture the life of his city as he felt it should be expressed.

The business theme in *The Cliff-Dwellers* certainly cannot be ignored, but it does not form the basis of Fuller's critical thrust against the romance. Rather, a conventional marriage motif is at the basis of his attack upon false ideality and upon the conventional claptrap of the popular fiction of his day. In "My Early Books" Fuller explained his intentions in *The Cliff-Dwellers:*

> The book asked this question: is it better for a young man to marry a girl who has pleasant, well-disposed family connections, yet who is rather flimsy and deficient herself, or for him to marry a girl who is much finer and stronger in herself yet who has a disadvantageous and even disreputable set of relatives? — the idea being that, even in informal America, marriage may be less a matter between individuals than between families.

Fuller recognized the potential for sentimentality in the many scenes he created. But his technique was to raise what are otherwise conventional expectations in the domestic and business lives of his characters, only to overturn them and satirize them. The marriage motif played a major role in the sentimental popular fiction of the 1890s; however, Fuller used the conventional plot for his own unconventional ends in *The Cliff-Dwellers.* Fairchild, a middle-aged cashier at the Underground National Bank, says in the first third of the novel: "Oh well . . . all of us are happily married or are going to be." Fuller then illustrates just how many unhappy marriages exist beneath the veneer of appearances. It seemed appropriate to Fuller that he should attempt to show the "local idealists" another side of life in their city, especially at a time when the great White City was attempting to improve upon its commercial and industrial image.

As the basis of the novel, the marriage motif assumes even much larger dimensions in *The Cliff-Dwellers* than Fuller admitted in his essay. There are thirteen married couples of various ages that play significant roles in the novel. Six of these couples are married in the course of the story. Two characters, George Ogden and Mary Brainard, are married twice. Some of the more important marital relationships are Mary Brainard's

ill-fated marriage to J. Russell Vibert, Burt Brainard's to Cornelia Mc-
Nabb, George McDowell's to Kitty Ogden, and finally Ogden's first marriage to Jessie Bradley and his second marriage to Abbie Brainard. The
stale, repressive marriage of Erastus and Abigail Brainard is contrasted
to the marriage of the socially prominent and successful businessman
Arthur J. Ingles and his wife Cecilia. Less important in the action of
the plot is the marriage of Jessie Bradley's parents, Mr. and Mrs. Daniel
Bradley, who represent in their unassuming manner a model of good
sense and decorum in the novel.

As Fuller describes the plot in "My Early Books," young George
Ogden, from a well-to-do New England background, has recently moved
to Chicago, which by the 1890s had become a vigorous, bustling industrial center. At twenty-four, and at the beginning of what he hopes will
become a successful business career, Ogden must choose between the
intelligent Abbie Brainard, who has a questionable family background,
and the somewhat shallow Jessie Bradley, who comes from a reputable
family. As it turns out, neither woman is the right choice for the un-
fortunate Ogden. Jessie is a prototype of that young woman Fuller described years before in his letters to the *Tribune* on the marriage question. She is extravagant, and her misguided social aspirations cause her
husband's social and financial ruin. After their divorce, Ogden marries
Abbie, the one woman he sought to avoid because of her father's reputa-
tion in Chicago.

Other marital relationships in the novel are no more successful than
Ogden's. Fuller shuns a sentimental treatment of his characters' problems. Instead he exposes the sordid facts that can surround both family
and business relationships. Burt Brainard's marriage to Cornelia Mc-
Nabb is plagued by disillusionment and failure. His parents' marriage
is a frigid relationship, a marriage in name only. Burt's father is cruel
and oppressive and has little regard for the feelings of others, including
his wife. The only successful marriage in the novel is that between Arthur and Cecilia Ingles. But Fuller makes it clear that even if they have
escaped the torment and financial ruin of the others in the novel, they
are in their own way partly responsible for the fate of the other characters. Ingles is the owner of the Clifton, the building at the center of
so much of the greed and corruption in the novel. As Fuller writes, "It
is for such a woman that one man builds a Clifton and that a hundred
others are martyred in it."

Just as important as the marital relationships in the novel is Brainard's relationship with Marcus, his artist son, who eventually kills his father. The parallel with Fuller's relationship with his father is unmistakable. It would be easy here, of course, to see the killing in merely psychoanalytic terms and to lay it at the feet of Fuller's own dark oedipal stirrings. Rather, far more significant, what emerges out of Fuller's use of his personal experience is the broader conflict between art and commerce that would preoccupy him for the remainder of his life. It was, after all, his father who pulled him out of school and tried to push him into business, which threw the young Fuller into protracted periods of depression. Just as it was George Fuller's firm opinion that a young man could do better than occupy his time with reading and writing, Brainard finds Marcus's desire to become an artist wasteful. Marcus's exile to the stockyards, where he is forced to design labels in order to feed himself, is the ultimate degradation of artistic talent in a capitalistic society. Fuller only narrowly escaped a similar fate in the banks of Chicago. In his darker characterizations of life in his city, Fuller would always relegate art to this subordinate role. Marcus's murder of his father and his suicide in the end of the novel were Fuller's way of dramatizing, though somewhat melodramatically, the conflict between art and commerce in his city.

In combining the commercial and the domestic themes, Fuller was able to expose more fully what he saw at the basis of life in his city. He laid bare the sordid facts of marriage and divorce. Behind the idealized image of the successful Chicago businessman, Fuller exposed the price that families and individuals paid for success. Like Theodore Dreiser after him, Fuller stripped away the thin veneer of sentimentality and false ideality and portrayed the problematic lives of his middle-class businessmen and their families.

Fuller even went out of his way several times to contrast his realistic story with the more popular romances of the period. About midway through the novel, Ogden mentions a romance that he had been reading entitled *A False Start* — a title foreshadowing his own first marriage. In discussing the romance with Abbie Brainard, Ogden criticizes the work as unnecessarily protracted, adding, "You know how they spin these things out." Also, one evening Ogden returns home to find Brower, his roommate, reading *Monte Cristo,* an allusion to Alexandre Dumas's historical romance. At the end, Ogden is reading another sentimental romance entitled *A Mistaken Marriage.* Again, the title of the romance is an apt summary of Ogden's own poor judgment. But Fuller makes it clear that Ogden is reading the romance only as an escape from his troubles, not as an honest confrontation with experience.

The Cliff-Dwellers's place in American literature distinguishes it not only from the nineteenth-century romance, but also in a way from the fiction of James and Howells: it lacks the moral order found in James's and Howells's fiction.[18] Isabel Archer in *Portrait of a Lady* and Kitty Ellison in *A Chance Acquaintance* are heroines who ultimately control their own destinies. They have choices. Yet external fact becomes the controlling force in *The Cliff-Dwellers,* however moral or sincere the characters' aspirations. The goals and ambitions, domestic and commercial, of Mary Brainard, her brother Burt, Cornelia McNabb, Eugene McDowell, and Kitty Ogden are all compromised by circumstances beyond their control. Whatever the good sense and virtue of Mr. and Mrs. Bradley, the moral turpitude of others in Chicago brings tragedy and unhappiness into their lives. Similarly, George Ogden finds himself buffeted about in the big city by forces far beyond his control. Ironically, in the end of the novel he marries Abbie Brainard, the woman he had initially rejected as socially unacceptable. His marriage to Abbie is a humbling compromise of his earlier principles.

With the publication of *The Cliff-Dwellers,* Fuller reveals a radical change in his approach to the novel. Going beyond the realism in the works of Hamlin Garland, Sarah Orne Jewett, and other local color writers of the period, he anticipated the literary naturalism that would become the basis of Theodore Dreiser's novels, beginning with *Sister Carrie.* Howells was right to compare Fuller to Zola and the realists on the Continent who were influenced by Charles Darwin and the theories of Herbert Spencer. In America *The Cliff-Dwellers* finds a place as well among the works of Jack London, Frank Norris, and Stephen Crane, whose *Maggie: A Girl of the Streets* appeared in 1893. Fuller surpassed in his novel what Dreiser would later define for the next generation as Howells's "conventional" and "uninformed" brand of literary realism.[19] Ultimately, in the end of *The Cliff-Dwellers,* Fuller offered no moral solution to the domestic and social problems that he exposed. This, perhaps more than anything, offended his conservative readers in the East and the Midwest.

But Fuller did not see the implications of his own story. *The Cheva-*

lier still loomed large in his imagination, and he would yet attempt to recapture some of the romance of his first book. He was not being coy when he wrote to Garland that he had not made a commitment to the realist school. The criticism from the East and his hometown did not please him. He felt that he had to soften some of that harsh realism that was the basis of his success in *The Cliff-Dwellers*. In his next work he wanted to appease his local critics, and perhaps more important, he wished to send a more presentable image of himself and of his city to the East.

II

At sunset on October 30, 1893, the World's Columbian Exposition officially closed its gates. As its overwrought fountains stopped flowing and its brilliant lights went out for the last time, the spirit that had inspired Chicago to build the fair also began to fade. At its close, the fair's builders and planners were unable to decide what to do with the colossal structures they had erected. The powerful men who had financed the fair discovered that there was no organization in their city to perpetuate the lofty ideal that the fair was supposed to represent. Various uses were proposed, but before anything decisive could be planned, with the grounds vacant and unused, fire broke out in January 1894 and destroyed a number of buildings. Over the next six months no decision was reached. Fire broke out again in midsummer and ravaged many of the most impressive structures. There was no realistic alternative, and demolition of the remaining buildings began. Pieces from some of them were preserved while others were sold as souvenirs. Other parts were given away to be used on buildings around the country. With a few exceptions, by mid-1896 most of the buildings had been razed.[20] Out of all the great structures, the Fine Arts Building was the only one preserved and now serves as Chicago's Museum of Science and Industry.

Though the fair lingered only in the memories of its supporters, it did have one long-term influence upon the cultural life of Chicago. The flurry of cultural activities surrounding the fair introduced Fuller to a small, elite group of Chicago artists, writers, and architects. Fuller and his friends began meeting casually in Lorado Taft's and Bessie Potter's studios on Friday afternoons after the matinee performances of Theodore Thomas's Chicago Orchestra. This "artistic gang," as Garland called them, soon organized themselves into a group called the Little Room, named after a short story by Madeline Yale Wynne. After the completion of the Fine Arts Building, at the corner of Michigan and Van Buren, the group moved to its permanent quarters in Ralph Clarkson's studio on the tenth floor.[21]

Among the original members of the group were Harriet Monroe, Lucy Monroe, Anna Morgan, Hamlin Garland, Roswell Field, Allen and Irving Pond, and Lorado Taft, all of whom would become Fuller's lifelong friends. During this period Roswell Field, brother of columnist Eugene Field, became an "intimate" friend.[22] It was among this group of close and wholly compatible Chicago artists, writers, and architects (Louis Sullivan would later join the group) that Fuller became known endearingly as "Henry B." He soon became the group's "dominating figure" and most admired member.[23] His opinion and participation were always sought. Even though over the years friends would find him elusive and private, Fuller seldom failed to take part in the group's discussions, lectures, or satirical plays.

Because of his close association with Chicago's art community, Fuller began to realize that there was another side to his city that was not nearly as corrupt or corrupting as the one he had portrayed in *The Cliff-Dwellers*. He still wished to send Norton the presentation copy he had promised him. As a result, in his next novel, begun early in 1894, he attempted to capture that far more benign and sophisticated side of life to be found in Chicago's art and cultural circles. By the second week in April he had finished an 85,000-word manuscript, entitled *With the Procession.*

Upon hearing that Fuller had another novel in progress, Howells offered to read the manuscript. When Howells returned his copy, he wrote, "It is all so good, that I have permitted myself a few grumbles on the margin."[24] After the appearance of *The Cliff-Dwellers,* Fuller had been hard on Howells in his letters to Louise. But his animosity dissipated quickly before Howells's continuing generosity. He could not avoid being impressed and a little touched by Howells's support and encouragement and wrote him to express his gratitude for what he called his "mastery of the Art of Kindness" toward young writers like himself.[25]

With his second and what he felt to be a far more successful Chicago novel completed, in late spring 1894 Fuller made a fourth trip abroad. He left no notebook of his tour. The only accounts of his trip are in his letters to Louise. He spent approximately six months, from early May to late October, traveling through England, Germany, Austria, and northern Italy. However, his tour was far from successful. Fuller became aware again of a problem that had bothered him while on his previous tours. Fuller admitted to Louise in a letter that he had become "fussy" and "overcritical" on his travels.[26] He finally had to admit to himself that he could never "identify with Europe." This was not the first time that Fuller had come to this conclusion and had become impatient with the form and manners of European culture. Europe had always loomed in his imagination as an escape from his native town. But his previous three trips, after his maiden tour of 1879, served only to reinforce the differences that separated his oftentimes overly fastidious American manners and his Protestant attitudes from those of European society.

When in Chicago Fuller would too often feel that Europe held the answer to his conflict with his city. But when abroad he always discovered that he felt alienated from Old World culture and missed his friends in Chicago. After this last tour, Fuller realized that Europe could never serve for him as anything more than a temporary salve for the wounds that commercial Chicago inflicted upon his genteel sensibilities. Now that he had earned a respectable place in Chicago's art colony, and especially now with the establishment of the Little Room, he would always be able to find friends with whom he could attend plays and concerts and discuss art and literature.

Upon his return home Fuller began proofreading the galleys of his latest novel. When it appeared in March 1895, *With the Procession* was greeted with far more acclaim and acceptance than *The Cliff-Dwellers*, and Fuller received numerous personal letters of congratulation. Writing for the *Critic*, Harriet Monroe praised the novel as "the strongest thing [Fuller] has ever written."[27] In *Harper's Weekly* Howells wrote a lengthy three-part review paying Fuller the ultimate compliment: "At present," Howells wrote, "we have no one to compare with [Fuller] in the East, in scale and quality of work."[28] Other eastern critics were not so complimentary. Nancy Banks wrote in the *Bookman*, "It is to be regretted that so artistic a book should be wholly a work of disintegration, of discontent and despair."[29] The realism in *With the Procession* still remained antithetical to that genteel sensibility.

During the first week of May, Fuller sent the presentation copy that he had promised his friend Charles Eliot Norton. Fuller wrote, "I have tried to keep in mind the suggestion which *The Cliff-Dwellers* prompted you to make, and hope to have avoided the extreme of violence which you deprecated in the closing portion of the book. Perhaps this second effort, too, is on a *fairer* social plane."[30] If Fuller was able to brush off Banks's review, however representative he felt it was, it is certain that Norton's reply to Fuller's gift copy and letter carried more weight. In a letter that bordered on impatience, Norton responded, "To be brief, I hold with the poets and the idealists; . . . I believe that your 'Chevalier' has done more for Chicago than any of the true Chicagoans whom you have given to us, 'twice as natural' as life."[31] Fuller was distraught over his response and felt a deep sense of frustration, especially after all he had done to make the novel more acceptable to Norton. On June 7, quoting from Norton's May 30 letter, Fuller wrote to Garland, "But what does C. E. Norton write? – 'a serious question whether such life (C. Dwellers and Procession) is fit subject for literary art.' What is a poor duck to do?"[32]

In the face of Howells's and Norton's responses to his two novels, Fuller found himself caught between the two warring poles in American letters. By now Howells had become a friend as well as his chief supporter in the East. In Chicago Garland had become another outspoken promoter of Fuller's book. But Fuller's own cultural and personal link to eastern Brahmin society and his desire to cater to that interest drew him in another direction, away from Howells and what was fast becoming the dominant mode in American fiction. He wished to please Norton as much as if not more than Howells, but this was not possible. It had now become clear to Fuller, with the appearance of his second realistic novel, that no form of literary realism, however toned down, would ever earn Norton's acceptance or praise.

At least Chicago's ruling class was not wholly displeased with Fuller's characterization of them. The story begins in November 1893, a week after "the spirit had taken its formal leave" from the great White City in Jackson Park, and it ends a year later in November 1894. The central theme of *With the Procession* is the overthrow of the old Chicago by the new emerging immigrant class that began to populate Chicago's neighborhoods after the Civil War. Representative of that virtuous old Chicago in the novel is Mrs. Granger Bates. She is also leader of the new Chicago, during and after the fair, in its efforts at cultural uplift. Her character is based upon the career of the renowned Mrs. Potter Palmer, leader of Chicago society throughout the 1890s.[33] Fuller's description of the Bates mansion derives from the Palmers' famous lakefront castle. The Bates mansion is an eclectic hodgepodge of styles – Turkish, Moorish, French, Spanish, Italian, and Japanese.[34] And like the Palmers' famous art collection and gallery, the Bates's "picture-gallery" is a collection of Europe's most outstanding painters.

The Bates represent those Chicagoans who built their lavish baroque domiciles on the fashionable Prairie Avenue and in the wealthy North Shore communities – Evanston, Kenilworth, Ravinia, and Lake Forest – during the three decades after the 1871 fire. As Fuller pointed out, the "weight of latter-day magnificence" was brought forward from the past by this rising middle class as an expression of their own power and wealth. They reasoned that like the ruling class of the Old World, they now had established their own empire, and they too deserved the appropriate symbols that represented their new status and power in modern society.

The Bates, and especially the Marshalls, find themselves in direct conflict with that new immigrant class in Chicago. David and Eliza Marshall have withdrawn from the social procession and have fallen behind their peers, to the chagrin of their upwardly mobile children. Fuller does not shrink from satirizing the pretensions of this younger generation of Chicagoans, with their materialistic values and pseudo-Europeanized manners. But most important, Fuller exposes the control that the immigrant element holds when the Marshalls' stable is vandalized by the Van Horn family. David discovers that the entire city government, from the Irish policeman who investigates the crime to the alderman and judge involved, is controlled by this new immigrant class. "It is not the old public I used to know twenty years ago," David says. "It has changed a good deal. It is better organized against us – banding together of petty officials with their whole contemptible following: steerage-rats that have left their noisome holds to swarm into our houses, over them, through them, everywhere."

In *With the Procession* Fuller found some room to sympathize with his hometown's older elite society. The fair was at least inspired by the right ideals, even if it did not change the makeup of commercial Chicago. To Fuller the city's general failure at cultural uplift was as much the fault of that emerging immigrant class as it was the money managers, like his father and grandfather. Fuller would always believe that democracy in anything but a limited sense was impossible. He held out little hope that the city's government—now controlled, so he believed, by the new immigrant class—would ever be reformed.

If there is a flaw in *With the Procession*, it is Fuller's flattering characterization of the "older settlers," the Bates and the Marshalls. He imagined that old Chicago was a "mere town," or in the homespun Eliza Marshall's imagination, "an arcadia" free from the corruption and materialistic values that dominate the Black City in his novels. David Marshall's obituary, which contains a detailed account of his long career in Chicago, ends the novel. Reading it, "A new and careless public was carried back once more to the early days whose revivification is always attempted for a preoccupied and unsympathetic community upon the passing away of another old settler. Then the frontier village lifts once more its bedraggled forlornness from the slime of its humble beginnings, and the lingering presence of the red man is again made manifest upon the grassy horizon." Even the American Indian is evoked here as a symbol of a simpler, unspoiled way of life in old Chicago.

But Fuller knew better than most of his contemporaries that the new immigrant class was no different from the old settlers. He realized that the same materialistic values and the same potential for corruption had dominated Chicago throughout its development. If Fuller was accurate in exposing the corruption that the new immigrant class brought to city government, he was well aware that only the names and accents had changed over two or three decades. Before the European immigrants and other workers flooded Chicago's neighborhoods, Fuller's own grandfather was developing the commercial resources of his newly adopted city. Judge Fuller's tactics had not differed greatly, when rights-of-way or zoning changes were needed to lay a new section of railroad track, from Erastus Brainard's lawlessness or David Marshall's extra-legal finagling.

Fuller's idealization of Chicago's past, on the whole, does not compromise the realistic thrust of the story. To soften somewhat his harsh social criticism, he added, as he had in *The Cliff-Dwellers*, a passing but humorous jab at the romance. When the pragmatic Roger marries off Sophie Leppin to save the fanciful Truesdale from a possible paternity suit, Truesdale is angry. He is embarrassed over "the vulgar ending of the episode . . . ; for it seemed to outrage all literary and artistic precedent. No farce in the Palais Royal had ever developed so grotesque a dénouement; no novel of Véron, of Belot, of Montépin could have ever followed a line of conduct so little *spiritual* as that taken by Sophie Leppin. What, then; were the books wrong, and only life true?"

But in spite of the ligher touches Fuller consciously added to his story, readers like Charles Eliot Norton still could not accept the realistic technique of the novel. As he had in *The Cliff-Dwellers,* Fuller again exposed in *With the Procession* the economic and social conditions that controlled the lives of his characters. Unfortunately, he could never remain content with such a bleak appraisal of his city. Like Norton, he was not convinced that illegitimate children, illicit affairs, divorce courts, the hypocrisy of the upper classes, and governmental corruption were all acceptable subjects for high art. Hereafter, to Howells's great disappointment, Fuller would hold to his earlier disclaimer that he should not be counted on as a hard-and-fast member of the realistic school of fiction.

6
Art and Imperialism

The 1890s brought Fuller the success and prominence that he had only dreamed of as a young man. By the middle of the decade and with the publication of his second Chicago novel, he had become a widely respected and established member of Chicago's art colony. He was pleased with the company in which he found himself, both as a member of the Little Room and as a welcomed guest in the art studios on the Midway and in the Fine Arts Building. Actually, he even became something of a gadabout – a side of his character and social life that has been obscured by his later critics. When Garland was away from Chicago in the East or abroad, Fuller would often write letters to him keeping him posted on the latest activities of Lorado Taft, Lucy and Harriet Monroe, Bessie Potter, Melville Stone, Harrison Rhodes, and a score of other artist and writer friends.[1] "For many years," Lorado Taft wrote of Fuller, "he averaged one visit a week to the Midway studios."[2] Later in *Under the Skylights* Fuller would satirize himself as an art-studio dawdler. When visiting the artists' studios, he would offer his always appreciated advice on his friends' work. He was especially interested in younger artists' progress and often scrutinized their canvases or sculptures. When in 1897 Lorado Taft established his art colony on the Rock River in Oregon, Illinois, Fuller became an enthusiastic supporter. At the camp he found a much-needed escape from urban Chicago, and he spent long weekends and entire weeks there with other writers and artists from Chicago.[3] Besides himself and Garland, chief among the camp's regular supporters were writers and artists like Charles Francis Browne, Charles Nixon, and Ralph Clarkson.[4]

By the mid-1890s Chicago had begun to provide Fuller with the cultural resources he demanded of a city. Yet his quarrel with Chicago did not end. Rather, the development of the arts, especially after the closing

of the Columbian Exposition, only seemed to magnify the distance between the White City and the Black City, as Fuller now referred to the
cultural and commercial flanks of his hometown. In 1895 he wrote to
Howells that he was "ashamed" of Chicago and considered it a "muck-
heap" which he sought to "edit" in his fiction.[5]

However, Fuller's troubles as a novelist went beyond his conflict with
the commercialism of his city. As a professional writer with four published volumes by 1895, Fuller had become very sensitive to criticism.
Beginning with *The Chatelaine*, he felt that too much bad opinion was
mixed with the good. After *With the Procession* was published, he became much more selective about where he would allow his name to appear. Now that he was widely known in literary circles, he was regularly
asked to write for journals or to provide biographical or pictorial information for articles on his works.[6] But if he did not know the editor of
the journal or a writer well enough to trust his or her judgment, he would
refuse to write or to send any information about himself. At this time
he also claimed to have stopped reading or collecting reviews of his books.
"Nothing goes now," he explained in a letter to Louise, "but letters from
authors and editors."[7] Even then, he would be very selective. In November 1895, still chafing from the reception of *The Chatelaine* and *The
Cliff-Dwellers*, Fuller wrote to Howells that a good writer needed "only
a dozen or so people: those, namely, who are in the same 'line,' who
apprehend his aims and his methods, and who can be counted upon,
he feels, to size up his work in gross and in detail."[8]

Partly because of this exclusivist if not elitist attitude, too many of
Fuller's critics and friends during his lifetime and after characterized
him as an aloof, self-confident writer who was not much concerned about
the public's opinion of his works. But Fuller was far more pragmatic
than his friends realized. By the mid-1890s Fuller's finances again began
to decline. To avoid a return to banking or to some other mundane oc-
cupation, he needed a regular income, especially now that he was no
longer living in his mother's house. He realized more than he ever admitted, even to his closest friends, that if he wished to continue as a
writer he had to rely upon editors and the general public to purchase
and to read his work.

Consequently, he was as capable as anyone else of living in the
dollars-and-cents world of his society. He was not above a publicity
stunt to promote the sale of one of his books. Before the publication

of *With the Procession* there was some confusion over its title. When it appeared, he wrote to Minna Smith at the *Boston Transcript,* "If you felt inclined to give the false title one week and come out in a correction the next, I might deplore the lack of moral principle involved, but should do nothing to prevent it."⁹ When *The Puppet Booth* appeared in 1896, he mailed a select list of editors and reviewers, many of them his friends and past supporters, to W. W. Ellsworth at the Century Company to suggest where review copies of the plays might be sent. He even suggested to Ellsworth that two copies be sent to the *Saturday Evening Herald* and the *Elite* because "these two reach society," and "perhaps society will henceforth buy instead of borrow."¹⁰ Fuller realized that if he were to create freely, he must be independent from the demands of the marketplace. But he learned first-hand the difficulty of that proposition in a capitalistic society.

Along with this cultivated image of aloofness was a feeling among Fuller's friends that in his personal relationships he was not as open as he could be. Even to someone like Hamlin Garland, who was among his closest friends, Fuller "remained a mystery, a familiar presence but a mystery nevertheless."¹¹ Fuller's wit and participation at social functions were a delight to his many friends. Yet whatever the occasion, by the end of the evening, very quietly and without giving notice, he would slip away to his roominghouse at 2831 Prairie Avenue, the exact location of which he never willingly divulged to anyone, not even to Garland. He was an inveterate walker, and his friends would often spot him walking alone in remote neighborhoods.¹² After his death Harriet Monroe wrote of Fuller's "great secret," that something which he held deep within him.¹³ He was a capable public speaker, and he lectured on art and literary topics before distinguished groups at the University of Chicago and the Midway studios. But his friends reported that during the late 1890s, in personal conversation Fuller often spoke with one hand partially covering his mouth, as though he wished to obscure some part of himself that might unexpectedly escape through a mistaken utterance or phrase.

What Fuller wished to hide hardly needs to be speculated upon now. Harriet Monroe went about as far as any of Fuller's contemporaries in suggesting that his homosexuality presented a major barrier to a more open intercourse with his society and more complete and open expression in his novels. Why Garland never implied as much as Monroe did in his published memoirs or why he never explicitly discussed it in his extensive private diary was no doubt owing to his sense of propriety.[14] Nowhere did he broach the subject. He laid the blame of Fuller's general dissatisfaction with life and his avoidance of society solely upon Fuller's unhappiness over his inescapable residence in Chicago. As Fuller's closest literary friend, Garland did Fuller a disservice by diverting the attention of his later critics and biographers from a major conflict that so profoundly influenced his life and his relationship with society.[15]

Fuller no doubt felt a double alienation: he loathed commercial Chicago, and he was no less embattled against a society that declared his sexual predilection immoral, as well as illegal. The one conflict was known to all who read his books, while the other remained a well-kept secret. But that sense of culpability which society had inflicted upon him at an early age and which he expressed in his early diaries underwent a transformation in his adult years. If he were going to be an honest writer, he felt that he should tell his whole story. This was not out of any morbid sense of self-deprecation, but instead grew from his own sense of outrage over contemporary moral standards. Until 1896 and the publication of his homosexual play, "At Saint Judas's" in *The Puppet Booth*, all of Fuller's references to his homosexuality remained private.

The possible influence of Oscar Wilde's widely publicized trial and conviction on May 25, 1895, upon the writing of the play cannot be established by any specific document. But it is no mere coincidence that Fuller wrote and elected to publish his play in the wake of Wilde's scandalous conflict with English society. Equally as important, Fuller realized that with "At Saint Judas's" he was making himself as vulnerable to moral censorship in the United States as Wilde had in England. Like his attack upon Chicago's idealized image of itself in his first two novels, Fuller's play about homosexuality was also a species of truth-telling, a way of exposing an issue that remained suppressed by contemporary moral standards in spite of its prevalence in all classes of society.

In the wake of Wilde's trial, Fuller took a grave risk in publishing his play, the first of its kind to be printed publicly in the United States. Like English law, Illinois state law made homosexuality a punishable offense. But Fuller's courage before the moral norms of his society must not be allowed to overshadow his ambivalence toward the decision to publish the play. He was wary of telling his whole story to a society that he felt would always be hostile to the truth about itself. In a letter to Charles Eliot Norton, Fuller confessed, "How can a man give himself to the public and hold himself back at the same time? How can he endure to walk barefooted over the rocky road of the everyday world?— and this world is very every-day indeed here in the West. How can he trust himself even to his friends, and what are the rights, in this matter, of his own sense of modesty?"[16]

Fuller's solution was to abandon realism entirely in *The Puppet Booth.* The overwrought symbolism of the plays lessens much of their impact, especially those that have a social or political theme. The homosexual theme in "At Saint Judas's" is equally embellished by the symbolic tapestry which Fuller wove around the relationship of the two young men in the play. The new form his plays took began with what he described as his first "Maeterlinckian fantasy," a one-act play entitled "O, That Way Madness Lies," which appeared in the *Chap-Book* in December 1895.[17] Fuller explained to Norton in a letter that he had "adopted this method as a species of self-defense: one must make his compromise with his own community."[18] Behind Fuller's defensive posture was, of course, the criticism he forced to endure over his first two Chicago novels. He was aware that more than in any of the other plays in the volume a sense of modesty and restraint had to prevail in his treatment of the homosexual theme. But he was also aware that his slight effort in "At Saint Judas's" to be honest with himself and his reading public could not serve as the final answer to the dilemma he faced as a writer.

By contemporary standards, "At Saint Judas's" is tame, though the theme was both unique and shocking to Fuller's readers. The play deals with the melodramatic end to a homosexual relationship. The setting is the vaulted sacristy of the church of Saint Judas's on the wedding day of the bridegroom. During the months preceding the marriage, Oliver, the best man and the bridegroom's now-betrayed lover, had done all he could to compromise the love between the bridegroom and his bride, Angela. He had been the anonymous source of several scurrilous stories about Angela, and he similarly had attempted to malign the bridegroom's character to her—all to no avail. In the sacristy the bridegroom discovers through Oliver's own admission that his former lover is responsible for the stories. As a last-ditch effort just before Angela arrives, Oliver attempts to plant the seed in the bridegroom's mind of Angela's unfaithfulness to him. When that fails too, Oliver tells his former lover, "No one loves you more than I" and then attempts to stand in the way to prevent the bridegroom from going to the altar. In a rage, the bridegroom demands that Oliver kill himself as "redemption" for the dishonor that he has brought upon both of them with his lies. The bridegroom leaves Oliver lying "in a pool of blood" as he goes to the altar to meet his bride.

The melodrama and violence in "At Saint Judas's," much like the ending of *The Cliff-Dwellers,* were Fuller's only means of resolving in his writing a conflict with the values of his society. The play's final scene, as with most homosexual writing before and even after World War II, suggests something like atonement, if not divine retribution, for the two young men's "deviant" sexual preference. There is a certain ambivalence at the center of the play that had always been a part of Fuller's life, socially as well as professionally. Fuller was outraged over Wilde's conviction and wished to defy his society's values with his play, but at the same time he was intimidated by the severe moral censorship of his day. In Oliver's violent death there is a sense that Fuller is doing something more than merely setting up a defense to soften or to deflect the shocking nature of his theme. Consciously or not, Fuller is acknowledging the moral impropriety and "sinfulness" of homosexuality and is attempting to redeem the two men. There is no overlooking that the ritual slaying takes place in the sacristy of a church. More than twenty years later, in *Bertram Cope's Year* Fuller would employ a nearly identical pattern in the attempted resolution of the homosexual theme in his novel. He would find then too that the risks were still as great for the homosexual writer. Caution would only breed equivocation.

The remainder of Fuller's one-act plays do not deserve much attention. Fuller was aware of the chance he was taking in his radical departure from the realistic form. His critics justifiably found the Maeterlinckian plays derivative and not the innovative works that Fuller thought they were. Before the end of the summer his worst fears were confirmed: the volume did not sell.

II

Following the publication of *The Puppet Booth* in the spring of 1896, Fuller began to lay plans for another European trip. The year before, in anticipation of visiting Scandinavia, encouraged largely by Louise's travels in northern Europe, Fuller had begun a short study of Norwegian. In hopes, too, of making a return trip to the Riviera, he also began in June a review of French and Italian. His study of Italian, it appears, revived his growing interest in contemporary Italian fiction, which he had planned to read while traveling through Italy. In May Howells returned his copy of Salvatore Farina's novel, *Il Signor Io,* which Fuller had sent to him the year before.[19] While Fuller was still planning his itinerary, he began in mid-July a translation of the novel, but worked on it for only one month before losing interest. His major concern throughout the summer was the sale of *The Puppet Booth,* which he had hoped would finance his tour. By the end of the summer he realized the fate of his latest volume and was forced to cut back on his travel plans. He moved up his departure date by two months and cut the Scandinavian countries and southern France entirely.[20]

Fuller spent five mostly enjoyable weeks in North Africa. From there, with an architecture student from New York whom he had met in Algiers, he traveled north to Palermo, where they separated. During a stretch of bad weather there, Fuller read several Italian novelists. In Rome, his next stop, he wrote to Lorado Taft that he had met Bessie Potter and another Chicago friend and was later invited to the studio of Larkin G. Mead, Howells's brother-in-law, where Bessie was working. He visited friends in Florence and then began his journey home. Upon his return to Chicago in late June, after a stopover in New York, he wrote to Garland, "No more Europe for a while. I guess it's done me all the good it can."[21] This time Fuller would honor his declaration.

Shortly after his return, Fuller resumed his translation of *Il Signor Io* and began translating a collection of Italian short stories.[22] But he could not find a publisher and was forced to abandon the idea.[23] Apparently, he was actively looking for some project that would put him back in print after the disappointment of *The Puppet Booth.* He returned briefly to novel writing, and by summer 1897 he completed the first four chapters of a story about Americans abroad, which he entitled "Oliver's Outing."

But for reasons he never explained, he lost interest in the manuscript and did not finish it. Instead, he put it aside and wrote an essay entitled "The Upward Movement in Chicago," which appeared in the *Atlantic Monthly* in October 1897. The upbeat, nearly propagandistic tone of the essay was Fuller's way of presenting a more favorable image of Chicago to the East and specifically to Charles Eliot Norton than he had in his last two novels. Fuller admitted that all too often life in Chicago was "a struggle for the bare necessities," and he acknowledged Chicago's "sense of shame and peril aroused by the comments of outside censors." Ironically, Fuller pointed out, the fair was the source of many of these comments and actually contributed to Chicago's negative image in the East, rather than changing it. For him the fair "was a period . . . of the city's greatest glory and of her deepest abasement." The fair was a "noble ideal," but it brought visitors from around the world to a city that was in its streets and buildings both unclean and ugly. But overall Fuller sidestepped the more obvious shortcomings of his city to emphasize to the East the advances that Chicago had made since the Great Fire of 1871.

The major endeavors had been made principally in the area of education, from cultural organizations to the establishment of libraries and John D. Rockefeller's University of Chicago. Fuller also pointed to "reform organizations," such as the Civic Federation, the Women's Club, the Citizens' Association, and the Municipal Voters' League. These groups were dedicated to reforming the general functioning of the city, from the cleanliness of its streets and bake-shops to reorganizing city elections. But foremost in Fuller's mind were what he termed Chicago's "four great libraries," the Public Library, the Newberry Library, the University of Chicago Library, and the John Crerar Library, now on the University of Chicago campus. Fuller also cited Chicago's many musical and literary societies, some of which dated back to the 1871 fire. The author of *The Cliff-Dwellers* and *With the Procession* must have shocked his readers by predicting Chicago's "final supremacy" in things cultural, economic, and political in the United States. He concluded that since "material prosperity is already won; a high intellectual status seems assured" for Chicago. In his final remarks, Fuller wished to reassure his artist friends in Chicago and to put his eastern audience on notice that, as it had done in the East, wealth would someday transform Chicago from a provincial town to a cultural center. But Fuller's complimentary attitude toward Chicago and its inhabitants would be short-lived.

In the meantime, he continued his writing and made plans for a tour of the American South. By the end of November 1897 he had written two short stories which he planned to publish the following March in a single volume of four works of short fiction entitled *From the Other*

Side. Fuller hoped to sell both these stories to magazines, but was able to place only one of them in the December *Atlantic* before his departure.

Before Fuller left on his southern tour, in October 1897 he began receiving the first of five letters from a homosexual friend, a young Englishman named Harold W. Curtis whom he had met in a brief stop in Sorrento on his last trip to Europe. After his tour abroad, Curtis traveled to Toronto, where he began studying at the Conservatory of Music in the fall of 1897. For both men their encounter in Sorrento was lamentably short, but Fuller had apparently told his friend that he was a writer. With some persistence Curtis managed to reach Fuller in mid-October through one of his New York publishers. When contacted, Fuller willingly resumed the relationship, though it never went beyond the photographs and five letters exchanged over the following six months. Although Fuller's letters were never preserved by Curtis, Fuller made a very conscious decision to preserve the Curtis letters in his personal papers. The letters are a poignant demonstration of that conflict within Fuller between his homosexuality and the values of American society at the time.

Probably in his early twenties, Curtis was hopelessly frustrated by his isolation in Toronto and was often tormented by his inability to fulfill his sexual needs. Although he had known Fuller only a few days in Sorrento, he considered Fuller his "confidant" and begged Fuller's indulgence in his letter. His first letter to Fuller was a testing of the waters to determine whether his former acquaintance cared to renew the relationship.[24] When Fuller responded encouragingly and promptly, Curtis replied that, now having reached Fuller directly, he felt he could "speak more openly" than in his previous letter, which had gone through Fuller's publisher. He explained that he was the only male in a class of twenty at the conservatory, but he hastened to add, "though I have no use for the opposite sex, I'm not afraid of it."[25] Earlier in the letter, while complaining to Fuller about the unavailability of men in Toronto who shared his own sexual predilection, he expressed his frustration: "I have tried very hard to get the upper hand but I think that it is impossible. The worst of it is that, though delightful in other ways, this town seems quite hopeless in that respect. It is bad that it is so, as I feel the necessity very often, I have no means of gratifying it, and see no chance of any." In two letters that followed in November, Curtis kept Fuller informed of the men he began to meet "of the right sort" and thanked Fuller for passing on a suggestion "re. commercial travelers."[26]

Because of Fuller's trip to the South in January 1898, there is a hiatus of more than three months in the Curtis correspondence. His next letter reached Fuller in March in Charleston, South Carolina, where he had been for approximately three weeks.[27] As in his other letters, in this letter Curtis mentioned another young man he had met and made more general references to his other liaisons, real and imaginary. But Fuller decided, and for good reason, to alter Curtis's text to obscure its meaning. In one passage Curtis referred to Fuller's last correspondence from Washington and wrote, "I am glad to hear such good accounts of Washington and hope someday I shall be able to sample the men in these as well as in other cities of the U.S.A." However, Fuller went back and altered Curtis's sentence so that it is impossible for the casual reader to grasp its meaning. Similarly, in the remainder of the letter Fuller very calculatedly changed letters, added words to sentences, and scribbled out, sometimes beyond recovery, entire passages where Curtis became too explicit in his descriptions. It takes a careful, labored reading to decipher Curtis's words.

Why Fuller went to such trouble to obscure the text in Curtis's fifth and last letter is not difficult to determine. He did not change the equally explicit and detailed texts of the other four letters because he had received them at his Prairie Avenue address. These letters were all safely tucked away in the privacy of his Chicago apartment. But the March letter reached Fuller in Charleston. By altering the text Fuller was assuring himself that if the letter were lost in transit, at a boardinghouse or at the home of a friend, its contents would certainly be lost upon any casual reader.

The question still remains why Fuller chose to keep any of the five letters at all. The answer lies in that appreciation for history he had begun cultivating as a young boy. As his personal reminiscences in "Allison Classical Academy" illustrate, he had brought that same historical perspective to his own past. As he read biographies of Europe's great writers, his belief in the biographer's ability to recover and illuminate the past was confirmed. At the end of his life when he and his works were all but forgotten, Fuller would often refer to his own literary revival, which he placed prophetically fifty years after his death. After winning accolades for his novels from such distinguished writers as William Dean Howells, Fuller believed that history would vindicate him. By 1895 when he felt that his place in American letters was established, he could refer to his "archives," in which he carefully saved his personal papers.[28] He knew that it would be only a matter of time and circumstances before his whole story, the one Victorian America would not allow him to tell fully, would be told. He was insuring his own accurate revival with the preservation of selected documents, like the Curtis letters, which held the truth about his own secret and about the complexity of his relationship with his society.

The Curtis correspondence was only a brief episode in Fuller's life at this time, and it ended as abruptly as it had begun. Before Curtis's last letter reached him in Charleston, Fuller had begun his tour of Washington. He then traveled through Richmond, Raleigh, Charleston, Savannah, and Nashville. His spending approximately a month in Washington and another in Charleston is largely why the last Curtis letter was able to reach him. He liked Charleston more than the other cities he visited. As a result he spent only a day in Savannah, and gave a week each to the other stops on his itinerary.[29]

Apparently, before Fuller left, Garland had written to Ellen Glasgow in Richmond to introduce Fuller and to inform her he would stop by for a short visit. In January 1897 *The Descendant,* Glasgow's first novel, appeared and created no little excitement among its readers and reviewers. Recognizing the work of a fellow realist, Garland was among her most enthusiastic supporters.[30] So with Garland's encouragement, some time in late January or early February, Fuller called three times at the Glasgow residence at One West Main Street.[31] Fuller managed to visit with Glasgow twice, but was disappointed when he was unable to have a satisfactory conversation with her on either occasion. Instead, he had to settle for discussing *The Descendant* with Mrs. Cary McCormack, Glasgow's widowed sister, and was forced to spend more time than he cared to with Francis Glasgow, Ellen's aging father.[32]

When he returned home during the first week in April 1897, Fuller received a short letter from Howells thanking him for the copy of *From the Other Side* which he had received from Fuller's publisher. The collection was subtitled *Stories of Transatlantic Travel* and contained four stories, "The Greatest of These" (1897), "What Youth Can Do" (1897), "The Pilgrim Sons" (1895), and the much earlier story "Pasquale's Picture" (1885). Even though Howells liked some of the new stories in the volume, he was clearly disappointed to discover that all of the stories were set abroad, either in Italy or in England. In his letter he made no effort to hide his total exasperation over Fuller's long abstinence from the sort of fiction he had created in his first two Chicago novels. "I wish I could see you," Howells wrote, "and I'll give you *a quattro occhi* how much your work contents and discontents me. You ought to do more of 'it'—more novels. You have done two of our best; you have no right to stop."[33]

But Fuller would remain resolute in his approach to his fiction. In "The Greatest of These," the first story in the volume, Fuller raises the issue of literary realism only to attack it. Through Stanhope, an American novelist traveling in Italy, Fuller creates a caricature of the practicing veritist. Notebook, in hand, like Fin-de-Siècle in *The Chatelaine,* he dispassionately records details and facts from life which he intends to use in his fiction. But Stanhope's realistic method is attacked by a more refined European type, Madame Brandt. She feels his method lacks any moral sense. Howells would have been chagrined if he had known that, in spite of all his support and encouragement, this was Fuller's capitulation to the East and to Norton specifically, who had criticized Fuller's first Chicago novel because it lacked a "moral lesson." In addition, "What Youth Can Do" and "Pasquale's Picture" were included in the volume to appeal more to that genteel East than to Howells's tastes. Their focus is upon Italy, and they avoid entirely the issue of literary realism.

By far the most successful story in the collection is "The Pilgrim Sons." Even Howells found it the "freshest" and "most adequately treated" story in the volume. Fuller's sense of irony and more convincing character development are at the basis of the story's success. James's influence is more apparent in "The Pilgrim Sons" than in anything Fuller had written since the publication of his first satires in *Life* years before. The story focuses upon three American families who renounce the United States for England in an effort to reclaim their lost English heritage.

The irony behind the families' moves is that, as Henry James made clear in so many of his novels and stories, the status of the rich transplanted American abroad is never secure. Mrs. Westgate says in "An International Episode," "There is some remarkably superior second-rate society . . . for strangers" in England. Likewise, Fuller's narrator, Theodore, referring to the two families that preceded him to England, observes, "Though they were of the first magnitude at home, they are but undistinguished stars of moderate lustre, in the great constellation of Old World society." But no matter: Theodore, his wife, and the others persist in their folly to settle into what their genealogist mockingly calls their "sawdust palace," that artificial society they have chosen over life in America.

Whatever Howells's opinion of "The Pilgrim Sons," *From the Other Side* did not sell, nor did it bring Fuller any greater notice. The reviews were short and unenthusiastic. The *Critic* noted that at least the collection was free from those "airy bubbles of imagination" which characterized Fuller's travel romances.[34] But as Howells believed, it was not the type of fiction that Fuller was capable of writing. At the book's center is a rejection of the tenets of Howellsian realism, in spite of the stories' realistic technique. Moreover, Fuller reserved the best qualities for his Europeans. Madame Brandt and Don Pietro are imaginative and sympathetic characters, but his Americans, such as Elizabeth Harkins, the bolt-and-padlock heiress from Birmingham in "What Youth Can Do," and the Pilgrim Sons, are wholly materialistic. The American writer Stanhope is little more than an uninspired literary realist. This much Howells must have recognized in Fuller's transatlantic stories, but he was too kind to be more forceful in his judgment.

III

Since his latest collection of stories failed to generate the sales Fuller had hoped for, he stayed close to Chicago during the following summer. He looked after the family property and finances that he was still obliged to oversee for his mother and nieces. As a break from his routine, he did manage to make several trips during the summer to Lorado Taft's camp on the Rock River. While there, among the tents and makeshift accommodations, Fuller made himself as comfortable as possible and joined the excitement and spirit of the new art colony. As the camp became more established, the members of the colony wished to have some writing done on the campgrounds to add to the work of the sculptors and painters. When the intentions seemed right to him, Fuller was always a willing participant. In July he solicited Garland to write something at the camp. Even though he had not yet written anything himself, he informed Garland in his letter, "While down there I read Miss

[Zulime] Taft a story I had written in your manner."[35] But he showed his friends that he was more than just a man of letters. He must have drawn chuckles from the young artists when one afternoon the otherwise genteel Fuller took off his suit of clothes, put on working garb, and clambered to the top of the colony's newly constructed kitchen to help shingle the roof.

For the next several years, visits to the camp became a welcome complement to Fuller's activities in Chicago, and his boyhood Coonie began to occupy less of his time.[36] He also began to rely upon the resort homes of his friends in Michigan, Indiana, and New York for trips away from Chicago. At this time too, his correspondence with Louise dropped off abruptly. The year before, he had written her a short note encouraging her to attend a lecture he was scheduled to give on the Italian dramatist Carlo Goldoni. But his friendships became more and more limited to his select group of writers and artists, which did not include Louise. The Little Room, Oregon, and studio life on the Midway and in the Fine Arts Building became the central focus of Fuller's active Chicago social life.

Fuller was well liked, and was among the chief supporters of the Little Room's weekly meetings and special events. In January 1899 he joined in the Little Room's "Twelfth Night Revel" and contributed his share to the banter and repartee which always characterized those occasions.[37] In another Little Room affair Fuller attended a costume party thrown in honor of his friend Hobart Chatfield-Taylor and went disguised as a "cockney bill distributor," a character from one of Chatfield-Taylor's works.[38] In recent years he had made many new friends among the younger, less established artists in town. In February 1899 he was invited to the Fine Arts Building by students to attend a more formal party. Later he wrote to Garland about a "fancy dress party" he attended "disguised as a gent."[39] To be respected and included among Chicago's young artists, in whose work he took such a deep personal interest, was a compliment Fuller did not take lightly.

When Howells visited Chicago in the fall of 1899, it was Fuller's turn to play host. He was eager to show Howells the "better side" of Chicago. He organized a luncheon for his friend and made a special effort to introduce him to George Ade, Will Payne, and other promising young midwestern writers.[40]

In the late 1890s Fuller became a well-known figure among the faculty and students at the University of Chicago. For the remainder of his life he would live in small boardinghouses which were nearly always within a reasonable distance from the campus. During this time Fuller became acquainted with Professors William Vaughn Moody, Robert Herrick, Robert Morss Lovett, and Myra Reynolds of the English Department. He also became good friends with French professor Elizabeth Wallace.[41] He was invited regularly to faculty teas and attended student plays, operettas, and even dances. In March 1899 he dined with Garland and Professors Reynolds and Wallace at Foster Hall. After dinner they attended a student comic opera production held in the gym. Later that same month Fuller returned to the campus in a more official capacity to lecture in Foster Hall "to fifty girls and six professors" on eighteenth-century Italian drama. His lecture was very well received. He was flattered when he was invited back to lecture to the faculty and postgraduate club. During this period Fuller continued to cultivate his association with Professor James Taft Hatfield, a member of the Little Room and the distinguished professor of German at Northwestern University in Evanston.

As Fuller's circle of friends in Chicago grew, so did his connections with the East and New York, where Howells was his chief supporter and promoter. Some time late in 1898 Howells, along with Francis Marion Crawford, recommended Fuller for membership in the National Institute of Arts and Letters.[42] Through the many dinners and functions that the institute sponsored, Fuller found himself more closely in touch with eastern society than he had been since his days in Boston. In early 1899 Walter Damrosch, Director of the Metropolitan Opera and also member of the National Institute, asked Fuller to write a libretto for an opera based on Edmond Rostand's *Cyrano de Bergerac*. At perhaps another time in his career, this would have been an easy matter for Fuller to decide. With the failure of his last two books, Fuller's literary stock, as well as income, was at its lowest in years. In late March a very concerned Fuller wrote a hasty note to Howells in "a frank appeal for advice." It seems that Fuller feared the loss of the support "of the good people down east" if he produced at that time an unoriginal piece.[43] In need of money, but not indifferent to his critics' opinion of his work, Fuller solicited Howells's professional advice about the impact of writing a libretto on his eastern friends and how much money he stood to earn by it. Apparently, Howells was not encouraging. Though

Fuller finished the libretto, the opera was never produced. The time he invested in the libretto caused a further drain on his dwindling financial reserves. Before the end of the year Fuller was forced to take a job writing editorials for the *Saturday Evening Post,* none of which would appear before 1900. This was the first job Fuller had held in nearly ten years.

IV

During this period Fuller spent much of his time away from his writing desk among professors, artists, and writers. In the spring of 1899 these associations were brought together in a common purpose. The previous May, acting upon Congress's declaration of war against Spain, Commodore George Dewey had attacked and annihilated the Spanish fleet stationed in Manila Bay in the Philippines. The "'splendid little war'" lasted only a few weeks. If Fuller was concerned about or opposed to Dewey's action, he did not discuss it in any of his letters. In 1898 there were few vocal opponents to America's involvement in Asia; the real opposition had to wait until the following year. Because of his new job as editorial writer for the *Post* and the mounting pressure to turn out a new volume of fiction, Fuller would not have been greatly concerned if the whole matter had ended with Dewey's short skirmish.[44] But in February 1899 the formerly exiled Philippine leader Emilio Aguinaldo clashed with American troops. It would take nearly two years and the loss of hundreds of lives before the conflict would end. The war's supporters who raised the patriotic battle cry "Remember the Maine" soon found themselves countered by a full-fledged, vocal, anti-imperialist movement.

Joining forces with Boston and New York, Chicago immediately organized its own anti-imperialist league. Fuller saw that among the movement's staunchest supports were his best friends Howells and Norton. Also included in the eastern leagues were William James, Charles W. Eliot, president of Harvard College, and Mark Twain. For the otherwise conservative Fuller, these names lent a certain sanction if not respectability to the ideals of the movement. But he did not have to rely upon the East for his support. At home he soon found himself surrounded by a group of equally distinguished and committed individuals. The effect of the anti-imperialist movement upon Chicago's citizens was

not unlike that of the fair. For six months the movement brought together the diverse elements of the city, from academicians, writers, and
artists, to ministers, businessmen, and social reformers, in one common
endeavor. Collectively, they urged President McKinley to stop the war
and return America to a more democratic foreign policy.[45]

Opposing a foreign policy that was "hostile to liberty," the Chicago
Anti-Imperialist League organized two mass meetings for April 30 and
May 7, 1899, in the Central Music Hall. As a member of the midwestern anti-imperialist movement, Fuller not only signed "The Call," urg-
ing all "lovers of liberty" to attend the public meetings scheduled, he
also added his name to the approximately one hundred vice-presidents
of the Chicago league.[46] Listed in the *Liberty Tract* with Fuller were
Little Room members William Morton Payne, James Hatfield, the Pond
brothers, and Sigmund Zeisler, who was among the six speakers at the
April 30 meeting. Not included in the published list were an additional
315 supporters. As one of the vice-presidents, Fuller was joined by a
distinguished group of Chicagoans: Dankmar Adler, Clarence Darrow,
Jane Addams, A. C. McClurg, and Charles Hutchinson, founder and
president of the Chicago Art Institute. From Chicago's universities
there came an outpouring of support. More than four hundred men and
women signed the *Liberty Tract,* while both meetings attracted more
than three thousand sympathizers to the Central Music Hall.

Fuller's role at the two "liberty meetings" in the spring and the two
national conferences held in Chicago in the fall was minimal and did
not go much beyond his signing the league's public call to oppose Mc-
Kinley's policy. At the meetings he listened to fiery moralistic and le-
galistic speeches punctuated by satirical poems read from the podium.
Inspired by the impassioned rhetoric of the meetings, Fuller wrote and
published at his own expense a pamphlet of satirical verse entitled *The
New Flag: Satires.*

The image of the flag in Fuller's title is taken from the predominant
role the banner played in the propaganda from the imperialist faction.
It became the chief symbol at the time in expansionist films supporting
the earlier Spanish-American conflict in Cuba. It was very likely that
Fuller saw at the Hopkins Theater in Chicago the year before at least
one of the imperialists' propaganda films in which the Spanish flag is
torn down and the new flag, the American flag, is dramatically raised.[47]

In the preface Fuller's answer to the imperialists' propaganda is to replace the American flag in McKinley's hand with the Jolly Roger.

As the bulk of the poems illustrate, for Fuller the war in the Philippines and in Cuba was less the compromise of democratic ideals than it was the avaricious, murderous extension of industrial capitalism. He opposed the American presence in the Philippines on moral rather than on political or legal grounds. The margins of the pamphlet contain quotations from the Bible that compare the imperialists to scribes and Pharisees. The poems themselves are often prefaced by quotations from Abraham Lincoln, who is portrayed as America's high priest of human rights and the archenemy of despotism. Fuller portrays the imperialists as the devil incarnate and as gluttonous hogs in quest of more land, foreign markets, or kickbacks at home.

For Fuller and his many associates in the league, the battle raging in the Philippines was brutal and racist. Fuller portrays the generals in command of the war effort as criminals who tolerated rape and other atrocities. Of General Lloyd Wheaton, Fuller writes, he gave "orders to leave no 'nigger' living." He calls Brigadier General Charles Eagan "McKinley's masterpiece / in Excrement." Alluding to the scandal involving the spoiled meat sent abroad to American soldiers, he names him "Canned Carrion Commissary Eagan."[48] Fuller refers again to the spoiled meat in his attack upon Russell Alger, McKinley's secretary of war: he "rides in a coffin-shaped tub; By Swift, Armour and Co. supplied."

Included in Fuller's broadside were other public figures like Henry Cabot Lodge, leader of the imperialist faction in Congress, and Senator Mark Hanna, longtime friend of McKinley and supporter of his foreign policy. In a short poem he attacked Rough Rider Teddy Roosevelt, whom he called Teddy the Terror. In other poems he ridiculed well-known Chicagoans like the Reverend Lyman Abbott, a widely respected Congregationalist minister and the man he had worked for in the 1880s at the Christian Union. He also attacked Professor Harry Pratt Judson, chairman of the political science department at the University of Chicago.

But the man whom Fuller singled out for special treatment among all of the professors at the University of Chicago was sociology professor Albion Small, considered among the most celebrated sociologists in America. When Fuller called him a "colossal dolt," he attacked one of the most distinguished members of the university faculty. In the margin

of one poem dedicated to Small, Fuller quotes Small as saying at an imperialist rally, "It's a crime to think nowadays." In another poem entitled "Ode to Small−Teenie−Weenie−Small," Fuller wrote,

> Professor Pudden Patum Small
> Says it's a crime to think at all−
> Which shows why Pudden Patum Small
> Of intellect imperial
> Is not what we exactly call
> A howling, tearing criminal.

In an image reminiscent of Pope's *Dunciad,* Fuller relegates Professor
Small to "the Paradise of Fools."

Included among the many loyalists supporting McKinley's policy were
Fuller's friends Melville E. Stone, one of the original founders of the
Little Room, and Walter Damrosch from New York. Damrosch wrote
a fifty-minute musical composition entitled "Manila Te Deum" honor-
ing Commodore Dewey's destruction of the Spanish fleet in the Philippines. It was played on the evening of May 1 at a loyalist gathering which
attracted approximately five thousand listeners to the auditorium in Chicago.[49] However, because of his friends' high visibility in the loyalist
camp, Fuller avoided attacking them in *The New Flag.* But it does appear that the division between the two factions in the Little Room would
come to alienate him for a short time from his friends anyway.

Years later Fuller would attempt to minimize the significance of *The
New Flag* in his career as a writer and would even deny ever having
written the volume. In the 1920s when Carl Van Vechten was writing
Excavations, he wrote to Fuller to confirm some sketchy evidence he
had about Fuller's attack upon McKinley and his administration. In return Fuller wrote very curtly, "I never attacked McKinley in print."[50]
But the war's impact upon Fuller cannot be overestimated. Ultimately,
his view of the war went far beyond William Vaughn Moody's claim
in one of his poems on the war that America had merely "stumbled in
the dark."[51] For Fuller the war in the Philippines represented less a
momentary lapse for his country than an inevitable extension of the commercial spirit he had observed around him in Chicago. His midwestern
hometown would never seem quite so local or so provincial to him again.
He came to believe that the anti-imperialists' failure to stop McKinley

in the summer of 1899 was not due to their lack of organization or even to their small numbers. Instead, he saw the war effort abroad as a dark force—Henry Adams called it the dynamo—that was ultimately greater than the ability of either side, the loyalists or the anti-imperialists, to control or even remotely influence.

The extremity of Fuller's invective in *The New Flag* is an index to the deep frustration that he felt over the direction his city and now more obviously the United States were taking. Fuller developed a brooding determinism about the future of his country that went beyond even his conservative views of social class. In his eulogy of the fin-de-siècle in the *Education,* Henry Adams would describe the controlling influence in his age as the forces of nature. Age, race, and environment became Fuller's doleful explanation for what he saw as the controlling and limiting forces in his generation. Referring to the war in a letter to Charles Eliot Norton, Fuller wrote, "Perhaps the whole matter is one of age and environment. . . . It is consoling to take, if one can, the view that as a mass, we may be blindly yet intuitively following a more or less predestined course."[52] Fuller once believed that moral censorship and perhaps a sound verbal thrashing might bring some satisfactory change to his city. Indeed, during and shortly after the fair Fuller believed that Chicago might yet earn the distinction of being something more than a brawling commercial center. That McKinley continued the war and ultimately suppressed Aguinaldo and his troops only confirmed Fuller's worst fears about the wholly materialistic orientation not only of his city but also of American society. He realized that the vulgar lust for money and empire was as indigenous to the highest public offices as it was on a smaller scale to the wards and precincts of Chicago's levee.

From this same deterministic position, while the war was still raging, Fuller launched yet another attack. This time he broadened his scope beyond the criticism he had hurled at selected politicians in *The New Flag* and turned his attack upon the whole of American culture and its dominant Anglo-Saxon population.

On Saturday afternoon, April 15, 1899, in Anna Morgan's studio in the Fine Arts Building, Fuller delivered a lecture entitled "Art in America." Basing his remarks upon Hippolyte Taine's scientific determinism, Fuller argued that Americans lacked the appropriate heredity, environment, and spirit to create or to appreciate great art. In his discussion Fuller used Chicago as an example of the compromise of aesthetic principles in this country. His main point about art bothered his audience less than the example he made of his hometown, and his remarks were soon distorted by the press.[53] Beginning the following day, and for nearly a week thereafter, the *Chicago Record,* the *Chicago Tribune,* the *Chicago Daily News,* the *Chicago Evening Post,* and the *Chicago Journal* all carried stories, letters, and editorials (some on the front page) vilifying Fuller for the "cruel sport" he had made of his hometown.[54] As the controversy escalated on the pages of Chicago's leading newspapers, the East even got wind of the verbal scrap, and the *New York Sun* published a highly critical article on Fuller's talk.[55]

The Sunday *Tribune* entitled one of its front-page articles "Calls Chicago a 'Horror,'" with Fuller's name in bold type under the title. In an editorial published the following day entitled "Pessimistic Mr. Fuller," the *Tribune* reprimanded Fuller for "lacking the local patriotism which a native Chicagoan should exhibit." It followed this with a reprint of the *New York Sun* article and another article entitled "Fuller in an Hornet's Nest," which included short interviews with some of Fuller's critics.[56] Among those interviewed were Fuller's friends Charles Hutchinson, president of the Art Institute, and General A. C. McClurg, both of whom tactfully disagreed with Fuller. However, more characteristic was the response of John McGovern, a local writer, who ended his derisive remarks by calling Fuller "effeminate."

That same week the *Chicago Daily News* entitled one short editorial "Mr. Fuller's Case of Dyspepsia."[57] The paper followed up that theme the next day with an editorial cartoon depicting a miniature Fuller in the hands of a giant personified Chicago who is force-feeding the helpless Fuller an oversize liver pill, presumably to curb his excessive flow of bile. The drawing appears between the last two lines of a satirical poem attacking Fuller.[58] The doggerel poem and cartoon injected a degree of levity into the otherwise hostile fusillade directed at Fuller by both editors and private citizens. But in characteristic form, Fuller did not shrink before his enemies' attacks.

In answer to what he felt were distortions of his remarks, Fuller decided to publish the entire text of his lecture. After some difficulty in placing his article, he finally persuaded James MacArthur to publish his lecture in the November issue of the *Bookman.*[59]

Judging from the full text of "Art in America," the press did in fact distort much of what Fuller intended in his talk. Missing from his

A Complaint and a Remedy

O Chicago, you are ugly, you are wicked, you
        are crass,
'Tis a pity that you cannot look into a looking-
        glass;
You are fat and you are filthy—hasn't Fuller
        told you so?
Go to, go to, Chicago—do not hesitate, but go!

O Chicago, you're disgraceful, you are every-
        thing that's vile,
And your future's dark according to the Fuller
        with his bile;
The survival of the fittest, it is plain, cannot
        apply
Unto you, O rude Chicago, or you'd go away
        and die.

O Chicago, what a pity that a city so debased
Should go on amassing money, letting Fullers
        go to waste;
O Chicago, for a moment set aside your grim
        "I Will!"
And persuade the brilliant Fuller to surround a
        liver pill.

Fuller and the Liver Pill (Chicago Daily News, *18 April 1899, p. 4*)

critics' attacks was a recognition that Fuller's rather free application of Taine's deterministic model was merely an excuse for him to expand his attack upon American imperialism, as he watched it develop in the war in the Philippines. Art would now suffer nationally as he once felt it was suffering only in Chicago. At the basis of the failure of art in the United States, Fuller reasoned, was America's mainstream Anglo-Saxon ancestry. But this was due less to genetic inheritance, Fuller argued, than to the cultural and political heritage that the English as empire builders and imperialists had bequeathed to their former subjects in the New World. "The place of the Anglo-Saxon in the world of today," Fuller wrote, "is determining itself with extreme clearness. We see ourselves . . . as a race of rulers and administrators, the Romans of the modern world. Our place is on the dais or under the canopy." Referring directly to the war in the Philippines, he wrote, it is "our easy conviction that the ark of the covenant rests in our keeping and that the brown man and the black can do no better for themselves—and for us—than to seek shelter under its protecting wings."

For the United States, as it had been for Britain, Fuller argued, the extension of its economic and political influence would only increase the already predominant role of commercialism in American life: "Today political dominance makes for commerce, and the question of commerce brings up the question of Philistinism." For years he had watched artistic standards being compromised by the marketplace. He deplored the unadorned designs of the modern skyscrapers that dominated the Loop District. In *Under the Skylights* he would write a more direct satire on the role of money in the artistic production of his Chicago friends. Americans, Fuller wrote, "are the best half-educated people in the world." For the rich man—the only individual in American society who can afford art—art only "acts as upholstery," mere adornment for the estate's manor or for the European villa. And before the great works that only the rich can afford, they stand "like so many snickering children." In this country, Fuller prophesied, philistinism will keep pace with the extension of the nation's markets abroad. Until "the acute national ambition to exploit the efforts of others" less fortunate is halted, Fuller concluded, art must "wait outside." Neither imperialistic nations nor their subjects could afford to pay the ever-inflating price of "a spreading industrialism."

Even after he had published the full text of "Art in America," Fuller was not ready to drop the theme of imperialism. Following his *Book-man* article, he published an editorial entitled "Why the Anglo-Saxon Is Disliked" in the January *Saturday Evening Post.* Here he focused again upon the racial theme of his *Bookman* article and restated his objection to the Anglo-Saxon American's ability to "subordinate passion" and to substitute in its place a "calculating" reserve.[60]

For a more private audience, he wrote a rough scenario of a satirical one-act "tragedy" for the entertainment of his artist friends and fellow anti-imperialists. The handwritten scenario, entitled "The Color Line," carried a dedication to Professor Elizabeth Wallace and was coauthored by Roswell Field, who wrote the lyrics, and Allen Spencer, who apparently provided musical accompaniment. The humorous piece took as its theme the prejudice that divides white and black people and was no doubt inspired by Fuller's outrage over the racist remarks made by McKinley's generals in the Philippines.

Fuller realized that he was joking about a serious subject in the midst of a mean national mood. Earlier in the year he had written to Norton, "The atmosphere of the country . . . is rather hostile."[60] In the face of the national and local controversies Fuller was involved in, he took some solace in believing, as he expressed it to Norton, "Still, I suppose, we shall all go on cultivating our little gardens, as before." For Norton that meant the cultivation of his tranquil nook at Shady Hill and the sequestered academic life at Harvard. Fuller's escape would have to be imaginative. In February 1900, he published in the *Century* a story entitled "Eliza Hepburn's Deliverance," which he described to Norton as "a sort of Italian rhapsody." Having written his first Italian story in approximately two years, he then committed himself to a full-length Italian romance he appropriately entitled *The Last Refuge.*

Fuller realized that once again he had broken ranks with the realists. Yet at the time and for several years after he would hold an inflated opinion of *The Last Refuge.* It must have chagrined Howells considerably to learn that in appreciation for his support of Fuller's entry into the National Institute, in which Fuller was officially enrolled in January 1900, he labeled *The Last Refuge* his "academy piece."[61] He wrote to R. W. Gilder at *Century Magazine* that the romance was "a reasonably unimpeachable work of art." Four years later he wrote to Will Payne, "It is the only one of my things that I set any great store by."[62] With this same confidence he attempted to have the work serialized in *Scrib-*

ner's and the *Century*, both of which rejected Fuller's offer before the *Living Age* reprinted a portion of the romance in 1901.[63] When Houghton, Mifflin and Company published the work in October 1900, the positive reviews it received seemed only to reinforce Fuller's high regard for his latest. The *Boston Journal*, the *New York Times*, and the *Chicago Evening Post* all had words of praise for *The Last Refuge*.[64]

Fuller's high opinion of his new Italian story was not justified; much of it was derived from his previous books and stories. It was neither an adequate summation of his best writing nor an advance over his previous romances. The plot takes Fuller's characters south, from Rome to Sicily, to many of the towns and monuments he had visited during his five trips abroad. The story begins in Rome with the middle-aged Freiherr von Kaltenau, otherwise known as Theodor Egmont. The Freiherr is a latter-day Cavaliere, but he finds himself in middle age without the enthusiasm and spark of youth that once inspired his appreciation of Old World culture. To remedy the sad decline in his imaginative faculties, the Freiherr seeks out and finds a "young Bacchus," Bruno de' Brunelli, through whose eyes he hopes to reclaim the spontaneity of youth. With his young companion, the Freiherr plans to travel south to the City of Happiness, that mythical Last Refuge located somewhere on the Sicilian coast. Along the way, they meet a whole cast of poorly drawn, one-dimensional characters, typical of those that made up Fuller's first two romances.

The political turmoil and the advance of materialism at the turn of the century forced Fuller to shy away momentarily from realism. However, the end of the 1890s also brought about the demise of the romance form for him. When *The Chatelaine* appeared, it had been criticized by some reviewers as little more than a poor imitation of his first work. Even then he suspected, without admitting it, that he had already exhausted the possibilities of the romance. Wholly derivative in content, *The Last Refuge* brought an abrupt end to Fuller's romance writing. His efforts to promote and defend his book fell upon deaf ears, and it failed to sell.

What remained for Fuller at the beginning of the twentieth century was a regrouping of his critical and imaginative powers and a return to Chicago as the most vital source he had for his books. If Fuller had already made his major contribution to the American novel, he was not yet ready to admit it to himself. But there is no overlooking the influence of the previous fifteen years upon Fuller's life and works. He could never be as optimistic again about his escape from the problems of his age as he had been for his characters in the end of *The Last Refuge*. His previous decade and a half as a fiction writer had been punctuated at one end by the murderous Haymarket riot and at the other by the protest against American imperialism in the Philippines. In between was what he felt to be the failure of the Columbian Exposition. As the decade came to a close, Fuller realized that his hometown was destined to follow that industrial course now laid bare by that broader, more far-reaching national policy represented by the Spanish-American War. Faded entirely now were the hopes he expressed in "The Upward Movement in Chicago" for a hometown that would dedicate itself to the arts as much as to commerce and industrialization.

7

A Decorous Realism

On January 9, 1900, Henry Fuller turned forty-three. He was still hopeful that his latest work, *The Last Refuge: A Sicilian Romance,* would breathe some life into his sagging career. Though his major contribution as a novelist lay behind him, he was forward-looking and had already begun work on his next Chicago book, *Under the Skylights.* In spite of the disappointing sales of his previous four books, he had not yet formally withdrawn from literature, as he would do before the end of the decade. Instead, he would redouble his efforts to regain some of the status that had marked his impressive beginning as a Chicago writer.

While he would never actually retreat from his ongoing quarrel with Chicago, he was no longer as committed to reforming Chicago as he had been during the previous two decades. His battle with nearly every Chicago newspaper over his lecture in Anna Morgan's studio affected Fuller more deeply than any other confrontation he had ever had with his critics. In a letter to English professor Robert Herrick at the University of Chicago, Fuller wrote, "Why should we goad Chicago too cruelly?—the poor place is 'too dead easy.' It is like a hippopotamus howling under hot pins; it makes the wretched beast so undignified."[1] But whatever his feelings for his hometown, he resolved to be more tactful in the future. "You may well recall my own experience last year," Fuller wrote to Herrick, alluding to his lecture at Morgan's studio. "I have about concluded that good-natured ridicule is the weapon." Approximately a year later, Fuller wrote to Garland and declined a speaking engagement with the excuse, "I'd rather keep out of sight—my rule for now and hereafter."[2] Between 1899 and 1901 Fuller also took a two years' leave of absence from his friends in the Little Room.[3] Because of his outspoken protest against the war, he may have offended the more hawkish members of the small club, like Melville E. Stone, who sup-

ported McKinley's policy. But more likely, he probably caused himself
even greater harm in the eyes of his many artist friends because of his
lecture. He felt it wise to allow some time to heal the wounds that his
remarks might have caused. When he did return to write about Chicago
in *Under the Skylights,* he would approach his city through the less direct form of literary satire.

To add to his weekly income, by the summer of 1900 Fuller began
writing editorials for the *Chicago Evening Post.* In the spring of 1902
he took over the literary supplement of the paper, holding this job until
March 1903. Besides his newspaper work, he still assumed the sole responsibility for his mother's property, from which he drew no income
for himself. Over the years Mary Josephine Fuller's arthritic condition
had worsened, and she relied more and more upon her son to attend
to family business. There were periods when Fuller was forced to spend
several weeks at a time with agents and lawyers arranging the sale of
his mother's property.[4] This Fuller sometimes did at the expense of his
own plans to visit with friends north of the city or in Manhattan. Though
tied to Chicago more than he cared to be, Fuller traveled often to his
friends' vacation homes for weekends and longer. In January 1901 one of
his younger sisters and her family moved to Kelsey, New York. Having
relatives in New York gave Fuller even more reason to make inexpensive trips to the East, where he could visit with the growing number
of friends he had made recently through the National Institute.

In the many essays written by his friends, Fuller was too often characterized as a solitary figure. But as one observed, "To those of us with
homes and families, the impulse was to think of him as lonely, but how
far this is from the truth."[5] What often gave rise to this notion was Fuller's
lack of domestic roots. His personal life did not have the stability that
was a part of middle-class family life. His residence at 2831 Prairie Avenue between 1894 and 1907 was the longest time Fuller would ever live
at one address since leaving his mother's house. For the remainder of
his life he would move no fewer than fifteen times. The small, one-room
apartments he rented in southside boarding houses were never adequate
for entertaining guests. Adding to his solitude was also the need to guard
his private life as a homosexual. Even so, over the next twenty years
Fuller would divide his usually busy weeks between his writing and
visiting with artists, writers, professors, and other members of Chicago's
upper-middle-class society. As Elizabeth Wallace writes of Fuller dur-

ing these years, he was "dreamy, vague, shy, and quizzical [and] murmured priceless phrases to those who had keen ears."[6] In December 1901 Harriet Monroe and Mrs. Franklin Head persuaded Fuller to attend, as he termed it, "a fandango" at the Friday Club. Fuller's desire to withdraw from the public gaze at this time applied more to formal speaking engagements than to social outings. After his reconciliation with the Little Room, he resumed his role as an enthusiastic supporter of the group's afternoon teas and convivial evening celebrations. In January 1902 the Little Room held its annual Twelfth Night gala organized around an Italian theme, replete with "spaghetti, Italian costumes, hand organs, . . . a Roman lottery," and with, no doubt, the group's favorite alcoholic beverage. Both Garland and Fuller considered sobriety among their many virtues, and like two teetotalers, they abstained during these functions. However, Fuller never refused to take his place among the chorus of singers that often surrounded concert pianist Fanny Bloomfield Zeisler at the grand piano.[7]

As he had with his brief membership in the Contributor's Club in the mid-nineties, Fuller again found himself associating with some of Chicago's wealthiest and most influential citizens. Numbered among his new acquaintances were the president and vice-president of the Chicago Art Institute, Charles Hutchinson and Martin Ryerson, two of the most respected businessmen in Chicago. They were among the original members of the University of Chicago Board of Trustees, which Ryerson presided over for thirty years.[8] In recent years Fuller had begun to spend a good deal more time at the Art Institute attending Lorado Taft's lectures and perusing the collection. He and Hutchinson were also members of the Chicago Anti-Imperialist League. Compared with some of the remarks made against Fuller over his lecture, Hutchinson's comments published in the *Post* were restrained. For Hutchinson's kindness Fuller would flatter him by placing him in one of the stories of *Under the Skylights*.

Fuller was not yet prepared to allow his declining finances and his tenuous literary stock to deny him what he believed was his legitimate place in Chicago's art community. He realized, however, that he needed a more reliable financial return on his fiction if he were going to survive as a writer. As a result, he decided that the short story held more financial potential than any of the forms he had written in before, including the novel. In January 1901 "Dr. Gowdy and the Squash" appeared in

Harper's Monthly. With this story he had already developed a new scheme for his next volume, *Under the Skylights,* which appeared in the fall of the same year. His new plan for short fiction was designed to increase its marketability in two ways: first by selling the stories individually to periodicals, and then by publishing them together in a single volume. As he later explained in "The Troubles of the Short Story," he wished to revive the sagging sales of collected volumes of stories. His intent was to bring two or three novelettes together with "a common background, a common environment and atmosphere, and to a certain extent a common range of characters." But for all his efforts, the form of *Under the Skylights* would prove less interesting to readers than the content. With the failure of his previous three volumes, Fuller wisely returned to Chicago and drew upon some of Chicago's best-known artists and citizens as models for his main characters—Lorado Taft, Hamlin Garland, Charles Hutchinson, and Mrs. Potter Palmer among them. As he described *Under the Skylights* to Garland, "It is a kind of Chicago 'Latin Quarter' chronicle."[9]

In June, before his collection appeared, Fuller wrote another article, "'Society' and the Arts," for the *Chicago Evening Post.* Without specifically mentioning his book, he attempted to prepare his readers for what he termed elsewhere the "admixture of satire, farce-comedy and sentiment" with which he treated his close friends and Chicago's upper-crust society in the stories.[10] He was desperately afraid that his latest treatment would be misread and rejected as just another of his intemperate attacks upon Chicago's art and business communities. In "'Society' and the Arts" Fuller complimented the relationship between business and the arts in Chicago. He directed his criticism toward what he referred to as Manhattan's "swell society," which reduced art and literature "to the level of house furnishing—ornaments for your mantel piece." Meanwhile, Fuller explained, Chicago had not yet had the time to develop a "flamboyant, plutocratic aristocracy." It must have come as no little surprise to some of Fuller's readers that the author of "Art in America" now actually believed that "local conditions for the person of talent are almost ideal." He had high praise for Chicago's wealthier citizens, whom he applauded for their generous economic support of the arts and especially for their afternoon and evening social affairs when they would invite "Mr. Talent" into their fashionable houses for lectures and readings. In wake of the personal attacks upon him, in Fuller's latest Chicago stories critical realism gave way to light satire. If this was a capitulation, it did not fail to pay certain literary dividends.

Fuller did assure his readers that it was only a matter of time before Chicago developed its own local version of Manhattan "swell society." But the generally flattering stance he took toward his midwestern home was not lost upon his readers. When *Under the Skylights* appeared in the fall, Chicago was pleased by Fuller's treatment of its more prominent businessmen, philanthropists, and artists. In its review of Fuller's latest, the *Chicago Tribune* was quick to point out that from the pen of the author who only two years before had written that Chicago could not create good art had come an amusing and touching portrayal of Chicago's art community.

The first story in the volume, "The Downfall of Abner Joyce," is a satirical treatment of Hamlin Garland's beginnings as a literary realist and of his corresponding rise to social prominence in Chicago. The story is set mainly in Chicago's art studios. Included in the story are fictionalized versions of many of Fuller's long-time friends: Stephen Giles (Lorado Taft), Medora Giles (Zulime Taft), Little O'Grady (Charles Francis Browne), and Daffingdon Dill (Ralph Clarkson).[11]

The major conflict in the "Downfall of Abner Joyce" is between the protagonist's rural heritage and the cosmopolitan society into which he is introduced by his newly won fame. Chief among those high society members from Chicago are Mr. and Mrs. Palmer Pence (Mr. and Mrs. Potter Palmer) and Mrs. Pence's niece, Clytie Summers (Julia Grant). The granddaughter of General Ulysses S. Grant, Julia was another well-known Chicago personage. The general's son, Frederick Dent Grant, married Mrs. Palmer's sister, Ida Honore.

Otherwise, more central to Abner Joyce's career and to the story are Mr. and Mrs. Leverett Whyland (Mr. and Mrs. Samuel Insull). Fuller could not have chosen a more fitting Chicagoan upon whom to base Whyland's character. Born in England, Samuel Insull had become known as the most powerful business magnate in America. He virtually monopolized the distribution of electrical power in Chicago. His power stations were the lifelines for the city's electrical lighting, its elevated train system, and nearly all its industry. He chaired in his lifetime sixty-five company directorships which regulated and operated utilities in twenty-three states.[12] He was so widely known that in a 1932 campaign speech Franklin Delano Roosevelt likened Samuel Insull to the "Ishmaels, whose hand is against everyman's." In the 1930s Insull would suffer a disgraceful fall from his position of power and wealth, but at the turn of the century, in Fuller's mind, his place in Chicago's high society was justified by his many charitable activities. Insull gave lavishly to civic and educational projects, the University of Chicago included. In the late twenties he organized his wealthy friends and nearly single-handedly directed the building of the Chicago Civic Opera House.[13]

By contrast to the wealth and power Whyland represents in the story, Abner Joyce is an outspoken supporter of the Readjusted Tax (Henry George's single tax) and is vehemently opposed to "that monster of inconsistency and injustice, the Unearned Increment." Leverett Whyland is Joyce's arch rival in the story on all these matters. In a confrontation with Whyland over the Readjusted Tax, both men air their differences. When Whyland invites the provincial Abner to lunch with him at his club, Abner recoils in horror from the thought of such an indulgence: "Club—fatal words; it chilled Abner in a second. He knew about clubs! Clubs were the places where the profligate children of Privilege drank improper drinks and told improper stories and kept improper hours. Abner, who was perfectly pure in word, thought and deed and always in bed betimes, shrank from a club as from a lazaret." For his abstemious ways Garland was well known and even ridiculed a little by his friends in Chicago. But the humor in Fuller's caricature of his friend is that Garland seldom if ever shrank from the club life and socials that threw him into the company of not only Chicago's but also New York's and London's high society. In just a few years Garland would establish the Cliff-Dwellers Club, named after Fuller's novel, in an effort to bring the wealthy businessmen of Chicago together with writers and artists.

Garland's fame, like Abner Joyce's, preceded him to Chicago. In a humorous piece in his column "Sharps and Flats" in the Chicago *Daily News,* Eugene Field hailed the coming of the virile realist to the blustery midwestern city.[14] Likewise, before moving to Chicago, Joyce had become famous with the publication of his first book, *This Weary World (Main Travelled Roads),* which treats the grim circumstances of rural life.

But despite the humor in the story, Fuller's parody of Garland's local-color writings was a truthful, though tactful, expression of his real opinion. Fuller's criticism in "Art and America" was directed in part at the provincialism and narrowness of American culture. He had always held a special contempt for the parochial local-color beginnings of critical

realism. Whenever Fuller had anything positive to say about the works
of writers like Mary Wilkins Freeman, Sarah Orne Jewett, or Bret Harte,
his criticism was always qualified by the view that their work was only
one small step on the road to a much larger, more sophisticated goal
in American letters. In his satire of his friend's work, Fuller wrote, "*This
Weary World* was grim and it was rugged. . . . Abner's intense earnest-
ness had left but little room for the graces." Later Fuller wrote, "Some
of these stories seemed to be written not so much by the hand as by
the fist, a fist quivering from the tension of muscles and sinews fully
ready to act for truth and right." Fuller characterizes Abner in the story
as a fire-breathing, radical populist, an advocate of tax reform and trial
marriages and an enemy of urban life and a friend of the rural poor.

But once in the big city, with the country life behind him, Joyce falls
prey to the comforts of his wealthy patrons and new friends. The climax of the story comes in a flurry of personal compromises by Joyce.
He is influenced by the wealth, comfort, and prestige of high society.
He marries the socially prominent Medora Giles and even promises her
that he will lay down his radical opinions on trial marriage. As Garland
did at the close of the nineties, Joyce turns from realism to the romance
with *My Lady's Honor*. In the final compromise of his rural heritage,
Abner writes *The Fumes of the Foundry*, a book about the growth of the
modern city. He even makes a sympathetic place for the Pences and
Whylands in his new book. As Fuller writes, "Yes, Abner had brought
down, one after another, all the pillars of the temple. . . . The pomp
and luxury of plutocracy enwrapped him, and he had a sudden sweet
shuddering vision of himself dining with still others of wealth just because they were wealthy, and prominent and successful. . . . He—a
great, original genius—had become just like other people. His downfall
was complete."

Fuller was able to get away with satirizing Garland and his other
friends largely because he reserved some of the most amusing lines for
himself and his own books. Included in the story was that "great studio
dawdler" and "alien romanticist," Adrian Bond (Fuller himself). Bond's
"thin hair was plastered . . . pitifully over his poor little skull," and he
always wore "a conventional society smirk." Poor Bond is shunned by
the rich and is described as being "too small," "meager," and "sapless,
like his books." Fuller describes Bond's early works as "slight, flimsy,
exotic, factitious." Bond is an unfulfilled writer, one who could never

bring himself to write that one great book on "local actualities," which he entitled *The City's Maw*. One afternoon while trying to encourage Bond to reject his idealized, exotic ways, Joyce finally gives up on him in exasperation: "Abner tossed his head with a suppressed snort; he felt but little inclined to give encouragement to this manikin, this tidier-up after studio teas, this futile spinner of sophistications." With that, Garland is allowed his licks too.

In both "Little O'Grady and the Grindstone" and "Dr. Gowdy and the Squash" Fuller attacks the influence of commercial interests upon the arts. In "Dr. Gowdy" he takes another good-humored swipe at Garland and the local color movement. In "Dr. Gowdy" the home art movement is represented by Abner Joyce, Adrian Bond, and Stephen Giles and their Western Art Association (Central Art Association).[15] Dr. Gowdy, the main character, is based in part upon the career of the Reverend Frank Wakeley Gunsaulus, at the time pastor of the Central Church in Chicago.[16] Like Dr. Gowdy, Gunsaulus was a widely respected minister in Chicago and was well known for his social gospel and his views on art. He was widely published and was identified with a group of Chicago writers and journalists that met regularly at McClurg's Book Store in what Eugene Field once named the "Saints' and Sinners' Corner."[17] In Fuller's story Dr. Gowdy's favorite artists are Phidias and Raphael, and he believes that nothing is "more calculated to ennoble and refine human nature than the practice of art itself."[18]

The story focuses upon Dr. Gowdy's opposition to Stiles's realistic squash paintings, framed in pieces of old fencing and with actual squash seeds pasted to the canvas. As Garland wrote of "Dr. Gowdy and the Squash," Fuller had put "a good deal of himself and his controversy with the colonels of militia and wholesale grocers on art matters" into the story.[19] The public outcry over Dr. Gowdy's condemnation of Jared Stiles's squash paintings, whose frames contained pieces of the original moss from the fence to enhance their local-color flavor, is reminiscent of Fuller's battle with the press over his "Art in America" lecture. The satire in the story is derived from Fuller's gentle attack upon the philistines in Chicago who would support art as ridiculous as Stiles's local-color paintings. Shortly after his lecture Fuller had complained to his friends that the press had grossly misrepresented his remarks.[20] After one of Dr. Gowdy's lectures, a newspaper, "by marvel of mutilation and misrepresentation, had put together a column to convey the impression that Dr. Gowdy was a carping Jeremiah, intent upon inflicting a deadly wound on local pride." Fuller was similarly accused for his lack of pride in his native town. Like his own lecture, Dr. Gowdy's becomes the subject of interviews held by a local newspaper: "Interviews continued. Generals [such as General A. C. McClurg], judges, merchants, capitalists – the whole trying tribe of 'prominent citizens' – were asked what they thought of such an attack on the fair name of the city by one of its own sons."

In league with Dr. Gowdy in the story is Mr. English (Charles Hutchinson), director of the local Art Academy (Chicago Art Institute). Fuller characterized his friend Hutchinson as the standard-bearer of good sense and judgment in the art establishment in Chicago. With Dr. Gowdy's support, Mr. English refuses to allow Stiles a room in the Art Academy for a one-man show of his realistic paintings of squash. Later with Dr. Gowdy's approval the New England–born Mr. English justifiably rejects a sculpture donated to the Art Academy by city officials. At the end of the story Fuller extends the final compliment to his friend Hutchinson when Dr. Gowdy comments on the program at the local Art Academy: "Here we have this magnificent school that for the past fifteen years has been offering the highest possible grade of art instruction." This was Fuller's way of making up for part of the damage he had done with his lecture.

In spite of the generally humorous tone in *Under the Skylights,* there is a far more serious theme running through the stories. Fuller realized that his city was undergoing a change; that was part of his concern in *With the Procession.* Beginning before the turn of the century and continuing in the next decade, one by one Chicago's wealthiest entrepreneurs, those who were at the ground breaking of the rebuilding of the city after the 1871 fire, would yield to time and the pressures of their own hectic careers. Before 1900, such famous Chicagoans as William B. Ogden, John Wentworth, Cyrus McCormick, and George Pullman had died. By 1903 Philip Armour, Gustavus Swift, and Potter Palmer would leave their vast wealth and commercial empires in the hands of less imaginative heirs. President William Rainey Harper of the University of Chicago and Marshall Field would also die before the end of the decade. While his friends Ryerson and Hutchinson would live on, as would Samuel Insull, Fuller realized that an important and distinct era of Chicago's history was coming to an end.

By the time of the publication of *Under the Skylights* (1901), there had been an important shift in Fuller's view of his city's business establishment. In *Under the Skylights* the older society that was once in the hands of private entrepreneurs is now replaced by a corporate capitalism, by anonymous boards of directors and by large, indifferent companies with certain unnamed ethnic elements at their controls. With this shift in the power structure in his city, the villains that emerge in the stories are the impersonal Board of Directors for the Grindstone National Bank and the unscrupulous Meyer, Van Horn and Company.[21] Both represent an overthrow of that magnanimous, quixotic individual entrepreneur. In their place are unreachable boards of directors and inscrutable corporations run by new faces and "foreign-sounding" names, such as Meyer and Van Horn. Even more important to Fuller, they have little interest in preserving that patronage of the arts represented by Mrs. Potter Palmer and Charles Hutchinson in the stories. It is not gratuitous that in the beginning of "Little O'Grady and the Grindstone," Mrs. Palmer Pence can catch only a glimpse of the distant, unapproachable board of directors of the Grindstone through an open door. In Fuller's view the old money is shut out, and in the end, in spite of Mrs. Pence's vast power and prestige, the board is indifferent to her efforts on behalf of Daffingdon Dill. The turn of the century brought with it the passing of an era in Chicago's history, and Fuller subtly caught that shift in his three stories.

There remained, however, a profound ambivalence in Fuller's attitude toward even the most generous patron of the arts in his city. He knew that the blame for Chicago's ugliness and dominant commercial spirit could not be laid exclusively at the feet of the new class of immigrants. Too deeply ingrained was his contempt for that early Chicago capitalist, symbolized by Erastus Brainard, whom he identified closely with the mentality of his father and grandfather. His feelings would always remain mixed. His father and grandfather were not as generous and as cosmopolitan as his friends Hutchinson and Ryerson. Their idealism and Hutchinson's sincere opposition to the war in the Philippines militated against Fuller's efforts to define a clear and consistent attitude toward the businessman in his literary works. At middle age, in contrast to his more independent youth, he was courting those whom he had so vigorously reproached in *The Cliff-Dwellers*. But one point would remain constant in Fuller's view of his city: whatever Chicago's cultural advances over the last two decades, he felt that his society was profoundly decadent. He felt that the new art encouraged by Chicago's older patrons would eventually suffer at the hands of the money changers in his city's temples of finance. If at this point in his life he found some virtue in his city and some of its older families, the emerging commercial class threatened to overthrow that older order.

II

In spite of the convincing stories in *Under the Skylights* and its positive reception among Fuller's friends, the collection failed to sell. Its local setting appeared to limit its appeal outside Chicago. In his next volume of short stories, *Waldo Trench and Others* (1908), Fuller would work for a broader scope in his collection by building his stories around a transatlantic theme. In the meantime, the short story published individually still seemed to Fuller to be a reliable, though limited, source of income. Besides the publication of "Dr. Gowdy and the Squash," before 1902 Fuller published four other stories, "Eliza Hepburn's Deliverance," "Miranda Harlow's Mortgage," "Striking an Average," and "A Lady of Quality," none of which were advances over his previous fiction. In July 1901 he returned to his Italian and published a translation of Antonio Fogazzaro's "The Visit from His Majesty" in the *World Review*. The hopes he once had of publishing a collection of translations from the Italian seemed to have fizzled to the appearance of this single story.

Fuller's lack of a secure income still remained a problem. In April 1902 he was forced to assume the literary editorship of the *Chicago Evening Post*. His contributions to the column actually began before he took over its editorship. Given a free hand as to what he could write, Fuller covered a wide variety of social, literary, and cultural issues, both local and national in scope. In a long essay entitled "Erroneous Ideas About Prospects for the Great American Novel" (1902), Fuller rejected the Howellsian position that if American fiction were ever to come of age, it had to return to home turf. Fuller wrote that the great American novel could never be local or parochial, just as Shakespeare and Dante in their works "range the centuries" and "ransack the world." In all, Fuller wrote nearly fifty columns for the *Post*, reviewing and discussing the works of writers as various as Booth Tarkington, Francis Marion Crawford, William Dean Howells, John Milton, Matilde Serao, Gabriele D'Annunzio, Jack London, Frank Norris, Henry James, Edith Wharton, James Lane Allen, Robert Louis Stevenson, George Gissing, and Rudyard Kipling. Overall, in his column Fuller chastised his city's excesses, complained of the adverse influence of the marketplace upon art and the novel, and attacked the lowbrow reading tastes of the American public.

Even though his new job made demands upon his time, Fuller was still able to maintain an active social life. He attended lectures at the University of Chicago and was a regular at the Little Room meetings. He spent a few hours every week at the Art Institute following lecture courses taught by Lorado Taft, Frederick Richardson, and Vachel Lindsay. He also spent many hours each week, winter and summer, in the parlors and on the lawns of his friends' homes in the fashionable North Shore communities of Evanston, Kenilworth, Winnetka, Highland Park, Ravinia, and Lake Forest.[22] He seldom refused a friend's invitation for an afternoon tea or an evening visit. He was always a welcome visitor at Professor James Taft Hatfield's homes in Evanston and Michigan, and he was a regular at Hobart Chatfield-Taylor's Fair Lawn home and Mary Aldis's theater, the Little Playhouse, in Lake Forest. He kept close tabs on I. K. Friedman's progress as a Chicago writer and often dined with him at his home in Winnetka. Anna Morgan, who had a house in Ravinia, once wrote of Fuller that he "always turned out to be the life of the party, cracking jokes as well as walnuts, popping corn with gusto, playing the piano, dancing the horn-pipe and generally cutting-up." To extend these frivolous afternoons and evenings Fuller often took a short walk to visit Ralph Fletcher Seymour, whose home adjoined Morgan's Eastgate Cottage.

When his North Shore friends were not having Fuller over for a social afternoon or evening, they expected his company at their resort homes for weekends or longer. In late spring and summer Fuller would often spend his weekends with the Hatfields at their Michigan resort, where he would "don dis-reputable overalls" and make himself handy and useful by repairing garden tools, furniture, and the family's boat.[23] He spent time, too, with the Hutchinsons and Ryersons at Lake Geneva in Wisconsin and with the Garlands at their home in West Salem. On the lake front near Highland Park, he hiked over the dunes with Jens Jenson, chief landscape architect of the West Park District in Chicago, and Everett Millard, a Chicago businessman and lawyer.[24] Once after inviting Fuller for a two-week visit to his home, Garland summed up what Fuller's company must have meant to all of his friends at the time: "He is seeing all that we do and all that we are in his own way. So quaint and bright and keen and incisive."[25]

Also beginning at this time and owing partly to his membership in the National Institute, Fuller began to make regular visits to New York City. Howells frequently invited Fuller east to attend Institute dinners. Though Garland did not take up permanent residence in New York until 1916, he was becoming disillusioned over the progress of the arts in Chicago. As early as 1903 he complained to Fuller that as soon as his finances would allow, he would establish a residence in New York.[26] In the late 1890s Fuller made the acquaintance of Frederick Richardson, a well-known Chicago artist and lecturer at the Art Institute between 1896 and 1903.[27] In 1903 Richardson decided to leave his native Chicago to set up a studio and a permanent residence in New York. Fuller now had one more good reason to escape Chicago and to visit New York.

Fuller's freedom to travel during this time was owing more to the extra time he had on his hands than to any great surplus of money. The only living accommodations he could afford or would ever be able to afford were one-room apartments in inexpensive southside boarding-houses with bathroom facilities down the hall. As Garland wrote of Fuller, "He lives in one little room and without the dignity which should be his."[28] He could not have failed to notice the contrast between his meager living conditions and his friends' fashionable North Shore homes and New York apartments. For many years to come he would restrict himself to one dress suit, which when torn or hopelessly worn would force him at times to cancel social engagements or turn down invitations until more auspicious times allowed him to replace his tattered clothing. His editorial job at the *Post*, which expired in March 1903, did not pay well, and he had to watch his expenditures very closely. As a result of his declining resources, a note of self-pity began to creep into his letters. He was forced once to miss a National Institute dinner in New York because he could not afford to replace his worn dress suit. In his answer to Garland's invitation to come east, Fuller was forced to decline and caricatured himself as "just a plain Western hobo."[29]

In February 1904 Mr. and Mrs. Bert L. Taylor, formerly of Chicago, invited Fuller to stay at their home in Cos Cob, Connecticut. At the same time other friends persuaded Fuller to stay at their apartment on Washington Square in New York. Shortly after he arrived in Manhattan, on February 7 he had lunch with Garland, Theodore Dreiser, and the novelist Irving Bacheller. As Garland described the affair, "Dreiser turned out to be a tall, thin, ugly and very uncouth fellow of serious not to say rebellious turn of mind. He was bitter over his treatment by Doubleday [the suppression of *Sister Carrie*] and disposed to take the world hardly—a vivid contrast to big sweet-minded Bacheller who is the personification of success. Fuller was very gay and witty and seemed to enjoy the whole day."[30] When Howells learned of Fuller's visit to New York, he promptly wrote a note asking him and Garland to meet him for lunch at the Century Club.[31] Whenever Fuller traveled east, Howells invited him out for lunch or dinner. He would never relent in his efforts to encourage Fuller to make the thousand-mile trip from Chicago to visit him. He always inquired after Fuller when he met Garland in New York, but Howells complained in a letter to Fuller that he would much rather speak to Fuller personally. Just before Fuller returned home in late February, Howells again asked that Fuller meet him for lunch at the Century Club. New York had become for Fuller, and would be for the remainder of his life, an escape from his daily routine as journalist and sometimes real-estate manager in Chicago. As he expressed it to Garland, he took no small interest in the "New York social whirl."[32] He always took special note of the writers he met there or read about in the *New York Times.*

Fuller's socializing with both the artist colony in Chicago and now with his New York acquaintances placed him in the midst of an even larger circle of friends. This much in his life kept him involved and his spirits high. Yet as a writer he began to realize that he was not keeping up with the trends in modern fiction. He looked on, somewhat helplessly, as the new psychological element in American fiction, increasingly exemplified by Henry James's fiction, made his own efforts seem outdated.

Fuller saw even in Howells's fiction at the time, specifically *The Son of Royal Langbrith,* this same drift toward the psychological novel. And he feared for his own future as a writer. "I suppose," he wrote to Howells, "it is because my apprehensions are stirred that I write at all." But he would never feel comfortable with the new trend in U.S. fiction.

The psychological probing of characters by the writer had always seemed to Fuller unhealthy, if not slightly immoral. Despite his interest in realism as a mode of truth-telling, he wished to maintain in his fiction that same propriety if not distance that he maintained for himself in his personal life: a privacy and an autonomy for the individual which could not be violated by either friends or society at large. The source of Fuller's point of view is not hard to define. Because of his homosexuality, he was forced to hold part of his life aloof and out of sight from his friends. Fuller's position in certain respects is parallel to that of his New England predecessor, Nathaniel Hawthorne. Psychological probing was to Fuller a violation of the heart, a violation of the sanctity and and privacy of the individual that was essential for a dignified life. Years before, in response to a letter from his childhood friend Louise, Fuller had written, "I don't know what you mean about 'reading a young girl's heart.' I have never tried that – have rather avoided it, in fact. . . . I might say I have rather avoided the reading of any heart, young or old, fine or super fine. . . . I don't want to violate anybody's personality."[33]

Fuller guarded his dark secret in a way that was typically Puritan, with the same sense of isolation and anguish that so many of Hawthorne's characters were forced to suffer. But as a writer Fuller failed to capitalize upon a theme that would have brought to his fiction in the twentieth century a depth and complexity that would have surpassed his own works of critical realism of the 1890s and would have put him in step with, as he termed it, the "new story." As a writer his position on the psychological novel would limit the scope of all else he would write over the next twenty-five years, including *Bertram Cope's Year*. As he explained to Howells, he saw American literature passing him by, and he relegated himself to a position on "the circumference of literature," with only an occasional contribution to the trend at its center.[34]

The fiction he would write over the next five years illustrates much of what Fuller said in his letter to Howells. By 1905 Fuller decided to return to the short story. His plan was to sell each story individually and then draw additional revenue by publishing them as a collection. None of the stories he wrote during this time advanced him as a writer, nor did he intend them to. He was testing the waters one last time to see if there was still a market for his work in American magazines.

By 1908 Fuller had enough stories for a volume, and Scribner agreed to publish the collection. It included one earlier story, "Eliza Hepburn's Deliverance," which had appeared in the *Century* in 1900. *Waldo Trench and Others* derives its chief unity from the setting of Americans in Europe, mainly Italy. As Fuller explained to Howells after the volume appeared, he strove only for a "decorous realism," a realism that fell far short of the stories Howells was still imploring Fuller to write.[35] In avoiding Chicago and in turning again to transatlantic themes, Fuller hoped to broaden his readership and possibly to bring a financial return on the volume. As he explained in a letter to R. W. Gilder, the editor of the *Century*, in their "technique and 'culture,' the stories should interest the highest class of readers."[36]

The stories in the volume are peopled with the usual naive Americans and crass businessmen. In the title story, "Waldo Trench Regains His Youth," Waldo Trench and other Americans almost compromise their American roots in a nearly fatal search for the past. But in the end Trench and his future fiancée save themselves by a quick return to the present and to their homeland. "A Coal from the Embers," by far the most interesting story in the volume, shows the influence of James's "Aspern Papers." In Fuller's story an American scholar attempts to acquire information for a biography of a deceased American poet from an American woman residing in Florence. In the five remaining stories, Fuller exploits the well-worn theme of the conflict between New and Old World culture.

Fuller was very apprehensive over the reception of his collection. He had not had a successful book in years. Even though *Scribner's Magazine* had published three of his stories, he was concerned that the other three had not sold. As his stories were going to press and before the reviews appeared, Fuller thought that with the little money his stories (published separately) had generated so far he could afford another trip to Italy. But on review of his finances he was forced to cancel his trip in early spring and spend the summer in Chicago. With this disappointment and his anxiety over his upcoming volume, Fuller was despondent. In June Garland wrote, after dinner "we sat talking the motives of life till nine o'clock. Fuller seems not to have any incentives left. Nothing interests him deeply. He said that he only lived in the hope of getting away to Italy. 'I'd never come back.' His attitude is absolutely hopeless."[37]

As the summer wore on, Fuller found some respite and distraction from his concerns. For the first time in nearly a decade, in July Fuller turned his attention once again to national politics. The owner of the *Chicago American*, William Randolph Hearst, called for an independent

national convention to be held in Chicago on July 27, 1908, to elect an
independent party ticket, with himself at its head, to run against the
major party candidates William Howard Taft and William Jennings
Bryan. As *Under the Skylights* illustrated just a few years before, Fuller
was strongly opposed to Chicago's entrenched political machine, controlled by new ethnic groups – the Irish in City Hall, Italians and Poles
in the wards – and its growing influence. He was equally scornful of the
alarming growth of big business and monopolies in America. So when
Hearst came forward with his broad reform platform and independent
ticket, Fuller did not hesitate to join forces with those Chicagoans and
friends who supported Hearst's latest political maneuver.

On that hot July afternoon in Convention Hall, Fuller sat in the front
row of the platform and joined five hundred other delegates in support
of Hearst. He listened as Hearst attacked the Republican party as the
"handmaiden of the trusts" and accused the Democrats of providing the
machinery and soldiers necessary to support the growth of trusts and
monopolies.[38] All of this struck an agreeable note in Fuller's mind. He
must have been moved to nod his approval when Hearst, in his assault
upon the Democratic party, singled out by name Chicagoans like Hinky
Dink Kenna, Bathhouse John Coughlin, Red Duffy, and Nigger Mike.
For years Fuller had been forced to observe the corrupting influence
that these men and others like them had had in Chicago politics. His
only protest in the past against this entrenched element in municipal
government had been made through his essays and Chicago stories.
Hearst provided Fuller with a public forum to demonstrate what he felt
was wrong with his city and the nation in general. His photograph appeared on the front page of one of Chicago's dailies on the following
morning.[39] Like the renegade protests and leagues that had sprung up
to oppose the Spanish-American War, Hearst's candidacy also provided
Fuller with that same sense of independence, separate from any long-
term established political structure, with which to express his protest.

The enthusiasm that the election year stirred in Fuller was fated not
to last. After the convention, Fuller spent the first week in August at
the Chatfield-Taylors' resort home in Michigan. *Waldo Trench* appeared
the following month in September.

Whatever encouragement Fuller may have felt over the publication
of his stories, his growing discontent with the short story, especially
when collected in a single volume, was only reinforced when *Waldo*

Trench did not sell. Though Fuller had not had high expectations for his collection, he did not expect it to fail as miserably as it did. By the end of February 1909 Scribner sent Fuller a meager check for a little over a hundred dollars and informed him that the book had fallen far short of the house's expectations.[40] In fact, when Fuller inquired a year later about the sales of his book, Scribner was forced to relay the devastating information that the book had not sold a single copy in the twelve months since their last correspondence.[41] The failure of *Waldo Trench* dealt a crushing blow to Fuller, especially at a time when he felt his creative resources flagging.

Some time in late 1908 or early 1909, Fuller made an effort to return to the novel. For his material he went back to his "Allison Classical Academy" diary. He attempted to fictionalize the events of his year at Allison in a work he entitled "Edmund Dalrymple." At the center of the story is the delicate, genteel Edmund Dalrymple (Fuller), poet and editor of the school periodical. However, Fuller refined out the explosive potential of the homosexual theme that underlay the younger Fuller's thin veneer of words. What remains in "Edmund Dalrymple" is an emasculated version of an otherwise valuable source of material for Fuller, especially at a time when he was in desperate need of a new direction in his fiction. What was obviously lacking in his story was that psychological dimension that Fuller had unconsciously brought to the original diary years before. He succeeded in creating only a caricature of himself in Edmund Dalrymple, a diffident, reserved youth. His efforts to exploit his early diary at this time is an expression of his futile search for new material, which he needed to keep himself alive as a writer. More significant, it points to the continuing importance of Fuller's desire to tell his whole story. He must have realized that he had obscured the only theme in the story that was worth developing. He was wise in not attempting to publish the manuscript.

The apprehension that Fuller had once expressed to Howells over his place in American fiction seemed now to be well founded. In January 1909 he wrote to Robert Johnson, Secretary of the National Institute of Arts and Letters, and submitted his resignation with the explanation, "I am no longer very active in literature."[42] Discouraged over his inability to change the direction of his fiction and over the failure of yet another volume, in early spring he wrote to Howells, "My interest in story writing gave its last gasp and decently composed its limbs for the last sleep."[43] He felt a sense of hopelessness over his future as a writer. To escape Chicago, in September he visited the Garlands in West Salem. After he left, Garland wrote in his diary, "He went in a rather depressed mood as if his trip here had been a failure. Little things annoyed him: the katydids, the children, the noises of the trains, and the lack of heat in his room. He is getting more and more 'notional' day by day and knows it and knows he can't help it. It is a sorrowful thing to us, not humorous. He is quite pitiful in his loneliness and essential hopelessness. He regards himself as a failure."[44] But Fuller's meager financial resources would never allow him to stop writing. He knew that there would always be a place for his essays and stories in local newspapers and eastern periodicals.

8

Delicate Affections and Dynamite

The failure of Waldo Trench and Others marked a decline in Fuller's career from which he would never recover. The two genres he had excelled in over the previous two decades as a writer, the short story and the novel, no longer seemed viable forms for him. He had long since come to accept the limitations of his European travel romances, though he would always count them among his best works. He failed, however, to recognize that *Under the Skylights* was the finest prose fiction he had written since his first two Chicago novels. His three long stories demonstrated the great potential that he found in Chicago as a subject, even if the volume did not sell. But he could not commit himself to the novel. Art for him had to aspire above the harshness of common experience. How to find that "ideality" among Chicago's stockyards and the commercialism of La Salle Street had always been and would continue to be Fuller's problem.

The two decades that followed were the most trying and difficult of Fuller's long life. The 1890s and the first decade of the twentieth century had been Fuller's most active and exciting years. But by 1910, the fifty-three-year-old Fuller found himself fighting a never-ending battle with loneliness and with his seriously declining finances. His life as a bachelor became more unsettled than ever before. He sought the least expensive rooms he could find on the south side. Over the next two decades he would move on an average of every two years from one boardinghouse to another in Hyde Park. Sometimes he stayed as briefly as three months in a room before packing his few belongings and moving. With the death of his mother in 1907 and the sale of the family home, Fuller was forced to rely more and more upon his friends to invite him over for special holidays such as Christmas, which always threatened to become for Fuller, as he once wrote, "a day of gloom."[1]

To alleviate some of the financial pressure, Fuller again took an editorial job, this time for the *Chicago Record Herald*.[2] With the time he had left over during the week he proofread his friends' manuscripts. At this time he helped edit Hobart Chatfield-Taylor's biography of Goldoni. As one of his friends reported, Fuller became a substitute for his friends' eyes. He often researched long hours in local libraries for them, as well as edited their texts. Because of his work at the *Record Herald* and the editorial work he took on for his friends, Fuller did not publish a single piece of fiction for nearly four years. In 1912 he contributed another article on the progress of the arts, commerce, and education in Chicago which appeared in the May *Century*. He also became a member of the advisory board on Harriet Monroe's newly established *Poetry: A Magazine of Verse*. Over the next ten to fifteen years he reported regularly to the *Poetry* office, where without pay he edited manuscripts and wrote rejections and acceptances to poets. He became familiar with Ezra Pound's work and his battle with Amy Lowell over imagism. Fuller eagerly supported Pound's theories, but he often cautioned Monroe not to turn her magazine over to any special literary interest.

In between work assignments and when he could afford to travel, Fuller still visited the homes of Mrs. J.W.A. Young and another friend, Max von Luttichau, at the Dunes on the southern end of Lake Michigan.[3] He remained close to Taft's art colony in Oregon and took extended weekends, summer and winter, at his North Shore friends' homes. Between 1912 and 1915 Fuller lived at 5428 Washington Avenue. When he could afford the time away from his desk, he visited Taft's studio on the Midway and the studios of Clarkson, Morgan, and younger artists at the Fine Arts Building. He remained a regular at Art Institute lectures and frequented the lecture halls at the University of Chicago. The Little Room still provided Fuller with a warm and welcome place to spend time with his long-established friends during the group's informal Friday afternoon teas and their more formal evening functions.

Through his wide association of friends in both New York and Chicago, Fuller never lost touch with the latest in both social and literary circles. As an editor of Monroe's *Poetry* magazine, he was at the center of nearly all the new movements that were beginning to change the face of modern poetry. He once admitted to a friend that his "'secret vice'" was keeping "abreast of the times."[4] After the attention that another Chicago writer, Edgar Lee Masters, received with his *Spoon River An-*

Caricature of Fuller

thology, and with the popularity that the new free verse form was enjoy-
ing at the time, Fuller tried his own hand at the new form. By February
1916 Fuller had made the acquaintance of Masters, whose *Spoon River*
had appeared the year before, and was invited to spend a Sunday afternoon with him at his home in Chicago.[5] Before that and as a preparation for his own free verse pieces, Fuller made an exhaustive study of
free verse, tracing its development historically in more than one foreign
language.[6] By February and his visit with Masters, Fuller had completed
twenty of a projected twenty-five pieces. He published several poems
in *Poetry,* the *New Republic,* and the *Chicago Tribune* before collecting
them in a single volume. As a reward for his hard work, the first consistent writing in years for Fuller, in the spring he allowed himself the

comfort of a trip south with Lorado Taft to Champaign and Urbana and the University of Illinois.[7]

Fuller's experiments with free verse were not nearly as forward-looking as they might have appeared to his readers at the time. He saw the new form as one possible way to solve his problem with the short story that he had been wrestling with for years. In September 1916 Fuller wrote to Houghton Mifflin, which had agreed to publish Fuller's collection of poems, "For years I have been trying to seize on some new vehicle, and to recapture a measure of that spontaneousness, momentum and careless sincerity of utterance which is almost every man's endowment — at the start."[8] In "A New Field for Free Verse," which appeared in the December *Dial,* Fuller complained of the "redundancies" of the short story form and argued that a five-thousand-word story could be handled just as effectively in eight or nine hundred words. He preferred that his own prosaic sketches be regarded not as "'poems' but as highly compressed short stories."[9] As Fuller explained in his essay, unlike Masters's poems, which he actually found too short, Fuller meant his free verse pieces to substitute for what he saw as the static and worn out form of the short story.

Fuller's poems appeared the following year in January 1917 under the title of *Lines Long and Short.* Their themes are mainly derived from Fuller's previously published works and contain little fresh material. Few reviewers were sympathetic to his experiments with the new free verse form. Howells, disappointed again that Fuller did not write a novel, did not give him any encouragement.[10] The collection did not go beyond a first edition, yet Fuller was not disappointed. After his collection had been accepted, he wrote to Houghton Mifflin that he "had no delusions about the profits of poetry."[11] He was simply gratified that he had been inspired by something fresh that had started him in what he believed was a new direction for his writing and thinking.

Even before the indifferent reviews of his poems appeared, Fuller had moved ahead with plans for his next novel, as well as ideas for several new essays. In addition to his article "A New Field for Free Verse," Fuller wrote fourteen reviews and two additional short articles for the *Dial* over the next three years. Among the articles for the *Dial* was a review of Amy Lowell's third annual volume, *Some Imagist Poets,* and a short essay entitled "A Plea for Shorter Novels," which would form the theoretical framework for his next experiment in fiction. The return of approximately twenty dollars an article was small, but he could not afford to turn down even the smallest payment.[12]

By the middle of June 1917, Fuller had completed over thirteen thousand words of his latest experiment in prose fiction. By August 1 Fuller wrote to Frederick Richardson that he had finished his novel, which he entitled *On the Stairs*. As he had written in "A Plea for Shorter Novels," scheduled to appear in the August 30 *Dial*, he limited his novel to no more than sixty thousand words.

When *On the Stairs* appeared in March, Fuller had included a short "Author's Note" in which he explained, "This volume may seem less a Novel than a Sketch of a Novel or a Study for a Novel. It might easily be amplified; but, like other recent works of mine, it was written in the conviction that story-telling, whatever form it takes, can be done with limits narrower than those now generally employed." To this end Fuller compresses four generations of characters in two families, spanning the years 1873 to 1916, and more than thirteen characters into two hundred and sixty-five pages.

In spite of the claims to innovation made in the "Author's Note," Fuller retreated again to familiar ground in both the plot and the characterization of *On the Stairs*. Raymond Prince aspires to become an artist and wishes to live abroad, hoping to immerse himself in Old World sophistication and culture. On the other hand, there is Johnny McComas, a hard-working lower-class boy who succeeds and becomes a wealthy Chicago banker. Also, through the device of his first-person narrator, George Waite, Fuller parodies, as he had termed it in an essay once, the "deadwood of 'punch' and 'climax'" in the novel. He eschews romantic entanglements by his characters and parodies the adventure story by staging a mock bank robbery which is stopped in mid-scene when George Waite breaks in, "I cannot compete with the films." As in *The Cliff-Dwellers*, included in the novel is an attack upon marriage and a realistic portrayal of all the potentially unpleasant social and domestic difficulties involved, from the divorce courts to child support.

The reviews of *On the Stairs* were mixed. Some found the novel "deadly dull," while others were mildly interested in Fuller's experiment. Only months before his untimely death, radical Randolph Bourne in a rave review of the novel praised Fuller's social realism and complimented him for having "the wisdom of a mind that has nothing to preach, no social problem to solve, [and] no moral to bequeath." Bourne went on to suggest that *On the Stairs* should serve as an example to the younger generation of novelists.[13]

But Fuller failed to read properly the experimental atmosphere of his own times. As Theodore Dreiser and a whole host of talented American writers would illustrate in the twenties, there was still room in American fiction for the kind of realistic novel Fuller had written in the 1890s. Otherwise, the radical changes that James Joyce, Virginia Woolf, and William Faulkner would bring to the novel in the twenties would go far beyond Fuller's experiment in merely shortening its length. Ironically, at a time when Fuller was advocating shortening the novel, John Dos Passos and James T. Farrell were writing multivolume novels containing hundreds of pages to cover the breadth of the social and spiritual lives of their characters in America. What Fuller offered in the name of experimentation in the novel was not the shifts in point of view that Joyce or Faulkner would provide, but a few ideas that Howells had expressed in his essays in the eighties and nineties. As Bourne pointed out in his review, the strength of *On the Stairs* lies in its uncompromising social realism. But Fuller fell back too comfortably upon some already well-worn formulas for both plot and character.

Rather than await the outcome of the sale of his latest novel, and no doubt anticipating its commercial failure, Fuller launched into another novel in January 1918. His spirits were down, and he was more than a little worried about his dwindling finances, which provided the major motivating force that kept him at his writing desk in his one-room apartment. He wrote swiftly, and by May 1 he had completed the final draft of his new novel, which he entitled *Bertram Cope's Year*.[14]

He was concerned, as always, over how his latest novel would be received by his readers. Unfortunately, it would prove to be his biggest failure in more than forty years of writing. It would also be the greatest personal blow Fuller had ever endured at the hands of his readers. He had put more of himself into *Bertram Cope's Year* than into any of his previous novels. It was here that he finally developed in a full-length work a homosexual theme.

For more than ten months Fuller's manuscript bounced from one New York publisher to another until he finally called the manuscript in and decided to print the novel himself. By the end of the ordeal Fuller was drained and angered. If his own financial status had not improved at the time, the novel probably would have never been published at all.

In early spring 1919, he arranged the sale of a Hyde Park building in which he was a part owner with his relatives. The money was a windfall for Fuller.[15] It was not much, but for the next few years it would provide him with money for board, entertainment, and even an occasional new suit of clothes. The sum he received enabled him to underwrite the publication of *Bertram Cope's Year*. To print the novel, which cost over eight hundred dollars, Fuller contracted the services of Chicago publisher Ralph Fletcher Seymour.[16] More than eighteen months after its completion, *Bertram Cope's Year* finally appeared in print. After the long ordeal of his search for a publisher, seeing the book through the press, and proofing his own galleys, he was discouraged and tired. An angry Fuller wrote to Richardson that *Bertram Cope's Year* would be "positively [his] last volume."[17]

The publication history of *Bertram Cope's Year* was not unusual for a homosexual novel in America.[18] The private publication of homosexual literature had become standard practice in societies that branded homosexuals as moral deviates and criminals. If Fuller could have known then the battle that other homosexual writers have fought and lost, he would have found some solace. The only fact that impressed him in his efforts to tell his whole story was his own profound isolation in his life-long struggle to break the silence that heterosexual society had forced upon him both as a social being and as a writer. *Bertram Cope's Year* is in the same truth-telling vein as *The Cliff-Dwellers* and *With the Procession*.

In one respect *Bertram Cope* is not a radical departure from Fuller's previous realistic fiction. Once again Fuller attacked ideality in romance fiction, an old theme in Fuller's realistic stories. Only this time the reality that he played off against the heterosexual courtship ritual in the story was not divorce, as it was in *The Cliff-Dwellers,* but rather Bertram Cope's homosexuality. There is in the novel an irreconcilable conflict between Cope and his three female admirers.

Cope is a twenty-four-year-old college instructor and graduate student working for an advanced degree at a small college (Northwestern University) in Churchton (Evanston). He is mercilessly pursued by three young females, Carolyn, Amy, and Hortense, who is the middle-aged Mrs. Phillips's niece. All three women are encouraged in their affection for Cope by the overzealous Mrs. Phillips, who has rented rooms to the three women in her spacious suburban home. Complicating Cope's life even further, Basil Randolph, an elderly art collector and stockbroker in the "Big Town" (Chicago), is equally infatuated with Cope. His plan is to entice the youthful Cope to live with him. But the self-centered Cope is not interested in establishing an intimate relationship with any of his admirers, including Basil Randolph. Indeed, he is hardly aware of their existence. His only concern is his homosexual relationship with Arthur Lemoyne, who lives in Wisconsin. Cope's problem is how he can afford to bring his companion to Churchton.

Cope is a weakly drawn character, but given the limitations that Fuller was working under, Cope's irresolute nature is somewhat understandable. A deeply probing psychological view of Cope's character and the conflict he faced as a homosexual in Churchton would have exposed far too much about him. A more socially assertive Cope would have caused him to challenge more directly and more openly the values of those around him, especially his female admirers. This would have been far too revealing and even dangerous for Fuller. He had observed the results of at least one open avowal of homosexuality in his lifetime in the persecution of Oscar Wilde. Fuller realized that if he exposed his protagonist more, according to contemporary views of homosexuality, Cope would have been judged either insane or morally decrepit. To have his novel read at all, the only route open to Fuller was a circuitous one, which ultimately damages Cope's characterization.

Fuller's strategy was not unusual for homosexual writers before World War II.[19] Though Cope does not live with the elderly Randolph, a living arrangement that would have been more difficult to rationalize, Cope does cohabit with Arthur. At the time it was no doubt easier for Fuller's readers to accept two young men living together. However, Fuller does make it clear that Cope's and Arthur's relationship goes beyond their being mere roommates or friends. In chapter 3 Fuller allows his reader a glimpse of Cope's letter to Arthur, who is in Wisconsin: "Several girls entertained me. They came on as thick as spatter. . . . It was all rather too much. I found myself preferring those hours together in dear old Winnebago." Later in the same chapter, after Mrs. Phillips again browbeats Cope into an insincere admission of his liking for the three women, he wonders how he could tell her "he had developed no particular dexterity in dealing with the younger members of the opposite sex?" By the end of the chapter, Cope finishes his letter to Arthur with, "You might as well come down. I miss you — even more than I thought I should." The chapter is neatly framed by Cope's letter and his open avowal of his preference for Arthur's company over that of the three young ladies, or any females, for that matter.

But however forthright and open Fuller was in chapter 3, by the end of his story he caves in to social pressure. As with the ending of his play "At Saint Judas's," there is a similar kind of atonement, even an attempted retraction of much of what Fuller had initially developed in Cope's character. After a production one evening at the university in which Arthur successfully plays a female role, his success goes to his head and he cannot restrain himself. Backstage "in his general state of ebulliency he endeavored to bestow a measure of upwelling femininity upon another performer who was in the dress of his own sex." The young man's reaction to Arthur's unsavory advance is violent, and Arthur sustains a bruise on his head from the shove that the young man gives him. The university and the town are scandalized by the incident. As a result, Arthur is banned from his dramatic society, loses his job, and is forced to leave Churchton and go back to Winnebago, his hometown.

Fuller uses Arthur's female costume and the backstage incident to draw the homosexual theme closer to the surface of his story. The implication of Arthur's actions were not lost upon the other characters in the novel, nor were they intended to be dismissed or ignored by the reader. But the incident becomes not a means to explore further the homosexual theme, but rather the very excuse Fuller needed to complicate and even cloud Cope's relationship with Arthur. Again its function in the novel is like the suicide at the end of "At Saint Judas's." Arthur is separated from Cope, and because of the embarrassment Arthur has caused everyone, in the end Cope breaks off his relationship with his impetuous friend. To complicate matters further, Fuller attempts to relieve Cope of any suspicion in his affair with Arthur. The chapter in which the incident occurs is entitled "Cope Gets New Light on His Chum," as though there is something about Arthur's character, presumably his homosexuality, that Cope had not known before. No less important, after Cope leaves Churchton to establish himself in a secure job in an eastern university, of his own will he writes a short note to Carolyn, one of his admirers, reviving in her the possibility that one day soon he may send for her. This letter and Cope's implied interest in a female after all were Fuller's way of setting out a smoke screen, of deflecting attention from his homosexual theme.

Fuller's efforts to soften the impact of his theme served only to weaken

his main character. Henry James, the better craftsman, more successfully handled the homosexual overtones in "The Turn of the Screw"
and "The Pupil" by thinly veiled innuendo and disguise. In "The Turn
of the Screw" the ghosts of Peter Quint and Miss Jessel represent pri-
mordial forces much larger than life that through the actions of the
governess have great power over the children. Fuller's efforts to disguise
his theme operate mainly through contradiction, which ultimately compromises the effectiveness of his characterization of Cope. Fuller's efforts
to give his reader a more psychologically probing view of Cope's mind
are finally tenuous and ambivalent. Even in those scenes when Cope
admits to Randolph that he had no plans for marriage, he adds that marriage may yet be possible on "some remote horizon, not yet in sight."
Later when Cope ruminates over his aversion to matrimony and his desire to live in a different manner, he qualifies his thoughts with "for
a while at least, and perhaps for always." By not being open and forthright in his characterization of Cope, Fuller was trying to keep his novel
within the moral boundaries of his times. He hoped to avoid sparking
the attack that his homosexual subject matter would otherwise cause.

The flaw in *Bertram Cope's Year* would not be worth dwelling upon
if it did not have significance for Fuller's own life as a writer and a
homosexual in Chicago. Ever since "Allison Classical Academy," he had
struggled with the problem of how he could more openly and satisfac-
torily treat homosexuality in his fiction. That he was finally ambivalent
in his treatment of it in *Bertram Cope's Year* reflects his lifelong conflict with society: his desire to tell his whole story while at the same
time maintaining his respectability in the eyes of his friends and readers. His unwillingness to develop his material as fully as he could have
is understandable, almost excusable, given the mores of his society. The
strength of his best fiction lay in its hard-hitting social realism. But that
depth of realism was not possible in Fuller's treatment of homosexual
characters. The risks in 1919 were still too great for the homosexual
writer.

When *Bertram Cope's Year* appeared in mid-October 1919, it was an
unqualified failure. It was scarcely noticed, and it did not sell. In the
only review that alluded to its homosexual subject matter, the critic for
the *Chicago Tribune* reported a conversation he had had with Fuller's
friend, Henry Kitchell Webster, who expressed surprise that "Mr. Fuller

should essay so delicate a theme."[20] As one critic recalled five years after the novel's publication, it "shocked Mr. Fuller's friends so painfully that they silenced it into limbo. It is a story, delicately done with the most exquisite taste, of a sublimated irregular affection. It received scant and unintelligent notice from the reviewers and, though it was filled with dynamite scrupulously packed, it fell as harmless as a dud, only to be whispered about here and there by grave people who wondered why Mr. Fuller should choose such a theme."[21] Fuller sent a copy to H. L. Mencken at *The Smart Set*. But even the acerbic Mencken, who was making a career out of attacking the Victorian and Puritanical values of the American bourgeoisie, was afraid to discuss the novel's homosexual subject. He wrote simply, "A very fair piece of writing, as novels go. A bit sly and *pizzicato;* even a bit distinguished."[22] That Fuller's society seldom even recognized the existence of homosexuality had been his problem all his life.

For any comments approaching what Fuller felt was intelligent criticism of the novel, he had to wait until *Bertram Cope* was all but forgotten. In 1922, in a general survey of Fuller's fiction, Carl Van Vechten wrote that Fuller's treatment of homosexuality in *Bertram Cope's Year* was "skillful," "refined," and "studiedly restrained."[23] Because of what he saw as Fuller's genteel sensibility, he felt that there were few American novelists who were able to treat such a delicate theme as successfully as Fuller had in his novel. Van Vechten recognized, too, the danger that any reference to homosexuality held for the American novelist. "If Theodore Dreiser had written this book," he wrote, "it would certainly have been suppressed. If Ben Hecht had written it, he would probably be languishing in jail. I cannot, indeed, think of another American writer who could have dealt with the subject so thoroughly, from so many angles, and yet have written it so discreetly." In June, the month after Van Vechten's article appeared, Fuller wrote to him, "I welcome your essay—the first general view and estimate of my work that I have ever met. My hair is not 'on end'—if you are referring to the section on Bertram Cope: your account of the book is the only intelligent one I have encountered.—I saw the 'Siege Perilous,' and said: 'I guess I can sit in it if I'm careful.' In fact, had sat in it once before, briefly but spectacularly."[24] He referred here to "At Saint Judas's." But the publication of his homosexual play, though perhaps a more daring move by Fuller given Oscar Wilde's persecution only one year earlier, could be easily ignored among the other eleven plays in *The Puppet Booth*. Unfortunately, little more had happened to *Bertram Cope's Year*.

In spite of the self-confidence in his letter to Van Vechten, Fuller had been more shocked and disappointed, as he watched his novel drop stillborn from the press, than he had been over the failure of any previous book. He reported to his friends that in his anger over the novel's failure he destroyed the manuscript and printer's copies.[25] In despair over his future career as a novelist, he carried through with his previous threat in a letter to Richardson that he would never write another novel. From his point of view, he had told the truth about himself, as delicately and as plainly as he could, and that was found wanting, even by his closest friends. With the failure of his two most recent experimental books, Fuller believed that he had nowhere to turn. He retired from novel writing. He wrote to Garland on May 22, 1920, "There seems to be no way for me to get read or paid, so—Shutters up."

II

By the summer of 1920, the sixty-three-year-old Fuller was content to become an onlooker in the literary scene in Chicago and America. Over the next ten years, his short stories, which appeared in the *Tribune*, *Harper's*, *Century*, and *Bookman*, were written merely for the money they could bring in. Out of the group of stories he wrote during this time, the most interesting, "The Big Show at Canberra" (1921), was never published. The story is set in the year 2008, when the novel has become an obsolete form and has been replaced by the cinema. In his story Fuller attacks "the manifold obtruding horrors of industrialization" in what he terms an "Imperial America," ruled by a dictator.

Fiction, he believed, had now moved beyond him and what he had to offer in his stories. In February 1921 he wrote to Garland, "Sometimes I try to console myself by saying that the new generation must have freedom to express itself: yet I feel that the new generation (with its most gifted spokesmen) is not American at all—just a shiny impudent hodge podge of low-grade foreigners. The decency and the modesty of the old Howells' day may well be emphasized."[26] In May 1920, William Dean Howells died. With Howells's death Fuller lost a lifelong friend and the man who had done the most to help launch him on his career as a writer. Fuller saw in the death of his friend the end of an era in American fiction. Years before, on the occasion of Howells's seventieth birthday, Fuller wrote to him, "For one full generation in American annals the dominant influence has been yours." He called this period after the Civil War the "Age of Howells." With Howells's death Fuller saw the older generation of writers being surpassed by a new generation in which, as he had once expressed it to Howells, "The decorous thing, decorously done, is rare and is becoming rarer."[27] And with this new generation Fuller also believed that there was little room for his fiction. It was some consolation to Fuller that he could link his best novels to the influence of someone as distinguished as Howells had been in his day.

Fuller was not entirely dissatisfied with the younger generation, and over the next decade, as a member of the advisory board of Monroe's *Poetry* and as an independent critic and reviewer, he found many young writers he could support. In essays and reviews he promoted writers like James Branch Cabell, Sinclair Lewis, Joseph Hergesheimer, Vachel Lindsay, Glenway Wescott, Thornton Wilder, Louis Bromfield, and, with the publication of *This Side of Paradise,* F. Scott Fitzgerald. His personal motto at this time became "Save the young."[28] He engaged in an active letter-writing and review campaign. In return, writers like Cabell, Wescott, Bromfield, and Wilder all wrote to Fuller acknowledging his place as the ground breaker in the form of the novel. In the late twenties Wescott wrote to Fuller, "You are the literary 'elder'" in America and assured him that he "carefully puzzled over" all of Fuller's criticism of his work.[29]

Having given up on fiction, Fuller was forced to rely upon book reviewing for income over the next ten years. Beginning in 1920, he would write more than 120 reviews. With his New York connections he would scatter them in the *Freeman,* the *Nation, Bookman, Commonweal,* the *New York Times,* and the *New York Herald Tribune.*

While his personal investments met some of his living expenses, his book reviews provided him with enough funds for the next few years to maintain an active social life. Fuller traveled to his friends' summer homes, stayed in the Garlands' apartment in New York, and made occasional trips with the Tafts. In the winter of 1923 he made a return trip with them to the South.

While on one of his many excursions to the Dunes the year before, the elderly Fuller met a twenty-year-old University of Illinois student named William Emery Shepherd. Their first meeting was limited to a brief conversation on the beach. After his return home to Chicago, Fuller went to considerable trouble to locate his young acquaintance's address at the university. When he received a letter from Fuller, Shepherd was surprised that Fuller had gone to such lengths to find him.[30] Over the next year they stayed in touch and made plans to meet at the Dunes. When their relationship developed and became more intimate, Shepherd would open his letters to the older Fuller with the endearing salutation "Dear Dunef'o'." On one occasion Fuller and Shepherd took a five-mile hike that ended at an abandoned house, in which they built a roaring fire in the fireplace to warm themselves. As Shepherd wrote of the experience afterwards to Fuller, "Two people before a fire – You know perfectly well this cannot be aught but communing friends. While I dreamed and warmed my damp, smoking stockened feet before that great log fire, you were in my mood with scintillations, inspired by a delightful five mile hike."[31] Because Shepherd attended the university in Champaign-Urbana, he and Fuller could visit only on weekends and during term breaks. But in the spring of 1924, the year that Shepherd graduated from the University of Illinois, a small number of Fuller's bonds came due, and he laid plans to take his young friend on a tour of Europe. Fuller's decision to take young Shepherd, whom Fuller described once as a "straight stepping young Methodist," was much like the wish of Freiherr of Kalteneau in *The Last Refuge* to travel with Bruno throughout Italy.[32] There was in Fuller's trip something of that same desire to recapture through his youthful friend the novelty and even awe that he had experienced as a young man on his first tour abroad.

The month before they sailed, Fuller expressed some reservations about undertaking such a trip at his age.[33] But he remained determined. In early June Fuller and Shepherd traveled to New York, where Fuller showed his "young gent" the sights, before they sailed for England on June 11.[34] Upon their arrival in England, they met Garland. It amused Fuller to report home to Richardson that Garland had helped him pick out a new suit of clothes for his European tour.[35] Fuller planned to travel in full regalia and to buy what he needed for his trip. After spending ten enjoyable days in London, the two men visited Cambridge and Oxford. From England they traveled to Paris, Switzerland, and northern Italy, where they visited, among other cities, Milan, Venice, and Verona.

By mid-July, little more than a month after they had started their journey, Fuller had become "travel worn" and bored. He complained to
Richardson, "I have seen very little that I haven't seen before." Even
though he was with his young friend, Fuller had little enthusiasm for
the monuments and cities they visited. By August Fuller and Shepherd
were both fatigued from their rigorous schedule, and they returned to
England. By September 10 they were aboard a ship bound for America.
Fuller wrote to Richardson that after taking care of some business in
New York, he would "depart westward, where [he would] spend the remainder of [his] natural life."[36]

The tour was too taxing for both men; even worse for Fuller, he spent
money he could have better used for his living expenses at home. Even
before he left, he knew that the trip would be a serious financial setback,
but he was also aware that his health was failing and that this was, as
he termed it, the "Last Call" for Europe.[37] His relationship with Shepherd would continue, but on a far more limited and less intimate basis.
The year following their return, Shepherd took a teaching job in Michigan city, Indiana, and in 1926 he returned to Chicago to teach at the
Chicago Teachers College, where he remained for two years. He and
Fuller visited occasionally. At this point in their relationship, whenever
Shepherd wrote, he addressed his elder friend as "Uncle Fuller."
Shepherd returned to Michigan City again for a year after he left his
position in Chicago, after which he settled permanently in San Diego,
California.[38]

Over the next four years Fuller would remain comfortable in his usually frugal manner. He kept in close touch with his friends and seldom
wanted for company. The only pieces of any significance that he wrote
during this period were two long essays published in the *New York Times
Book Review* entitled "The Melting Pot Begins to Smell" and "America's Coming of Age." In these he recapitulated his scorn of commercialism. He advised younger writers to look to Twain, Whitman, and
Howells for their influences and standards, not to Hollywood and popular culture.

Because of his success in publishing regularly in newspapers and journals like the *Times*, Fuller was encouraged by his friends to return to
writing fiction. As a result, one afternoon he confessed privately to a
fellow Little Room member, Mary Hastings Bradley, "I have yielded
to my friends and have become a working man again."[39]

On December 30, 1928, Fuller began his fourth travel romance, entitled *Gardens of This World*. In a burst of energy Fuller wrote twenty-four chapters and more than 51,000 words by January 28. By February 4 the typewritten manuscript was in New York and was being considered by Latham and Knopf for publication.[40]

Gardens of This World was simply a sentimental journey through his previous romances for the aged Fuller. He does draw in a small way upon his most recent tour of Europe for a more up-to-date view of life abroad. Otherwise, *Gardens of This World* is staffed largely with Fuller's characters from his first three travel books. They are older, but they are without any cynicism or disillusionment over the changes that time had brought to Europe.

Fuller's intent was merely to reacquaint himself for one last time with the characters he had enjoyed creating so many years ago. Whether or not the romance sold did not concern him at all. His heart was weakening, and he knew he had little time left. Even before *Gardens of This World* was accepted by Knopf, Fuller began on February 12, 1929, a new novel he entitled *Not on the Screen*. As he had on his last, Fuller worked consistently on the manuscript and finished it by the second week in April.[41] "It's Chicago to-day," Fuller wrote to Garland, "Clubs, opera, football, teas, prize-fights, police, bathing parties, 'orgies,' etc. etc. That is to say it's a *righthanded* version of a lefthanded 'film' society-story."[42] Drawing upon his more than twenty years of serious movie-going in Chicago, Fuller attempted to exploit the new cinematic art form in his novel. Replacing the sentimental romance as his target, Fuller aimed his satire at the form of the silent screen in America.

By conscious design, Fuller followed a conventional plot in *Not on the Screen*. There is an unscrupulous villain in one Robert F. Sherrill, mortgage broker and financial adviser to the fashionable Trent family. There is also Sherrill's lower-class kept woman, Claire Basquin, with whom Sherrill is loath to be seen in polite society. The protagonist, Embert Howell, is the familiar young country boy who moves to the big city to make his fortune. Once there, he meets the upper-class Trents: Catherine, a pretentious, bejeweled widow; and Evelyn, her youthful, clever daughter. There are fights in the story, imagined and real, as good always vanquishes evil. Fuller even delivers the orgy that he promises the reader at the beginning of the novel. To compete with the new fast tempo of the cinema, Fuller brings the automobile into the action. For more than ten years, the automobile had been the source of much slapstick comedy in the cinema.

The main thrust of Fuller's novel parodies what he saw as the idealized images of life that filmmakers cast upon the silver screen. Throughout, in asides to the main action of the story, Fuller suggests the romanticized cinematic possibilities in many scenes only to back away and give his more realistic view of experience. To that idealized image of the human body that Hollywood's stars bring to the screen, Fuller adds his own touch of satire. At a bathing party, rather than the comely shapes of cinematic heroes and heroines, Fuller's "young women were overplump" and the "young men were flat-chested and scrawny." The promised climax is "not the vast, elaborated orgy that gives you scores of odalisques on divans, attentive slaves in numbers, and wine poured lavishly from empty goblets, with a Sardanapalus of some age and country for a centre." Rather, it is a late-night party on "the restricted scale of modern living." In another scene at a tea in a fashionable neighborhood in Chicago, Fuller suggests that some of the more prominent guests could have been viewed more dramatically "in a close-up."

Overall, *Not on the Screen* is an interesting experiment. It points to the influence that the cinema was beginning to have upon American literature of the twenties. Fuller's novel exhibits much of the wit and satire that characterized *Under the Skylights* over two decades before. Here again Fuller had focused upon experiences that he knew well, even if character development is sacrificed in favor of his attack upon the cinema.

Fuller was exuberant over his imaginative reawakening. He wrote to Richardson that he was in a "social whirl" once again. In April before a somber Little Room gathering, Fuller spoke at a memorial service for his friend A. B. Pond, the architect, who died the month before. In the afternoon he attended a concert, a tea where Thornton Wilder spoke on his novel *The Bridge of San Luis Rey,* and an exhibit at the Arts Club. Later that evening his took I. K. Pond over to Anna Morgan's for dinner. At the end of the week he was asked again to speak at a memorial service for his friend Pond at the City Club, where he shared the podium with Jane Addams and other distinguished Chicagoans gathered to honor the late architect. In the midst of his social activities the aging

Fuller sketched the beginning of yet another travel romance. For new materials he even spoke of going to Paris the following year. He wrote to Richardson that he was making his "last howl for fame."

But Fuller's health would not allow him to fulfill his extravagant plans. On June 2, a Sunday, he suffered a slight stroke, and the Tafts and the Hatfields had to rush him to the hospital. He rebounded from this episode and traveled the following Tuesday and Wednesday to Indiana and Michigan for a visit. By the end of June the plans for his third romance were set aside when the proofs for *Gardens of This World* arrived from Knopf. His work restricted him for a large part of every day to his small upstairs room at 5411 Harper Street. He was not totally satisfied with *Gardens of This World.* But after reading the proofs he was still gratified over his accomplishment at this point in his life: "I'm still surprised to have done, at 72," he wrote to Richardson, "such a wonderful, lovely, beautiful, exquisite, varied, and altogether glorious book (Gardens); still more so to have turned round, within a week, and have done another of the exactly opposite kind." Even so, he did not have high expectations for his last two books. A week later he wrote, and somewhat prophetically, to Richardson, "But don't talk about 'acclaim'—there never has been any, and there never will be. Not for another generation."[43] He knew that after his June stroke his health was on the decline, never to improve. All he asked was to make a "credible finish" as a writer and to leave a little money for his young nieces. Little more than a month later, during an unbearable siege of heat, Fuller's weak heart gave out, and on July 29, while sitting up in an armchair overlooking the sunbaked street below, he died quietly in his room, alone.[44]

As his friend Professor Robert Morss Lovett wrote shortly after Fuller's death, Fuller's passing was not a loss for Chicago literature. He had not fulfilled the great promise that critics like William Dean Howells saw in his first two Chicago novels. Fuller had made his contribution in the 1890s, and in the next three decades he had not followed up on the innovations he had made in the novel. Like so many of his previous works, his last two, appearing posthumously, did not sell and were not reprinted after the first limited editions were published.

What remains of Fuller's contribution to American fiction is found in *The Cliff-Dwellers, With the Procession, Under the Skylights,* and *Bertram Cope's Year,* in spite of its flaws. In 1932 Theodore Dreiser paid

Fuller a high compliment in calling him the "father of American realism." He wrote, "Fuller appears to have introduced for the first time the purely American realistic novel. In it he pictures the era following the Civil War, and through the labors and psychology of his characters and the post–Civil War commercial and social atmospheres, we are permitted to glimpse the true Chicago American scene of the day."[45] Fuller approached the quality of his first two Chicago novels again only in *Under the Skylights* and *Bertram Cope's Year*. A month before his death, in an assessment of his own career, he compared his success in the 1890s with Thornton Wilder's recent acclaim with *The Bridge of San Luis Rey:* "It all reminds me of another young Middle-Westerner who, at the age of twenty-eight or thereabouts, after a year or so in Italy, attempted in his turn a lofty flight, doing it all his own way and not giving a damn for the previous performances of others." But the aged Fuller was puzzled, if not a little angered, that what was being acclaimed in the 1920s as good literature had been scorned in his own day. "The reception accorded *The Bridge* amazed me," he went on in his letter. "Have such things a public, after all. Was I forty years too soon? Is civilization so long delayed, finally overtaking us? If that happens, I shall lop off twenty years and try again."[46] But it was less the hounding that Fuller took from his critics that turned him away from the dominant literary mode of the period than it was his own disenchantment with his industrial age. He repeatedly attempted to find an alternative in fiction to the chaos of the pit and the stench of Chicago's stockyards.

But his relationship with Chicago cannot be wholly explained by his simple dislike for his city's commercial and industrial face. Too often, throughout his life and after, Fuller's critics and biographers laid the sole blame for his uneven career on his disdain for commercial Chicago. What was consistently missing in this point of view was a consideration of Fuller's homosexuality. No less than the materialistic values of his era, Fuller's homosexuality held him back from full participation in his society, whether in Chicago, New York, or Boston. Long before Fuller was old enough to understand the effects of industrialism on his society, as his "Allison Classical Academy" diary illustrates, he was already forced to guard his own emotions and thoughts. He felt compelled at times to withdraw from the society of his peers. He was always forced to hold back part of himself, and he too often was forced to view his society and even close friends from a distance. His friends never failed to sense this in the man so many of them admired, but whom so many found somewhat mysterious and elusive. As Fuller wrote of "Tobias Holt, Bachelor" in *Lines Long and Short,*

> Yes, perhaps he did
> Come through all right —
> With much or little sympathy —
> To take up, with what zest he could,
> The frantic role
> Of buying favors from a cooling world.

Notes

Bibliography

Index

Notes

Complete bibliographical information for Fuller's works is given in the bibliography.

Introduction

1. Edmund Wilson, "Henry Blake Fuller: The Art of Making It Flat." *New Yorker*, 23 May 1970, pp. 112–16, 120–39.
2. In Clara Marburg Kirk and Rudolf Kirk, eds., *Criticism and Fiction and Other Essays by W. D. Howells* (New York: New York University Press, 1959), p. 231.
3. Larzer Ziff, *The American 1890s: Life and Times of a Lost Generation* (New York: Viking Press, 1966), p. 108.
4. William Dean Howells letter to Fuller, 26 May 1895, Morris Library, Southern Illinois University.
5. Kenny J. Williams, *In the City of Men* (Nashville: Townsend Press, 1974), p. 4.
6. Richard Hofstadter, *The Age of Reform* (New York: Vintage Books, 1955), p. 141.
7. Jay Martin, *Harvests of Change: American Literature 1865–1914* (Englewood Cliffs, N.J.: Prentice-Hall, 1967), p. 249.
8. Theodore Dreiser, "The Great American Novel," *American Spectator*, 1 Nov. 1932, p. 1.
9. Frederick J. Hoffman, *The Modern Novel in America* (Chicago: Henry Regnery Co., 1951), p. 28.
10. Robert L. Beisner, "1898 and 1968: The Anti-Imperialists and the Doves," *Political Science Quarterly* 85 (June 1970), 187–216.
11. Fuller letter to H. L. Mencken, 6 Oct. 1919, Fuller Papers, Newberry Library, Chicago.
12. H. L. Mencken, "The Flood of Fiction," *The Smart Set* 61 (Jan. 1920), 138–44.

Chapter 1. The Marriage Question

1. "A Year in Europe," 13 Nov. 1879, 1:86.
2. Family Genealogy, typescript attached to Fuller letter to Hamlin Garland, 24 Aug. 1928, University of Southern California Library.
3. *City Council Journal of Proceedings*, Chicago Historical Society, 1859–1879.
4. A. T. Andreas, *History of Chicago* (Chicago: A. T. Andreas Publishers, 1884), 3:243.
5. "Obituary: Judge Henry Fuller," *Chicago Tribune*, 24 June 1879, p. 8.
6. Andreas, *History of Chicago* 2:119, 517.

7. "Obituary: Judge Henry Fuller."
8. Andreas, *History of Chicago* 2:119.
9. Constance Griffin, *Henry Blake Fuller: A Critical Biography* (Philadelphia: University of Pennsylvania Press, 1939), p. 2.
10. Interview with Helen Ranney, Henry Fuller's niece, Chicago, 1975 and 1976.
11. Fuller letter to Louise Washburn, 31 July 1880.
12. Fuller letter to Van Wyck Brooks, 21 June 1922.
13. The full title on F. C. Burnand's play is *The White Fawn: Or, The Lovers of Prince Buttercup and the Princess Daisy.* Burnand, editor of *Punch* 1880–1906, wrote burlesques and was associated with Arthur Sullivan before Sullivan's rise to fame with W. S. Gilbert.
14. "Toy Village Theatricals," p. 1.
15. Anna Morgan, ed., *henry b. fuller* (Chicago: Ralph Fletcher Seymour, 1929), pp. 19, 27.
16. *On the Stairs,* p. 20.
17. "School Notebook," 1868–1870.
18. "A Legacy to Posterity."
19. Fuller letter to Washburn, 27 Sept. 1873.
20. "Edmund Dalrymple."
21. Fuller letter to Washburn, 27 Sept. 1873.
22. See Christopher Isherwood's *Christopher and His Kind* (New York: Farrar, Straus, & Giroux, 1976), p. 11. Isherwood expresses here a revealing perspective on his view of women which I found applicable to Fuller's relationship with women.
23. See Kenneth Scambray, "He Caught It For This: Four Letters by Henry Blake Fuller," *American Literary Realism* 13 (Autumn 1980), 266–69, in which I describe in detail the contents of the letters.
24. Morgan, ed., *henry b. fuller,* pp. 20–21.
25. Diary for 25 Aug. 1876–24 Feb. 1879.
26. Ibid.

Chapter 2. Italy: From Etruria to Naples

1. Interviews with Helen Ranney, 1975 and 1976, Chicago.
2. Fuller letter to Louise Washburn, 19 Oct. 1879.
3. Interviews with Helen Ranney.
4. *On the Stairs,* p. 28.
5. Bessie Pierce, *A History of Chicago,* vol. 3: *The Rise of a Modern City 1871–1893* (New York: Alfred A. Knopf, 1957), p. 536.
6. Lloyd Wendt and Herman Kogan, *Lords of the Levee* (New York: Bobbs Merrill, 1943).
7. "A Legacy to Posterity," 10 Aug. 1876.
8. Diary for 25 Aug., 1876–24 Feb. 1879. Entry dated 29 Oct. 1876.
9. Diary for the American Centennial Exposition.
10. Carl Condit, *The Chicago School of Architecture* (Chicago: University of Chicago Press, 1964).
11. Two playbills dated 9 June and 7 July 1879 from Haverly's Theater for *H.M.S. Pinafore* performed by the Chicago Church Choir Company, Newberry Library.

12. George P. Upton, *Musical Memories* (A. C. McClurg, 1908), pp. 148–49.
13. "A Year in Europe," vol. 1, 25 Aug. 1876.
14. Ibid.
15. "English Railways," "Paris," and "Parisian Oddities."
16. Fuller letter to Washburn, 19 Oct. 1879.
17. At this time Bishop Cheney was the bishop of the Reformed Episcopal Church in Chicago.
18. Paul R. Baker, "The Italian People," in *The Fortunate Pilgrims: Americans in Italy 1800–1860,* (Cambridge, Mass.: Harvard University Press, 1964), pp. 80–104.
19. Fuller letter to Washburn, 29 Nov. 1879.
20. Fuller letter to Washburn, 24 Dec. 1879.
21. Fuller letter to Washburn, 13 Jan. 1880.
22. "A Year in Europe," vol. 2. Unless otherwise indicated, all quotations hereafter are from volume 2.
23. Fuller letter to Washburn, 24 Dec. 1879.
24. Fuller letters to Washburn, 18 May and 6 April 1880.

Chapter 3. Boston: Vulgar Dollars

1. Fuller letters to Louise Washburn, 24 Dec. 1879 and 13 Jan. 1880.
2. Fuller letter to Washburn, 10 June 1880.
3. Telephone interview, 1976, Mrs. George White (formerly Mrs. Lawrence Washburn), daughter-in-law of Mrs. Roland Tileston, Pebble Beach, California. Telephone interview also with Mr. Edward Story Washburn, son of Mrs. Tileston, Woodside, California. Mrs. Tileston's first husband, Edward Washburn, was Louise Washburn's nephew. In November 1929, approximately four months after Fuller's death, Louise Washburn, then approaching her seventies, moved to Pasadena, California, to be near her relatives. Before her death in June 1947 in a Pasadena hospital, Louise apparently talked a great deal about her friendship with Henry Fuller to Mrs. Tileston, who related her conversations to Mrs. George White and to her son Edward Washburn. Louise's relationship with Fuller begins to taper off in the mid-nineties. No reference to her in any of Fuller's letters or documents appears after 1898 until Anna Morgan published *henry b. fuller* in 1929. In that volume Louise's only contribution was a photograph of Fuller and a four-line poem that Fuller wrote and sent to her in the 1880s. Both are now in the Huntington Library. It is certain that Fuller did maintain some sort of contact with Louise during his later years, but nothing like the companionship that they shared during their teens and twenties.
4. Fuller letter to Washburn, 24 Dec. 1879.
5. *On the Stairs*, p. 107.
6. Diary for 25 Aug. 1876–24 Feb. 1879.
7. Emmett Dedmon, *Fabulous Chicago* (New York: Random House, 1953), p. 204. See also Bernard Bowron, *Henry B. Fuller of Chicago: The Ordeal of a Genteel Realist in an Ungenteel America* (Westport, Conn.: Greenwood Press, 1974), p. 71.
8. "The Ballade of the Touriste"; "The Ballade of the Bank-Teller."
9. Ernest Thompson letter to Fuller, 6 Aug. 1883, Newberry Library.

10. Ticket stub dated 19 Apr. 1883, Berg Collection, New York Public Library.
11. Fuller letter to Washburn, 5 May 1883.
12. Fuller letter to Washburn, 16 June 1883. Mary Agnes Tincker wrote *Signor Monaldini's Niece* (1879).
13. Fuller letter to Washburn, 16 June 1883. Frank Lee Benedict was a popular southern writer of the period.
14. Fuller letter to Washburn, 1 Aug. 1883.
15. Ibid.
16. Fuller letter to Washburn, mid-Sept. 1883.
17. Ibid.
18. Fuller letter to Washburn, 12 April 1884.
19. Fuller letter to Washburn, 12 Nov. 1883. Attached to Fuller's letter is a chart of the churches he visited and the dates of the services he attended.
20. "Are Publishers Unjust to Young and Unknown Authors?"
21. Fuller letter to Washburn, 20 April 1884. "G. W." possibly refers to George Woodberry.
22. Ibid.
23. Fuller letter to Washburn, 10 Aug. 1894.
24. Fuller letter to Washburn, 3 April 1884.
25. Fuller letter to Washburn, 12 April 1884.
26. Ibid.
27. Fuller letter to Washburn, 13 July 1885.
28. Obituary, no date [1885], Chicago Historical Society.
29. Interview with Mary Hastings Bradley, 1976, Chicago.
30. Fuller letter to Washburn, 12 Nov. 1883.
31. Family Ledger, Helen Ranney, Chicago. Now in the Newberry Library.
32. William Dean Howells, "Henry James, Jr.," *Century* 25 (Nov. 1882), 25–29.
33. Quoted in Mary Reid, "Henry B. Fuller," *Book Buyer* 12 (Jan. 1896), p. 822. The letter Reid quotes is lost.
34. Lydia Blood is from Howells's *The Lady of Aroostook* (1879); Isabel Archer is from James's *The Portrait of a Lady* (1881).
35. Fuller letter to William Dean Howells, 4 Mar. 1909.
36. Reid, "Henry B. Fuller."

Chapter 4. The Chevalier of Vain Thoughts

1. In "My Early Books" Fuller recounts selected incidents surrounding the writing and publication of his books up to 1900.
2. Review of *The Chevalier of Pensieri-Vani*, *Critic*, 25 July 1891, p. 43.
3. Mrs. Emma Cheney letter to Fuller, 21 Oct. 1884, Newberry Library; Fuller letter to Louise Washburn, 13 July 1885.
4. "Howells or James?" p. 163.
5. "The American School of Fiction," ed. Darrel Abel, *American Literary Realism* 3 (Summer 1970), 250.
6. Fuller letter to Washburn, 22 Dec. 1887.
7. Ibid.
8. While the libretto of "Mariquita: Opera in Three Acts" is undated, the score is dated

31 July 1890 on p. 65. However, this date was obviously written on the manuscript several years after it was completed. My date of 1888 comes from a rough draft outline of "Mariquita" in the New York Public Library Manuscripts and Archives division. There is also some evidence that Fuller copyrighted "Mariquita," but a search of the files of the Copyright Office of the Library of Congress failed to locate any entry for the opera between 1870–1937. Contrary to Bernard Bowron's dating, the New York Public Library manuscript dates "Mariquita" later than "Pipistrello" (see *Henry Blake Fuller of Chicago*, pp. 86–87).

9. Miscellaneous notes for Fuller operas, New York Public Library.

10. I am grateful to Mr. Robert Gay and his students in the Northwestern University Opera Workshop, 1976, for these insights into Fuller's two operettas.

11. For plot summaries of both operas, see Constance Griffin, *Henry Blake Fuller: A Critical Biography* (Philadelphia: University of Pennsylvania Press, 1939), pp. 22–26.

12. See "No. 2 Duet Fairy and Mother," MS, Newberry Library; and fragment entitled "Falkenfels," New York Public Library.

13. Fuller letter to Minna Smith, 24 May 1891, Newberry Library.

14. "My Early Books," pp. 1–2; see also Fuller letter to Clifford Irving in *henry b. fuller,* ed. Anna Morgan (Chicago: Ralph Fletcher Seymour, 1929), p. 132.

15. Charles Eliot Norton letter to Fuller, 3 Dec. 1890. Original enclosed in Fuller's copy of *The Chevalier,* owned by Helen Ranney, Chicago. Copy in the Newberry Library.

16. Fuller letter to Norton, 6 Dec. 1890.

17. James Russell Lowell letter to Norton, 26 Dec. 1890. Original enclosed in Fuller's copy of *The Chevalier.* Copy in the Newberry Library.

18. See advertisement for *The Chevalier of Pensieri-Vani,* Huntington Library.

19. Fuller letter to Lowell, 12 Feb. 1891.

20. Review of *The Chevalier of Pensieri-Vani, Boston Evening Transcript,* 12 Feb. 1891, Newberry Library.

21. See collection of reviews of *The Chevalier,* Newberry Library.

22. Fuller letter to Norton, 24 Nov. 1891.

23. Review, "The Chevalier of Pensieri-Vani," Newberry Library. Another review in the collection described the romance as "a sort of nineteenth-century *Sentimental Journey.*" See Bowron, *Henry Blake Fuller of Chicago,* p. 79; Larzer Ziff, *The American 1890s* (New York: Viking, 1968), p. 109.

24. Ferdinand Gregorovius, *Rome and Medieval Culture,* ed. K. F. Morrison (Chicago: University of Chicago Press, 1971). The original work, entitled *History of Rome in the Middle Ages,* was published in 1871. Gregorovius's history gained notoriety in 1874 when Pope Pio Nono placed his work on the Index of Prohibited Books ("Editor's Introduction," pp. xvii–xix). In *On the Stairs* Fuller wrote that Raymond Prince "got hold of Gregorovius, with his 'City of Rome in the Middle Ages'–though his teacher did not know of this" (p. 14). Fuller probably read the history in preparation for his first or possibly second trip abroad.

25. Interview with Helen Ranney, 1976, Chicago.

26. Fuller letter to Norton, 12 Nov. 1892.

27. Fuller letter to Norton, 10 Dec. 1891; Fuller informed Norton that he had attended "a little literary gathering" in Chicago.

28. Eugene Field letter to Fuller, Dec. 1891, Southern Illinois University Library.

29. Anna Morgan, *My Chicago* (Chicago: Ralph Fletcher Seymour, 1918), p. 188, quoted in Kenny Williams, *In the City of Men*, p. 63.
30. Fuller letter to Smith, 7 Aug. 1891, Boston Public Library.
31. "My Early Books," p. 4.
32. Fuller letter to Smith, 7 Aug. 1891.
33. Fuller letter to Norton, 24 Nov. 1891.
34. "The Lounger," *Critic* 20 (16 June 1892), 39.
35. "Is a Chicago Novelist," *Chicago Herald*, 28 Feb. 1892, Newberry Library. This article incorrectly reported that Fuller was "on a commission, literary and pictorial" in Spain for *Century* Magazine.
36. Fragment, Fuller letter to Washburn, unsigned and undated.
37. *Critic* 21 (21 Oct. 1892), p. 186; reprinted from the *Boston Transcript*. This is a short paragraph reporting a brief visit by Fuller to Boston.
38. Fuller letter to Norton, 12 Nov. 1892.
39. Ibid. Fuller letter to Norton, 8 July 1892.
40. Fuller letter to Norton, 12 Nov. 1892.
41. Reviews of *The Chatelaine of La Trinité: Boston Evening Transcript*, 10 Dec. 1892; *Critic*, 5 Nov. 1892, p. 248, Newberry Library.
42. "Book Notes," *Harvard Monthly*, Dec. 1892, pp. 128–30.
43. "Today's Literature," *Chicago Tribune*, 22 Oct. 1892, Newberry Library.
44. Review of *The Chatelaine*, 1 Jan. 1893, p. 22.
45. Fuller letter to Norton, 12 Nov. 1892.
46. Ibid.

Chapter 5. Chicago: The Black City versus the White City

1. Fuller letter to Charles Eliot Norton, 12 Nov. 1892.
2. Fuller letter to Louise Washburn, 21 Aug. 1893.
3. Fuller letter to Washburn, 9 Oct. 1891.
4. David Burg, *Chicago's White City of 1893* (Lexington: University Press of Kentucky, 1976).
5. Fuller letter to Washburn, 30 Jan. 1893.
6. Fuller letter to Minna Smith, 4 July 1893, Newberry Library.
7. Lucy Monroe, "Chicago Letter," *Critic*, 2 Sept. 1893, pp. 157–58. This was the second of two reviews by Lucy Monroe, Harriet Monroe's sister, and the second of the three reviews of *The Cliff-Dwellers* that the *Critic* would publish. See also Lucy Monroe, "Chicago Letters," 18 Mar. 1893, p. 168; and "the Cliff-Dwellers," 7 Oct. 1893, p. 221 (unsigned).
8. Review of *The Cliff-Dwellers*, "A New American Novelist," [London] *Times*, 13 Aug. 1895, Newberry Library.
9. Fuller letter to Norton, 30 Oct. 1893.
10. Norton letter to Fuller, in *Letters of Charles Eliot Norton*, ed. Sara Norton Howe and M. A. De Wolfe Howe (Boston and New York: Houghton Mifflin, 1913), 2:218.
11. H. H. Boyesen letter to Fuller, 3 Mar. 1894, Newberry Library.
12. Hamlin Garland, *Roadside Meetings of a Literary Nomad* (New York: Macmillan, 1930), p. 266; and Garland letter to Fuller, 17 Jan. 1894, Newberry Library.

13. William Dean Howells, "The Cliff-Dwellers," *Harper's Bazar,* 18 Oct. 1893, p. 863.
14. Fuller letter to William Dean Howells, 3 Nov. 1894.
15. Garland, *Roadside Meetings of a Literary Nomad,* p. 267.
16. Fuller letter to Washburn, 25 Dec. 1893.
17. Ibid.
18. Frederick J. Hoffman, *The Modern Novel in America 1900–1950* (Chicago: Regnery Publishers, 1951), p. 19.
19. Theodore Dreiser, "The Great American Novel," *American Spectator,* 1 Nov. 1932, p. 1.
20. Burg, *Chicago's White City of 1893,* p. 288.
21. For the origins of the Little Room, see Anna Morgan, *My Chicago* (Chicago: Ralph Fletcher Seymour, 1918), p. 188. Bernard Duffey, *The Chicago Renaissance* (East Lansing: Michigan State College Press, 1954), pp. 51–57; Kenny J. Williams, *In the City of Men* (Nashville: Townsend Press, 1974), pp. 63–64; Hamlin Garland, *A Daughter of the Middle Border,* p. 9.
22. Garland, *A Daughter of the Middle Border,* p. 9.
23. Emmett Dedmon, *Fabulous Chicago* (New York: Random House, 1953), p. 206.
24. Howells letter to Fuller, 8 Jan. 1894, Houghton Library, Harvard University.
25. Fuller letter to Washburn, 10 Aug. 1894.
26. Ibid.
27. Harriet Monroe, "Chicago Letters," *Critic,* 1 Mar. 1895, pp. 167–68; See also Lucy Monroe, "Chicago Letters," *Critic,* 18 May 1895, pp. 370–71.
28. W. D. Howells, *Harper's Weekly,* 1 June 1895, Newberry Library.
29. Nancy Banks, "Henry Blake Fuller," *Bookman* 2 (Aug.–Sept. 1895), 15–17.
30. Fuller letter to Norton, 6 May 1895.
31. *Letters of Charles Eliot Norton,* ed. Howe and Howe, 2:225.
32. Fuller letter to Hamlin Garland, 7 June 1895.
33. Aline B. Saarinen, *The Proud Possessors* (New York: Random House, (1958). See also Ishbel Ross, *Silhouette in Diamonds: The Life of Mrs. Potter Palmer* (New York: Arno Press, 1975), p. 111.
34. Ross, *Silhouette in Diamonds,* pp. 53–56. Fuller does not give an accurate description of the Palmer castle in his novel, but he was careful to insert all the elements that composed the eclectic style of the Palmers' famous house. In addition to his personal association with the Palmers in organizations such as the Contributor's Club, Fuller could not have escaped knowing about the house. As Ross writes, "No private home in Chicago's history was so much discussed." The mansion was demolished in 1950.

Chapter 6. Art and Imperialism

1. For example, Fuller letter to Hamlin Garland, 15 Sept. 1899.
2. Quoted in Anna Morgan, ed., *henry b. fuller* (Chicago: Ralph Fletcher Seymour, 1929), p. 94.
3. "Lorado Taft Again Honors Town of Oregon," *Illinois Historical Society Journal,* 1911–1912, p. 601.
4. Fuller letter to Garland, 7 July 1899.
5. Fuller letter to William Dean Howells, 3 June 1895.
6. Fuller letter to W. E. Ambler, 21 Oct. 1896.

7. Fuller letter to Louise Washburn, 20 June 1895.

8. Fuller letter to Howells, 3 Nov. 1895.

9. Fuller letter to Minna Smith, 2 Jan. 1895, Columbia University Library.

10. Fuller letter to W. W. Ellsworth, 21 Apr. 1896.

11. Hamlin Garland, *Roadside Meetings of a Literary Nomad* (New York: Macmillan, 1930), p. 271.

12. Donald Culross Peattie, "Henry Blake Fuller," *Reading and Collecting* 2 (Jan. 1938), 19–20.

13. Harriet Monroe, *A Poet's Life: Seventy Years in a Changing World* (New York: Macmillan, 1938). See also Harriet Monroe, "A Tribute to Henry B. Fuller," *Poetry* 35 (Oct. 1929), 34–41.

14. Donald Pizer, ed., *Hamlin Garland's Diaries* (San Marino, Calif.: Huntington Library, 1968). Garland's unpublished diaries are in the Huntington Library.

15. The biographies in question here are Constance Griffin, *Henry Blake Fuller* (Philadelphia: University of Pennsylvania Press, 1939); Bernard R. Bowron, *Henry Blake Fuller of Chicago* (Westport, Conn.: Greenwood Press, 1974); and John Pilkington, Jr., *Henry Blake Fuller* (New York: Twayne, 1970). Drawing upon Fuller's biographers, the literary historians of the period all reflect the same general view. Edmund Wilson's essay on Fuller, "Henry Blake Fuller: The Art of Making it Flat," *New Yorker*, 23 May 1970, pp. 112–16, 120–39, was the first to suggest the possible effects of Fuller's homosexuality upon his life and works. Since then there have been some informative works on homosexual literature in America that have briefly discussed Fuller's work. See Roger Austen, *Playing the Game: The Homosexual Novel in America* (New York: Bobbs-Merrill, 1977), pp. 27–30; Georges-Michel Sarotte, *Like Brother, Like Lover* (New York: Doubleday, 1978), pp. 14–15.

16. Fuller letter to Charles Eliot Norton, 6 Apr. 1898.

17. In "My Early Books" Fuller suggests the influence of the Belgian playwright upon his plays. Fuller wrote but never published a fourteenth play entitled "The Red Carpet," later published in Griffin's *Henry Blake Fuller*, pp. 77–86.

18. Fuller letter to Norton, 6 Apr. 1898.

19. Fuller letter to Washburn, 22 June 1896.

20. Ibid.

21. Fuller letter to Garland, 22 June 1897.

22. Fuller translated stories by Vittorio Bersezio, Enrico Castelnuovo, Antonio Fogazzaro, Carlo Placci, Gerolamo Rovetta, Matilde Serao, and Giovanni Verga.

23. Fuller letter to Norton, 17 Mar. 1898. With slightly more success, Fuller also set to work on translations of Carlo Goldoni's *The Fan* and *The Coffee House*. Of the two, *The Fan* was produced first on 14 April 1898 by Anna Morgan's students at the Grand Opera House in Chicago. See playbill, Huntington Library. The week before, Fuller was invited to present an introductory lecture for the event. The following year Fuller's translation was edited and produced again by a New York–based drama school. See receipt for royalties paid to Fuller by the Schubert Theatrical Company, Newberry Library. Otherwise, over the next decade and a half both translations would undergo periodic revivals.

24. Harold W. Curtis letter to Fuller, 17 Oct. 1897, Newberry Library.

25. Curtis letter to Fuller, 23 Oct. 1897.

26. Curtis letters to Fuller, 2 and 24 Nov. 1897.
27. Curtis letter to Fuller, 1 Mar. 1898.
28. Fuller letter to Washburn, 20 June 1895.
29. Fuller letter to Washburn, 1 Mar. 1898.
30. Fuller letter to Garland, 22 June 1897.
31. E. Stanley Godbold, Jr., *Ellen Glasgow and the Woman Within* (Baton Rouge: Louisiana State University Press, 1972), pp. 42–43.
32. Fuller letter to Garland, 15 Feb. 1898.
33. William Dean Howells letter to Fuller, 31 Mar. 1898, Southern Illinois University Library.
34. Review of "From the Other Side," *Critic*, 18 May 1898, pp. 345–46.
35. Fuller letter to Garland, 29 July 1899. Apparently, the story Fuller referred to in his letter was lost. Zulime Taft married Garland on 18 November 1899. Jean Holloway, *Hamlin Garland: A Biography* (Austin: University of Texas Press, 1960), pp. 159–63.
36. Fuller letter to Garland, 8 Sept. 1899. In his letter Fuller expressed his displeasure with some of the artists in Taft's camp who "have no idea as to how to conduct a career."
37. Fuller letter to Garland, 24 Jan. 1899.
38. Fuller letter to Garland, 28 May 1898 or 1899.
39. Fuller letter to Garland, 15 Feb. 1899.
40. Fuller letter to Richard Watson Gilder, 25 Oct. 1899. For a detailed discussion of Howells's lecture tour, see Robert Rowlette, "William Dean Howells' Midwestern Lecture Tour," *American Literary Realism* 10 (1977), 125–67.
41. Fuller letter to Garland, 27 Feb. 1899, and letter dated Wednesday P.M.
42. "My Early Books," p. 8.
43. Fuller letter to Howells, 23 Mar. 1899.
44. Samuel Eliot Morison, *The Oxford History of the American People* (New York: Oxford University Press, 1965), pp. 799–810.
45. See E. Berkeley Tompkins, "The Old Guard: A Study of the Anti-Imperialist Leadership," *The Historian: A Journal of History* 30 (May 1968), 366–88; Fred Harrington, "The Anti-Imperialist Movement in the United States," *Mississippi Historical Review* 22 (Sept. 1935), 211–30; Maria C. Lanzer, "The Anti-Imperialist League," *Philippine Social Science Review* 3–4 (1930–32), 7–36; Robert L. Beisner, "1898 and 1968: The Anti-Imperialists and the Doves," *Political Science Quarterly* 85 (June 1970), 187–216; James A. Zimmerman, "The Chicago Liberty and Loyalty Meetings, 1899: Public Attitudes Toward the Philippine-American War," *North Dakota Quarterly* 43 (Autumn 1975), 29–37.
46. *Liberty Tracts*, No. 1, the Chicago Liberty Meeting, published by the Central Anti-Imperialist League, Tacoma Building, Chicago, 1899. A copy is in the Joseph Regenstein Library, University of Chicago. Hamlin Garland's name did not appear in the published list because he was in Europe at the time. Holloway, *Hamlin Garland*, 156–57. However, Robert L. Beisner in "1898 and 1968" lists Garland as a supporter of the Chicago league.
47. "Tearing Down the Spanish Flag," *New York Times*, 20 Mar. 1898, p. 9. Films of the Spanish-American War were shown later that same year in Chicago; see ads in the *Chicago Daily News*, 12 July 1898, p. 12.
48. The Chicago Historical Society has a rare copy of *The New Flag: Satires*.

49. Zimmerman, "The Chicago Liberty and Loyalty Meetings."
50. Fuller letter to Carl Van Vechten, 21 June 1922.
51. William Vaughn Moody, "An Ode in Time of Hesitation," and "On a Soldier Fallen in the Philippines."
52. Fuller letter to Norton, 8 Sept. 1899.
53. After the story broke, Fuller wrote to Garland, "Don't be misled by newspaper reports and comments about my little address. I have made a two weeks' sensation but it was not local at all" (10 May 1899).
54. See, for example, "Mr. Fuller on Chicago," *Chicago Record*, 17 Apr. 1899, p. 4.
55. "The Chevalier of Vain Thoughts," reprinted in the *Chicago Tribune*, 21 Apr. 1899, p. 7.
56. "Pessimistic Mr. Fuller," *Chicago Tribune*, 16 Apr. 1899, p. 1; "Fuller in an Hornet's Nest," ibid., 17 Apr. 1899, p. 5.
57. "Mr. Fuller's Case of Dyspepsia," *Chicago Daily News*, 17 Apr. 1899, p. 4.
58. "A Complaint and a Remedy," *Chicago Daily News*, 18 Apr. 1899, p. 4.
59. See Jeanette Gilder letters to Fuller, 20 Apr., 2 May, and 8 May 1899, Newberry Library.
60. Fuller letter to Norton, 8 Sept. 1899.
61. Fuller letter to Hamilton W. Mabie, secretary of the National Institute, 24 Jan. 1900.
62. Fuller letter to Gilder, 3 Mar. 1900; Fuller letter to William Morton Payne, 15 Aug. 1904.
63. Fuller letter to *Scribner's Magazine*, 4 Mar. 1900, Princeton University Library; Fuller letter to R. U. Johnson, associate editor of the *Century*, 12 Mar. 1900. The selection was entitled "A Lady of Quality," reprinted in *The Living Age*, 2 Feb. 1901, pp. 328–30.
64. Reviews of *The Last Refuge*, most of them undated [1900?], Newberry Library.

Chapter 7. A Decorous Realism

1. Fuller letter to Robert Herrick, 1 Aug. 1900.
2. Fuller letter to Hamlin Garland, 11 Mar. 1901.
3. Fuller letter to Garland, 16 Dec. 1901.
4. Ibid.
5. Anna Morgan, ed., *henry b. fuller* (Chicago: Ralph Fletcher Seymour, 1929), p. 118.
6. Elizabeth Wallace, *The Unending Journey* (Minneapolis: University of Minnesota Press, 1952), p. 127.
7. Fuller letter to Garland, 12 Jan. 1902.
8. Richard Storr, *A History of the University of Chicago: Harper's University: The Beginnings* (Chicago: University of Chicago Press, 1966).
9. Hamlin Garland, *Companions on the Trail* (New York: Macmillan, 1931), pp. 62–64, 97.
10. Fuller letter to *Century Magazine*, 30 May 1901.
11. C. J. Bullus, "Artists of Chicago: No. 96, Oliver Dennet Grover," *Chicago Daily News*, 22 July 19–, Chicago Historical Society. This is a short article on the competing factions in the Chicago art colony.
12. Samuel Eliot Morison, *Oxford History of the American People* (New York: Oxford University Press, 1965), p. 939.

13. Forrest McDonald, *Insull* (Chicago: University of Chicago Press, 1962).

14. Jean Holloway, *Hamlin Garland: A Biography* (Austin: University of Texas Press, 1960), pp. 84–85.

15. Donald Pizer, ed., *Hamlin Garland's Diaries* (San Marino, Calif.: Huntington Library, 1968), p. 14.

16. Gunsaulus was pastor of the Plymouth Congregational Church between 1887 and 1899, when he became pastor of the Central Church in Chicago (*The Elite of Chicago: 1887–1888* [Chicago: The Elite Publishing Company, 1887]).

17. Emmett Dedmon, *Fabulous Chicago* (New York: Random House, 1953), p. 186.

18. Gunsaulus published a book of poems entitled *Phidias and Other Poems* (1891) and was well known for his historical romance *Monk and Knight* (1891).

19. Pizer, ed., *Hamlin Garland's Diaries*, p. 15.

20. Fuller letter to Garland, 10 May 1899; Fuller letter to Charles Eliot Norton, 8 Sept. 1899.

21. Too often Fuller caricatures Chicago's immigrant population. Jews were by no means singled out, but they were a part of the fast rising immigrant class with which Fuller did not totally sympathize, as he makes clear in *With the Procession* as well. In "Little O'Grady" one of the board members is named Simon Rosenberg, whom Fuller caricatures as a Jewish tenement owner. At a board meeting Rosenberg is voted down by the other board members when he proposes that they make room for a few tenants in the new bank building.

22. Anna Morgan, "Henry Blake Fuller and the North Shore," unpublished, Newberry Library.

23. Ibid.

24. Carl Condit, *The Chicago School of Architecture* (Chicago: University of Chicago Press, 1964), p. 193.

25. Hamlin Garland, diary for 20 Sept. 1900, MS, Huntington Library.

26. Hamlin Garland, *A Daughter of the Middle Border* (New York: Macmillan, 1921), p. 271.

27. Richardson (1862–1937) was also a member of the art staff of the *Chicago Daily News* for more than fifteen years. His cartoons appeared regularly in the *Daily News*, and a collection was published in 1889. He studied in Europe, and one of his paintings was hung in the Paris salon of 1889. He was also an illustrator of children's books (*New York Times* obituary; "Vignettes of Western Artists," *Sketch Book*, Sept. 1903, Art Division file, New York Public Library).

28. Pizer, ed., *Hamlin Garland's Diaries*, p. 133.

29. Fuller letter to Garland, 12 Jan. 1902.

30. Pizer, ed., *Hamlin Garland's Diaries*, p. 123.

31. William Dean Howells's letters to Fuller, 10 Feb. and 26 Feb. 1904, Southern Illinois University Library.

32. Fuller letter to Garland, 18 Jan. 1904.

33. Fuller letter to Louise Washburn, undated, Sunday [after 1888].

34. Fuller letter to William Dean Howells, 11 Jan. 1904.

35. Fuller letter to Howells, 4 Mar. 1909.

36. Fuller letter to Richard Watson Gilder, 9 Sept. 1906.

37. Pizer, ed., *Hamlin Garland's Diaries*, p. 134.

38. Mrs. Freemont Older, *William Randolph Hearst: American* (New York: Appleton-

Century, 1936), p. 320; John Tebbel, *Life and Good Times of William Randolph Hearst* (New York: E. P. Dutton, 1952), p. 214; John Winkler, *William Randolph Hearst: A New Appraisal* (New York: Hastings House, 1955), p. 158.

39. Fuller letter to A. B. Pond, 24 Aug. 1908.
40. Scribner's letter to Fuller, 24 Feb. 1909, Princeton University Library.
41. Scribner's letter to Fuller, 26 Feb. 1910.
42. Fuller letter to Robert Underwood Johnson, Jan. 1909, American Academy of Arts and Letters.
43. Fuller letter to Howells, 16 Apr. 1909.
44. Pizer, ed., *Hamlin Garland's Diaries*, p. 134.

Chapter 8. Delicate Affections and Dynamite

1. Fuller letter to Frederick Richardson, 27 Dec. 1913.
2. Constance Griffin, *Henry Blake Fuller* (Philadelphia: University of Pennsylvania Press, 1939), p. 134.
3. Fuller letter to Hamlin Garland, 19 July 1912.
4. Anna Morgan, ed., *henry b. fuller* (Chicago: Ralph Fletcher Seymour, 1929), p. 103.
5. Fuller letter to Garland, 19 Feb. 1916.
6. Fuller letter to Rudolph Altrocchi, 23 Feb. 1916.
7. Fuller letter to Garland, 23 May 1916.
8. Fuller letter to Houghton Mifflin Publishing Co., 4 Sept. 1916.
9. Fuller letter to Robert Bridges, editor of *Scribner's Magazine*, 20 Jan. 1916.
10. Mildred Howells, ed., *Life in Letters of William Dean Howells* (New York: Doubleday and Doran, 1928), 2:304.
11. Fuller letter to Houghton-Mifflin, 4 Sept. 1916.
12. Fuller letters to Richardson, 15 Oct. and 22 Dec. 1917; Fuller letter to William E. Symonds.
13. Randolph Bourne, review of *On the Stairs, Dial,* 25 Apr. 1918, pp. 405–07.
14. Fuller letter to Richardson, 10 Apr. 1918; Fuller letter to Garland, 4 Apr. 1916.
15. Fuller letter to Richardson, 4 June 1919.
16. Receipts, Newberry Library.
17. Fuller letter to Richardson, 24 July 1919.
18. See Roger Austen, *Playing the Game: The Homosexual Novel in America* (New York: Bobbs-Merrill, 1977), pp. 1–53.
19. Ibid., pp. xi–xv.
20. Review of *Bertram Cope's Year, Chicago Tribune* [1919?], Newberry Library.
21. John Farrar, "The Literary Spotlight," *Bookman* 57 (Feb. 1924), 649.
22. "The Flood of Fiction, *The Smart Set* 61 (Jan. 1920), 141.
23. "Henry Blake Fuller," *Double Dealer* 3 (May 1922), 295.
24. Fuller letter to Carl Van Vechten, 13 June 1922.
25. Griffin, *Henry Blake Fuller*, p. 67.
26. Fuller letter to Garland, 21 Feb. 1921.
27. Fuller letter to William Dean Howells, 27 Feb. 1907.
28. Fuller letter to Van Vechten, 27 June 1922.

29. Glenway Wescott letter to Fuller, 2 Sept. 1926(?)–1929(?), Newberry Library.
30. William Emery Shepherd letter to Fuller, 8 Oct. 1922, Newberry Library; see Shepherd's account of their meeting in Morgan, ed., *henry b. fuller,* p. 119.
31. Shepherd letter to Fuller, 11 Dec. 1923.
32. Fuller letter to Van Vechten, 12 Mar. 1924.
33. Fuller letter to Garland, 1 May 1924; Fuller letter to Richardson, 8 Apr. 1924.
34. Fuller letter to Richardson, 8 Apr. 1924.
35. Fuller letter to Richardson, 29 June 1924.
36. Fuller letter to Richardson, 18 July 1924.
37. Fuller letter to Richardson, 8 Apr. 1924.
38. See Shepherd letters to Fuller; Shepherd letter to the California State Teachers' Retirement System, 3 Feb. 1968, Shepherd Estate. I located the bedridden Mr. Shepherd in San Diego in 1977, but he was unable to speak to me about his friendship with Fuller. After I had an opportunity to read through a vast amount of papers and notebooks that Mr. Shepherd had collected over the years, he died in August 1977, little more than a month after I had visited him. When I returned to his house the following year to examine further the papers in his estate, I discovered that they had all been taken; there is now no record of their whereabouts. My thanks here to Richard Kinney, Jr., of Willes & Circuit Law Offices, San Diego, California, and to Mr. John Westwood, Conservator of the Person for Mr. Shepherd, for their cooperation.
39. Interview with Mary Hastings Bradley, 1976, Chicago.
40. Fuller letters to Garland, 8 Jan. and 4 Feb. 1929.
41. Fuller letter to Richardson, 15 Apr. 1929.
42. Fuller letter to Garland, 10 June 1929.
43. These last days of Fuller's life are chronicled in seven letters he wrote to Richardson between 15 Apr. and 27 June 1929.
44. For an account of Fuller's death, see Joseph A. Matter, *Henry Blake Fuller* (Chicago: Chicago Literary Club, 1965), pp. 27–28.
45. Theodore Dreiser, "The Great American Novel," *American Spectator* 1 (Dec. 1932), 1. Reprinted in *The American Spectator Year Book,* ed. G. J. Nathan (New York: Frederick A. Stokes, 1934), pp. 16–125.
46. Morgan, ed., *henry b. fuller,* p. 132; Fuller letter to Clifford Raymond, 17 July 1929.

Bibliography

Locations of Manuscript Collections

American Academy and Institute of Arts and Letters Archives, New York.
Boston Public Library, Department of Rare Books.
University of Chicago Library, Department of Special Collections, Robert Herrick Papers.
Columbia University, Rare Book and Manuscript Library.
Harvard University, Houghton Library.
Huntington Library, San Marino, Calif., Department of Manuscripts.
Newberry Library, Chicago, Henry Blake Fuller Papers.
New York Public Library, Manuscripts and Archives Division, Astor, Lenox, and Tilden
    Foundations, Henry W. and Albert A. Berg Collection.
Princeton University Library.
University of Southern California Library, Hamlin Garland Collection.
Southern Illinois University Library, Morris Library, Special Collections, Letters of Henry
    Blake Fuller, Mark Turbyfill Papers, and Letters of William Dean Howells.
University of Virginia Library, Clifton Waller Barrett Library, Henry Blake Fuller Collection.
Yale University, Beinecke Rare Book and Manuscript Library, Collection of American
    Literature.

Primary Works
Novels

The Chevalier of Pensieri-Vani with Frequent References to the Prorege of Arcopia. [Stanton
    Page, pseud.] Boston: J. G. Cupples, 1890.
The Chevalier of Pensieri-Vani. 4th ed. rev. New York: The Century Company, 1892. Added
    chapter: "Siena: A Vain Abasement."
The Chatelaine of La Trinité. New York: The Century Company, 1892. Serialized in *Cen-
    tury Magazine* 44 (May–Oct. 1892).
The Cliff-Dwellers: A Novel. New York: Harper and Brothers Publishers, 1895. Serialized
    in *Harper's Weekly* 37 (June–Aug. 1893).
With the Procession: A Novel. New York, Harper and Brothers Publishers, 1895. Rpt. Chi-
    cago: University of Chicago Press, 1965.
The Last Refuge: A Sicilian Romance. Boston: Houghton Mifflin, 1900.
On the Stairs. Boston: Houghton Mifflin, 1918.

179

Bertram Cope's Year: A Novel. Chicago: Ralph Fletcher Seymour (Alderbrink Press), 1919.
Gardens of This World. New York: Alfred A. Knopf, 1929.
Not on the Screen. New York: Alfred A. Knopf, 1930.

Collected Plays

The Puppet-Booth: Twelve Plays. New York: The Century Company, 1896. Contents: "The
  Cure of Souls," "On the Whirlwind," "The Love of Love," "Afterglow," "The Ship
  Comes In," "At Saint Judas's," "The Light That Always Is," "The Dead-and-Alive,"
  "Northern Lights," "The Story-Spinner," "The Stranger Within the Gates," "In Such
  a Night."

Collected Short Stories

From the Other Side: Stories of Transatlantic Travel. Boston: Houghton Mifflin, 1898. Contents: "The Greatest of These," "What Youth Can Do," "The Pilgrim Sons," "Pasquale's Picture."
Under the Skylights. New York: D. Appleton and Company, 1901. Contents: "The Downfall of Abner Joyce," "Little O'Grady vs. the Grindstone," "Dr. Gowdy and the Squash."
Waldo Trench and Others: Stories of Americans in Italy. New York: Charles Scribner's Sons,
  1908. Contents: "Waldo Trench Regains His Youth," "New Wine," "A Coal from the
  Embers," "For the Faith," "Eliza Hepburn's Deliverance," "Addolorata's Intervention,"
  "The House-Cat."

Collected Poems

The New Flag: Satires. Chicago, 1899. (Chicago Historical Society).
Lines Long and Short: Biographical Sketches in Various Rhythms. Boston: Houghton Mifflin,
  1917. Contents: "Tobias Holt, Bachelor," "Rigmarole," "Patience," "Aridity," "Veils,"
  "The Two Apprentices," "Delicacy," "Postponement," "Polly Greene," "Manners,"
  "Death of Aunt Juliana," "Charm," "Whisperings," "Alonzo Grout," "Victory," "In-
  terlude," "The Statue," "The 'Art of Life,'" "The Alien," "Toward Childhood," "The
  Outsider," "Glare," "The Day of Danger," "Chameleon," "Deliquescence."

Essays and Letters to the Editor

"You'll Catch It for This." *Chicago Tribune,* 4 Sept. 1875, p. 2. Signed "Harry B. Free."
"Not a Bit Scared." *Chicago Tribune,* 11 Sept. 1875, p. 7. Signed "Harry B. Free."
"This Young Man Needs Taking Down." *Chicago Tribune,* 19 Sept. 1875, p. 6. Signed
  "Harry B. Free."
"Compliments of H.B.F. and Some More Allusions." *Chicago Tribune,* 30 Oct. 1875, p. 8.
  Signed "Harry B. Free."
"English Railways." *Chicago Tribune,* 20 Nov. 1879, p. 9. Signed "H. F."
"Paris." *Chicago Tribune,* 2 Dec. 1879, p. 9. Signed "H. F."
"Parisian Oddities." *Chicago Tribune,* 28 Dec. 1879, p. 7. Signed "H. F."
"The American School of Fiction" (1886). Ed. Darrel Abel. *American Literary Realism*
  3 (Summer 1970), 248–57.
"World's Fair Architecture." *Morning News Record,* 14 Sept. 1892, p. 4; 16 Sept. 1892,
  p. 4; 20 Sept. 1892, p. 4.

"Westminster Abbey." *Century* 55 (Mar. 1893), 700–18.

"Some Exposition Pictures." *Chicago Record,* 22 May 1893, p. 4.

"Mural Painting at the Fair." *Chicago Record,* 25 May 1893, p. 4; 26 May 1893, p. 4.

"Holy Week in Seville." *Contributor's Magazine,* 22 Apr. 1893, pp. 2–7.

"Minor Buildings at the Fair." *Chicago Record,* 2 June 1893, p. 4; 5 June 1893, p. 4.

"Photographers at the Fair." *Chicago Record,* 10 Aug. 1893, p. 4; 11 Aug. 1893, p. 4; 23 Aug. 1893, p. 4.

"Howells or James?" (1895). Ed. Darrel Abel. *Modern Fiction Studies* 3 (Summer 1957), 160–64.

"Mr. Fuller on Italian Fiction." *Critic* 30 (29 May 1897), 365–66.

"Easter in Florence." *Parish Messenger* 9 (June 1897), 12–13.

"The Upward Movement in Chicago." *Atlantic* 80 (Oct. 1897), 534–47.

"Art in America." *Bookman,* 10 (Nov. 1899), 218–24.

"Why the Anglo-Saxon Is Disliked." *Saturday Evening Post,* 6 Jan. 1900, p. 590.

"The Modern Man and Nature." *Saturday Evening Post,* 20 Jan. 1900, p. 638.

"How to Make Good Aldermen." *Saturday Evening Post,* 14 Apr. 1900, p. 950.

"A National Park at Lake Itasca." *Saturday Evening Post,* 21 Apr. 1900, p. 974.

"Civic Federation and Literature." *Chicago Evening Post,* 14 July 1900, p. 8.

"The Shortcomings of Our Architects." *Saturday Evening Post,* 6 Oct. 1900, p. 12.

"Howells Plays Professor Wendell." *Chicago Post,* 6 Apr. 1901, p. 13.

"As to 'Best Selling' Novels." *Chicago Post,* 13 Apr. 1901, p. 13.

"Chicago as a Country Town." *Chicago Post,* 27 Apr. 1901, p. 6.

"Our 'Young Lady Novelist.'" *Chicago Post,* 1 June 1901, p. 6.

"Literature and the Market." *Chicago Post,* 8 June 1901, p. 6.

"An Artistic Round Robin." *Chicago Post,* 15 June 1901, p. 6.

"'Society' and the Arts." *Chicago Post,* 29 June 1901, p. 6.

"Reflections on Comic Opera." *Chicago Post,* 6 July 1901, p. 6.

"Suggestions to Literati." *Chicago Post,* 20 July 1901, p. 6.

"Billboards and the Remedy." *Chicago Post,* 27 July 1901, p. 6.

"For Revival of the 'Patron.'" *Chicago Post,* 3 Aug. 1901, p. 6.

"Mediocrity in Literature." *Chicago Post,* 10 Aug. 1901, p. 6.

"Great Italian Novelist (Antonio Fogazzaro)." *Chicago Post,* 17 Aug. 1901, p. 6.

"Literature and Democracy." *Chicago Post,* 31 Aug. 1901, p. 6.

"The Troubles of the Short Story." *Chicago Post,* 7 Sept. 1901, p. 6.

"The Novels of Matilde Serao." *Chicago Post,* 14 Sept. 1901, p. 6.

"The Vitality of Romanticism." *Chicago Post,* 21 Sept. 1901, p. 6.

"Processions and Pantheons." *Chicago Post,* 28 Sept. 1901, p. 6.

"Our National Literature Suffers from Our National Prosperity." *Chicago Evening Post,* 10 May 1902, sec. 2, p. 13.

"Erroneous Ideas About Prospects for the 'Great American Novel.'" *Chicago Evening Post,* 17 May 1902, sec. 2, p. 9.

"New and Representative Type of American Fiction Developing." *Chicago Evening Post,* 24 May 1902, sec. 2, p. 1.

"Development of Popular Literature Through Present Deluge of Books." *Chicago Evening Post,* 31 May 1902, sec. 2, p. 9.

"Weakening of National Spirit Under International Influences." *Chicago Evening Post,* 7 June 1902, sec. 2, p. 1.

"Is Great Literature of the Future to Come from American Continent?" *Chicago Evening Post,* 14 June 1902, sec. 2, p. 9.

"How Shall the Author and His Book Be Treated by the Modern Publisher?" *Chicago Evening Post,* 28 June 1902, p. 4.

"Frank Norris and Jack London on Literary Art and the Multitude." *Chicago Evening Post,* 6 Sept. 1902, sec. 2, p. 9.

"Increase in American Fiction of Aristocratic Social Ideals." *Chicago Evening Post,* 8 Nov. 1902, sec. 2, p. 9.

"Preoccupations of the Specialist vs. the Broader Interests of the Laity." *Chicago Evening Post,* 15 Nov. 1902, sec. 2, p. 9.

"Prospects for a Radical Change in the General Nature of Fiction." *Chicago Evening Post,* 27 Dec. 1902, p. 5.

"Need in This Novel-Writing Age for a University of Fiction." *Chicago Evening Post,* 3 Jan. 1903, p. 5.

"American Manners Do Not Exist, Says Critic of Contemporary Novel." *Chicago Evening Post,* 10 Jan. 1903, p. 4.

"Why the American Reading Public Neglects the Printed Drama." *Chicago Evening Post,* 24 Jan. 1903, p. 4.

"Are Publishers Unjust to Young and Unknown Authors?" *Chicago Evening Post,* 7 Feb. 1903, p. 4.

"An Industrial Utopia (Gary, Indiana)." *Harper's Weekly,* 12 Oct. 1907, pp. 1482–83, 1495.

"Notes on Lorado Taft." *Century* 76 (Aug. 1908), 618–21.

"Chicago." *Century* 84 (May 1912), 25–33.

"A New Field for Free Verse." *Dial,* 14 Dec. 1916, pp. 515–17.

"New Forms of Short Fiction." *Dial,* 8 Mar. 1917, pp. 167–69.

"A Plea for Shorter Novels." *Dial,* 30 Aug. 1917, pp. 139–41.

"Development of Arts and Letters." *The Centennial History of Illinois,* vol. 4: *The Industrial State 1870–1893,* ed. Ernest Ludlow Bogart and Charles Manfred Thompson. Springfield: Illinois Centennial Commission, 1920, pp. 188–216.

"Chicago Poets." *New York Evening Post Literary Review* 10 Dec. 1921, pp. 249–50.

"Chicago Novelists." *New York Evening Post Literary Review,* 18 Mar. 1922, pp. 501–02.

"The Melting Pot Begins to Smell." *New York Times Book Review* 21 Dec. 1924, p. 2.

"The Americanization of Europe's Youth." *New York Times Magazine,* 25 Jan. 1925, p. 15. Rev. and ed. version entitled "Europe After Thirty Years," ed. John Pilkington, *University of Mississippi Studies in English* 8 (1967), 35–42.

"America's Coming of Age." *New York Times Book Review,* 3 May 1925, p. 2.

Uncollected Poems

"'We Girls.'" *Chicago Tribune,* 23 Feb. 1879, p. 11. Signed "X."

"'We Girls'–II." *Chicago Tribune,* 2 Mar. 1879, p. 10. Signed "X."

"'We Girls'–III." *Chicago Tribune,* 9 Mar. 1879, p. 11. Signed "X."

"'We Girls'–IV." *Chicago Tribune,* 16 Mar. 1879, p. 10. Signed "X."

"'We Girls'–V." *Chicago Tribune,* 23 Mar. 1879, p. 12. Signed "X."

"The Ballade of the Touriste." *Puck*, 20 July 1881, p. 339. Unsigned.
"The Ballade of the Bank-Teller." *Puck*, 7 Sept. 1881, p. 451. Unsigned.
"Some Day (Revised Edition)." *Life*, 27 Mar. 1884, p. 173. Signed "B. F."
"Pensieri Privati." Selections published in Constance Griffin, *Henry Blake Fuller: A Critical Biography*. Philadelphia: University of Pennsylvania Press, 1939, pp. 7–8.

Uncollected Short Stories

"A Transcontinental Episode, Or, Metamorphoses at Muggins' Misery: A Co-Operative Novel by Bret James and Henry Harte," *Life*, 24 and 31 Jan. 1884, pp. 47–49, 62–63. Signed "B. F."
"A Story of Naphtha: A Tale of Culture, Fashion and Duplicity by Elizabeth Hodgson Phelps and Frances Stuart Burnett." *Life*, 3 and 10 Apr. 1884, pp. 187–89, 201–02. Signed "Blake Fuller."
"The Long and the Short of It: A New England Idyl." *Life*, 26 June 1884, pp. 355–57. Signed "Blake Fuller."
"The Romance of a Middle-Aged Merchant and His Female Private Secretary." *Chicago Tribune*, 4 Oct. 1884, p. 16. Unsigned.
"Miranda Harlow's Mortgage." *Atlantic* 86 (Nov. 1900), 671–75.
"Striking an Average." *Saturday Evening Post*, 25 May 1901, pp. 3–5, 14–15. Rpt. in *The Great Modern American Stories: An Anthology*, ed. William Dean Howells. New York: Boni and Liveright, 1920, pp. 267–87.
"Under the Crest of Shishaldin." *Everybody's* 16 (June 1907), 809–15.
"'Make Way for the Young.'" *Scribner's* 46 (Nov. 1909), 625–33.
"The Life-Tale of Pearl McRoy." *Everybody's* 23 (Sept. 1910), 380–89. Rpt. in *Scholastic* 6 (18 Apr. 1925), 3–4, 30–32.
"'Silence.'" *Scribner's* 48 (Oct. 1910), 430–41.
"Quartette." *Harper's* 121 (Nov. 1910), 934–38.
"Milk." *Chicago Sunday Tribune*, 27 Nov. 1921, sec. 5, p. 7.
"His Little Life." *Chicago Sunday Tribune*, 1 Jan. 1922, sec. 5, p. 7.
"Responsibility." *Chicago Sunday Tribune*, 19 Mar. 1922, sec. 5, pp. 8, 10.
"The Few Days of Little Fiji." *Chicago Sunday Tribune*, 21 May 1922, sec. 5, pp. 2, 5.
"The Thirteenth Goddess." *Harper's* 148 (Dec. 1923), 125–27.
"The Covered Pushcart." *Harper's* 149 (June 1924), 130–32.
"Turn and Turn About, Or, More Informally, Being the Other Fellow." *Chicago Sunday Tribune*, 22 June 1924, sec. 5, p. 8.
"Errol's Voice." *Century* 108 (Aug. 1924), 527–35.
"The Duchess Visits Her Home Town." *Bookman* 60 (Dec. 1924), 413–16.
"Carl Carlsen's Progress" (1894–1907). Published in Constance Griffin, *Henry B. Fuller: A Critical Biography*. Philadelphia: University of Pennsylvania Press, 1939, pp. 87–91.

Uncollected Plays

"O, That Way Madness Lies: a Play for Marionettes." *Chap-Book*, 1 Dec. 1895, pp. 71–80.
"The Red Carpet" (1896). Published in Constance Griffin, *Henry Blake Fuller: A Critical Biography*. Philadelphia: University of Pennsylvania Press, 1939, pp. 77–86.

184   *Bibliography*

Selected Book Reviews

"D'Annunzio's Cruel Perfidy." (*The Flame*, by Gabriele D'Annunzio.) *Chicago Evening Post*, 9 June 1900, p. 7.

"Taft's 'Solitude of the Soul.'" (*"Solitude of the Soul" [Sculpture]*, by Lorado Taft.) *Chicago Post*, 20 Apr. 1901, p. 6.

"Three Glimpses Across the Sea." (*Crucial Instances*, by Edith Wharton.) *Chicago Post*, 4 May 1901, p. 6.

"D'Annunzio in a New Phase." (*The Song of Garibaldi* and other works by Gabriele D'Annunzio.) *Chicago Post*, 18 May 1901, p. 6.

"Gissing's 'By the Ionian Sea.'" (*By the Ionian Sea*, by George Gissing.) *Chicago Post*, 24 Aug. 1901, p. 6.

"Review of New Books." (*The Valley of Decision*, by Edith Wharton.) *Chicago Evening Post*, 5 Mar. 1902, p. 5.

"'The Captain of the Gray-Horse Troop.'" (*The Captain of the Gray-Horse Troop*, by Hamlin Garland.) *Chicago Evening Post*, 29 Mar. 1902, sec. 2, p. 11.

"W. D. Howells's Return to Fiction in His New Novel 'The Kentons.'" (*The Kentons*, by William Dean Howells.) *Chicago Evening Post*, 26 Apr. 1902, sec. 2, p. 9.

"Ten Centuries of Russian Literature Reviewed in Weiner's 'Anthology.'" (*Anthology of Russian Literature*, vol. 1, ed. Leo Weiner.) *Chicago Evening Post*, 12 July 1902, p. 4.

"Work of the 'Landscape Architect' and His Opportunities East and West." (*Charles Elliot: Landscape Architect*, by Charles William Elliot.) *Chicago Evening Post*, 26 July 1902, p. 4.

"Russian Novelist Deals Vividly with the Italian Renaissance." (*The Romance of Leonardo Da Vinci*, by Dmitri Merejkowski.) *Chicago Evening Post*, 2 Aug. 1902, p. 4.

"D'Annunzio's Dramatic Masterpiece Blends Archaeology and Passion." (*The Dead City*, by Gabriele D'Annunzio.) *Chicago Evening Post*, 9 Aug. 1902, p. 4.

"Kipling's Tasteless, Ill-Considered Employment of the Keats Legend." (*Wireless*, by Rudyard Kipling.) *Chicago Evening Post*, 16 Aug. 1902, p. 4.

"Herbert Paul Waxes Enthusiastic with Matthew Arnold as Theme." (*Matthew Arnold*, by Herbert Paul.) *Chicago Evening Post*, 23 Aug. 1902, p. 4.

"Latest Novel of Henry James Is a Typical Example of His Art." (*The Wings of the Dove*, by Henry James.) *Chicago Evening Post*, 30 Aug. 1902, p. 4.

"Varying Aspect of Parody Displayed in Recent Work by Harte and Seaman." (*Condensed Novels*, by Bret Harte; *Borrowed Plumes* by Owen Seaman.) *Chicago Evening Post*, 11 Oct. 1902, sec. 2, p. 9.

"Marion Crawford's Latest Novel Deals with Modern Roman Society." (*Cecilia*, by Francis Marion Crawford.) *Chicago Evening Post*, 1 Nov. 1902, sec. 2, p. 9.

"Dumas's Latest Biographer Defends His Methods and Morals." (*Alexandre Dumas: His Life and Works*, by Arthur Davidson.) *Chicago Evening Post*, 22 Nov. 1902, sec. 2, p. 9.

"Tolstoy as Man and Artist Weighed by Dmitri Merejkowski." (*Tolstoy as Man and Artist*, by Dmitri Merejkowski.) *Chicago Evening Post*, 6 Dec. 1902, sec. 2, p. 13.

"Variorum and Definitive Edition of the Works of Edward Fitzgerald." (*Variorum and Definitive Edition of the Poetical and Prose Writings of Edward Fitzgerald*, ed. George Bentham.) *Chicago Evening Post*, 13 Dec. 1902, sec. 2, p. 9.

"Long-Forgotten Romance by John Milton Is Brought to Light." (*Nova Solyma,* by John Milton.) *Chicago Evening Post,* 31 Jan. 1903, p. 4.

"First Complete Life of Mazzini, The Great Italian Republican." (*Mazzini,* by Bolton King.) *Chicago Evening Post,* 14 Mar. 1903, sec. 2, p. 9.

"Studies of Darker Aspects of Life in Russian Steppe and British Capital." (*Maxim Gorky: His Life and Writings,* by Emile Joseph Dillon.) *Chicago Evening Post,* 21 Mar. 1903, sec. 2, p. 1.

"'William Wetmore Story and His Friends.'" (*William Wetmore Story and His Friends,* by Henry James.) *Interior* 34 (3 Dec. 1903), 1600.

"'The Divine Comedy of Dante Alighieri.'" (*The Divine Comedy,* by Dante Alighieri, trans. Henry Johnson.) *Poetry* 9 (Nov. 1916), 104–05.

"Embracing the Realities." (*Twilight in Italy* and *The Prussian Officer,* by D. H. Lawrence.) *Dial,* 22 Mar. 1917, pp. 237–38.

"An Idol of the Parnassians." (*Edgar Allan Poe,* by Hans Heinz Ewers.) *Dial,* 17 May 1917, pp. 433–34.

"The Classical Stage of Japan." (*"Noh" or Accomplishment: A Study of the Classical Stage of Japan,* by Ernest Fenollosa and Ezra Pound.) *Dial,* 13 Sept. 1917, pp. 209–10.

"The Imagists." (*Some Imagist Poets: 1917,* ed. Amy Lowell.) *Dial,* 27 Sept. 1917, pp. 271–72.

"Tendencies in Modern American Poetry." (*Tendencies in Modern American Poetry,* by Amy Lowell.) *Dial,* 8 Nov. 1917, pp. 444–45.

"Rebecca West Novelist." (*The Return of the Soldier,* by Rebecca West.) *Dial,* 28 Mar. 1918), pp. 299–300.

"The Theory of Fiction." (*The Modern Novel,* by Wilson Follett; *A Manual of the Art of Fiction,* by Clayton Hamilton.) *Dial,* 22 Feb. 1919, pp. 193–94.

"Coleridge and Wordsworth." (*Coleridge's Biographia Literaria with Wordsworth's Preface and Essays on Poetry,* ed. George Sampson.) *Poetry* 18 (June 1921), 167–68.

"The Eminent Victoria." (*Queen Victoria,* by Lytton Strachey.) *Freeman,* 31 Aug. 1921, pp. 594–95.

"Three Generations." (*A Daughter of the Middle Border,* by Hamlin Garland.) *Freeman,* 9 Nov. 1921, pp. 210–11.

"Planner of Cities." (*Daniel H. Burnham: Architect, Planner of Cities,* by Charles Moore.) *Nation,* 8 Feb. 1922, pp. 116–17.

"Sardinian Days." (*Sea and Sardinia,* by D. H. Lawrence.) *Freeman,* 1 Mar. 1922, pp. 595–96.

"The Art of Fiction-Writing." (*The Craft of Fiction,* by Percy Lubbock.) *Freeman,* 3 May 1922, pp. 189–90.

"The Crocean Dante." (*The Poetry of Dante,* by Benedetto Croce.) *Freeman,* 31 May 1922, pp. 282–84.

"Dante in English Rhyme." (*The Divine Comedy of Dante Alighieri,* trans. Melville Best Anderson.) *Poetry* 20 (June 1922), 165–68.

"A Maker of America." (*A Life of George Westinghouse,* by Henry Prout.) *Freeman,* 7 June 1922, p. 308.

"The Last Half." (*Senescence: The Last Half of Life,* by G. Stanley Hall.) *Nation,* 9 Aug. 1922, pp. 150–51.

"The Italian Renaissance." (*Aspects of the Italian Renaissance,* by Rachel Annand Taylor.) *Freeman,* 11 July 1923, pp. 428–29.

"Hamlin Garland's Book on the Indian." (*The Book of the American Indian*, by Hamlin Garland.) *New York Herald Tribune Books*, 30 Sept. 1923, p. 6.

"Early American Architecture." (*Domestic Architecture of the American Colonies and of the Early Republic*, by Fiske Kimball.) *Freeman*, 16 Jan. 1924, pp. 453–54.

"The Color of a Great City." (*The Color of a Great City*, by Theodore Dreiser.) *New Republic*, 30 Jan. 1924, pp. 263–64.

"The Real Sarah Bernhardt." (*The Real Sarah Bernhardt*, by Mme Pierre Berton and Basil Wood.) *New Republic*, 7 May 1924, pp. 290–91.

"The Risorgimento." (*Mazzini*, by Edyth Hinkley.) *New York Herald Tribune Books*, 19 Oct. 1924, p. 4.

"True Arnold Bennett." (*Elsie and the Child*, by Arnold Bennett.) *Saturday Review of Literature*, 29 Nov. 1924, p. 319.

"Eugene Field." (*Eugene Field's Creative Years*, by Charles Dennis.) *Nation*, 10 Dec. 1924, pp. 650–52.

"Straws and Prayer-Books." (*Straws and Prayer-Books*, by James Branch Cabell.) *New Republic*, 31 Dec. 1924, pp. 151–52.

"James Huneker, Critic, Enthusiast and 'Steeplejack.'" (*Intimate Letters of James Gibbons Huneker*, ed. Josephine Huneker.) *New York Times Book Review* 4 Jan. 1925, p. 3.

"Dialogues and Spotlights." (*The Literary Spotlight*, ed. John Farrar.) *New Republic*, 7 Jan. 1925, p. 180.

"Mr. Ellis's Parting Shots." (*Impressions and Comments/Third and Final Series*, by Havelock Ellis.) *Bookman* 60 (Feb. 1925), 771–72.

"Mr. Brooks on the Thwarted Career of Henry James." (*The Pilgrimage of Henry James*, by Van Wyck Brooks.) *New York Times Book Review*, 19 Apr. 1925, pp. 4–5.

"Crepitant Fantasy." (*Firecrackers*, by Carl Van Vechten.) *Saturday Review of Literature*, 15 Aug. 1925, p. 39.

"The Great Victorian Novelists Were City-Bred." (*Charles Dickens and Other Victorians*, by Arthur Quiller-Couch.) *New York Times Book Review*, 30 Aug. 1925, p. 4.

"Contemporaries." (*James Branch Cabell*, by Carl Van Doren; *Theodore Dreiser*, by Burton Rascoe.) *New Republic*, 16 Sept. 1925, p. 104.

"These Twain." (*Wanderings*, by Robert Herrick.) *New Republic*, 21 Oct. 1925, pp. 236–37.

"R. L. Stevenson, Man or Myth?" (*The Works of Robert Louis Stevenson/South Seas Edition*.) *New York Times Book Review*, 29 Nov. 1925, pp. 1, 20.

"Mr. Wells Insists on Making the World Over." (*The World of William Clissold*, by H. G. Wells.) *Literary Digest International Book Review* 4 (Nov. 1926), 755–56.

"Sharps and Flats." (*Life of Eugene Field*, by Slason Thompson.) *New York Herald Tribune Books*, 30 Jan. 1927, p. 3.

"The Bromfield Saga." (*The Green Bay Tree, Possession*, and *Early Autumn*, by Louis Bromfield.) *Bookman* 65 (Apr. 1927), 200–03.

"Mr. Lowes on Coleridge." (*The Road to Xanadu*, by John Livingston Lowes.) *Poetry* 30 (Aug. 1927), 283–85.

Published Translations

"The Visit from His Majesty" ("La Visita di Sua Maesta"), by Antonio Fogazzaro. *World Review*, 27 July 1901, pp. 607–09.

The Coffee-House (*La Bottega del Caffe*), play by Carlo Goldoni. New York: Samuel French, 1925.
The Fan (*Il Ventaglio*), play by Carlo Goldoni. New York: Samuel French, 1925.

Unpublished Translations

With one exception, the partial translation of *Il Signor Io,* Fuller's translations are dated 1897. All are in the Fuller Papers, Newberry Library. See Swanson, "A Checklist of the Writings of Henry Blake Fuller."

"Aradolfi's Novel" ("Il Romanzo"), by Carlo Placci. MS, 27 pp.
"The Cavaliers of the 'Immacolata'" ("I Cavalieri Dell' Immacolata"), by Enrico Castelnuovo. MS, 85 pp.
"Domenico's Duel" ("Stonella Vecchia"), by Gerolamo Rovetta. MS, 59 pp.
"The Fairy in the Mirror" ("Il Folletto Nello Specchio"), by Antonio Fogazzaro. MS, 12 pp.
"Grandmother's Gossip" ("Le Chiacchiere Della Nonna"), by Enrico Castelnuovo. MS, 35 pp.
"I Would Kill Him Again!" [no Italian title], by Vittorio Bersezio. MS, 43 pp.
"Lisa's Watch" ("L'Orologio di Lisa"), by Antonio Fogazzaro. MS, 34 pp.
"The Loves of an Egoist" (partial translation of *Il Signor Io*) by Salvatore Farina. MS dated 18 July 1896–10 Aug. 1896, 163 pp.
"A Matrimonial Joke" ("Una Cella"), by Carlo Placci. MS, 38 pp.
"The Mystery" ("Il Mistero"), by Giovanni Verga. MS, 19 pp.
"Signora Cherubina and Her 'Democracy'" ("La Democrazia Della Signora Cherubina"), by Enrico Castelnuovo. MS, 24 pp.
"A Story from Greece" ("Novella Greca"), by Matilde Serao. MS, 21 pp.
"The Toymaker" ("Un Inventore"), by Matilde Serao. MS, 22 pp.

Selected Unpublished Works

"The White Swan." MS, 2 pp., 1866. University of Virginia Library.
"A Feast for the Gods." MS, 6 pp., 1876. Newberry Library.
"Toy Village Theatricals." MS, [late 1870s]. Newberry Library.
"Howells or James?" [1885?] Ed. Darrel Abel. *Modern Fiction Studies* 3 (1957), 160–64.
"Pipistrello: Opera in Three Acts." MS, libretto, 62 pp.; score, 115 pp., 1887. Newberry Library.
"Mariquita: Opera in Three Acts." MS, libretto, 69 pp.; score, 104 pp., 1888. Newberry Library.
"Our Lady of Light." MS, 29 pp., unfinished, 1892. Newberry Library.
"Cyrano de Bergerac: Opera in Three Acts." MS, 94 pp., 1899. Based on the French of Edmond Rostand. Newberry Library.
"The Color-Line." MS, 3 pp., 11 Dec. 1899. University of Virginia Library.
"My Early Books." TS, 8 pp., [n.d.]. Newberry Library.
"Oliver's Outing." MS, 41 pp., unfinished, 1899. University of Virginia Library.
"Edmund Dalrymple." MS, 127 pp., 8 Sept. 1904. Newberry Library.
"Valentino." MS, 12 pp., 1901. Newberry Library.

Diaries and Notebooks

1868–1870	"School Notebook." MS, 2 vols., Newberry Library.
1869	"Private Diary," diary for 23 Feb. 1869–June 1869. MS, 2 vols., 40 pp.
1871–1872	"Odds and Ends," diary for 4 Nov. 1871–4 Nov. 1872. MS, 16 pp.
1874–1879	"A Legacy to Posterity," diary for 11 July 1874–14 Aug. 1879. MS, 76 pp. Newberry Library.
1875–1876	"Allison Classical Academy," diary for 28 Feb. 1875–21 July 1876. MS, 2 vols., 220 pp.
1876	Diary for the American Centennial Exposition, Philadelphia, 5–25 Oct. 1876. MS, 38 pp. Newberry Library.
1876–1879	Diary for 25 Aug. 1876–24 Feb. 1879. MS, 46 pp. Newberry Library.
1879–1880	"A Year in Europe," diary for European trip 19 Aug. 1879–1 Sept. 1880. MS, 3 vols., 439 pp. Newberry Library.
1883	Diary for European trip, 14 Apr. 1883–1 May 1883. MS, 34 pp.
1891–1892	Diary for European trip, 31 Dec. 1891–1892. MS, 23 pp.
1890s	Notebook. MS, 58 pp.

Collections of Letters

To Rudolph Altrocchi, University of Chicago Library.

To W. E. Ambler, Chicago Historical Society.

To H. H. Boyesen, University of Virginia Library.

To Robert Bridges, *Scribner's Magazine,* Princeton University Library.

To Van Wyck Brooks, University of Pennsylvania Library.

To *Century Magazine,* Century Collection, Newberry Library.

To Theodore Dreiser, University of Pennsylvania Library.

To W. W. Ellsworth, Yale University Library.

To Hamlin Garland, University of Southern California Library.

To Richard Watson Gilder, Century Collection, Newberry Library.

To Robert Herrick, University of Chicago Library.

To Houghton-Mifflin Publishing Company, Southern Illinois University Library.

To William Dean Howells, Houghton Library, Harvard University.

To James Gibbons Huneker, Newberry Library.

To Robert Underwood Johnson, American Academy of Arts and Letters; Century Collection, Newberry Library.

To James Russell Lowell, University of Virginia Library.

To Hamilton W. Mabie, American Academy of Arts and Letters.

To H. L. Mencken, Newberry Library.

To Harriet Monroe, University of Chicago Library.

To Anna Morgan, Newberry Library; Southern Illinois University Library.

To Charles Eliot Norton, Houghton Library, Harvard University.

To William Morton Payne, University of Virginia Library.

To A. B. Pond, Newberry Library.

To Burton Rascoe, University of Pennsylvania Library.

To Frederick Richardson, New York Public Library.

To Minna Smith, Boston Public Library; Columbia University Library; Dartmouth College Library; Newberry Library.

To William E. Symonds, Knox College, Galesburg, Ill., Symonds Papers.

To Lorado Taft, Chicago Historical Society.

To Carl Van Vechten, Yale University Library.

To Van Wyck Brooks, Yale University Library.

To Louise Washburn, Huntington Library.

Selected Secondary Works

Andreas, A. T. *History of Chicago.* 3 vols. Chicago: A. T. Andreas Publishing Company, 1884.

Austen, Roger. *Playing the Game: the Homosexual Novel in America.* New York: Bobbs-Merrill Company, 1977.

Bowron, Bernard R. *Henry Blake Fuller of Chicago: The Ordeal of a Genteel Realist in an Ungenteel America.* Westport, Conn.: Greenwood Press, 1974.

Burg, David. *Chicago's White City of 1893.* Lexington: University Press of Kentucky, 1976.

Cady, Edwin H. *The Light of Common Day: Realism in American Fiction.* Bloomington: Indiana University Press, 1971.

———. *The Realist at War: The Mature Years, 1885-1920, of William Dean Howells.* Syracuse: University of Syracuse, 1958.

Carter, Everett. *Howells and the Age of Realism.* Philadelphia: J. B. Lippincott, 1954.

Condit, Carl. *The Chicago School of Architecture.* Chicago: University of Chicago Press, 1964.

Couser, G. Thomas. "Art in Chicago: Fuller's *With the Procession.*" *American Literary Realism* 13 (Spring 1980), 31-40.

Dedmon, Emmett. *Fabulous Chicago.* New York: Random House, 1953.

Dell, Floyd. "Chicago in Fiction." *Bookman* 38 (November 1913), pp. 275-77.

Dondore, Dorothy Anne. *The Prairie and the Making of Middle America.* Cedar Rapids: Torch Press, 1926.

Dreiser, Theodore. "The Great American Novel." *American Spectator* 1 (November 1932), 1-2.

Duffey, Bernard. *Chicago Renaissance in American Letters.* East Lansing: Michigan State College Press, 1954.

Elias, Robert H. *Letters of Theodore Dreiser.* 3 vols. Philadelphia: University of Pennsylvania Press, 1959.

Farrar, John. "The Literary Spotlight." *Bookman* 57 (February 1924), 645-49.

Garland, Hamlin. *A Daughter of the Middle Border.* New York: Macmillan, 1921.

———. *Afternoon Neighbors.* New York: Macmillan, 1934.

———. *Companions on the Trail.* New York: Macmillan, 1932.

———. *My Friendly Contemporaries.* New York: The Macmillan Company, 1932.

———. *Roadside Meetings of a Literary Nomad.* New York: Macmillan, 1930.

Gilbert, Paul, and Bryson, Charles Lee. *Chicago and Its Makers.* Chicago: Felix Mendelsohn, 1929.

Griffin, Constance. *Henry Blake Fuller: A Critical Biography.* Philadelphia: University of Pennsylvania Press, 1939.

Hansen, Harry. *Mid West Portraits*. New York: Farrar and Rinehart, 1923.

Hays, Samuel P. *The Response to Industrialism: 1885–1914*. Chicago: University of Chicago Press, 1957.

Hoffman, Frederick, *The Modern Novel in America*. Chicago: H. Regnery, 1956.

Holloway, Jean. *Hamlin Garland: A Biography*. Austin: University of Texas, 1960.

Howe, M. A. De Wolfe, and Sara Norton, eds. *Letters of Charles Eliot Norton*, vol. 2. Boston and New York: Houghton-Mifflin, 1913.

Howells, Mildred, ed. *Life in Letters of William Dean Howells*, vol. 2. New York: Doubleday and Doran, 1928.

Howells, William Dean. "The Chicago School of Fiction." *North American Review* 176 (May 1903), 739–46.

———. *Heroines of Fiction*. New York: Harper and Brothers, 1901.

Huneker, James. "James Huneker's Bitter Criticism of Our Neglect of a Great American Masterpiece." *Current Opinion* 50 (January 1916), 52.

Huneker, Josephine, ed. *The Intimate Letters of James Gibbons Huneker*. New York: Boni and Liveright, 1954.

Jones, Llewellyn. "Chicago – Our Literary Crater." *Bookman* 60 (January 1925), 565–67.

Kazin, Alfred. *On Native Grounds*. New York: Harcourt, Brace, 1945.

Kramer, Dale. *Chicago Renaissance*. New York: Appleton Century, 1966.

Lovett, Robert M. "Fuller of Chicago." *New Republic*, 21 August 1929, pp. 16–18.

Martin, Jay. *Harvests of Change: American Literature 1865–1914*. Englewood Cliffs, N.J.: Prentice-Hall, 1967.

McDonald, Forrest. *Insull*. Chicago: University of Chicago Press, 1962.

Monroe, Harriet. *A Poet's Life*. New York: The Macmillan Company, 1938.

———. "Henry Blake Fuller." *Poetry: A Magazine of Verse*, 35 (October 1938), pp. 34–41.

Morgan, Anna, ed. *henry b. fuller*. Chicago: Ralph Fletcher Seymour, 1929.

———. *My Chicago*. Chicago: Ralph Fletcher Seymour, 1918.

Murray, Donald M. "Henry Blake Fuller, Friend of Howells." *The South Atlantic Quarterly* 52 (January–October 1952), 430–44.

Nevius, Blake. *Robert Herrick: The Development of a Novelist*. Berkeley and Los Angeles: University of California Press, 1962.

Oppenheim, J. H. "Autopsy on Chicago." *The American Mercury* 40 (April 1937), 455–61.

Peattie, Donald Culross. "Henry Blake Fuller." *Reading and Collecting* 2 (January 1938), 19–20.

Pierce, Bessie L. *A History of Chicago*. 3 vols. New York and London: Alfred A. Knopf, 1937.

Pilkington, John, Jr. *Henry Blake Fuller*. New York: Twayne Publishing, 1970.

Putnam, Samuel. "Chicago, An Obituary." *The American Mercury* 8 (August 1926), 417–25.

Redd, Penelope. "Henry Blake Fuller." *Scholastic*, 18 April, 1925, p. 5.

Reid, Mary. "A Glance at Recent Western Literature." *Midland Monthly* 5–7 (1896), 413–25.

———. "Among the Chicago Writers." *Midland Monthly* 3–4 (1895), 491–504.

———. "Henry Blake Fuller." *The Book Buyer* 12 (January 1896), 821–22.

Repplier, Agnes. *Essays in Miniature*. New York: C. L. Webster, 1892.

Ross, Ishbel. *Silhouette in Diamonds: The Life of Mrs. Potter Palmer*. New York: Arno Press, 1975.

Saarinen, Aline B. *The Proud Possessors.* New York: Random House, 1958.

Sarotte, Georges-Michel. *Like Brother, Like Lover.* New York: Doubleday, 1978.

Scambray, Kenneth. "From Etruria to Naples: Italy in the Works of Henry Blake Fuller." *Italian Americana* 3 (December 1976), 56–71.

———. "He Caught It for This: Four Letters by Henry Blake Fuller." *American Literary Realism* 13 (Autumn 1980), 266–69.

———. "The Romance in Decline: Realism in Henry Blake Fuller's *The Cliff-Dwellers.*" *North Dakota Quarterly* 46 (Spring 1978), 19–28.

Schultz, Victor. "Henry Blake Fuller: Civilized Chicagoan." *Bookman* 70 (September 1930), 34–38.

Storr, Richard. *A History of the University of Chicago: Harper's University – The Beginnings.* Chicago: University of Chicago Press, 1960.

Swanson, Jeffrey. "A Check List of the Writings of Henry Blake Fuller (1857-1929)." *American Literary Realism* 7 (Summer 1974), 211–43.

———. "Flesh, Fish or Fowl: Henry Blake Fuller's Attitudes Towards Realism and Romanticism." *American Literary Realism* 7 (Summer 1974), 195–210.

Szuberla, Guy. "Henry Blake Fuller and the 'New Immigrant.'" *American Literature* 53 (May 1981), 246–65.

Tomsich, John. *A Genteel Endeavor: American Culture and Politics in the Gilded Age.* Stanford, Calif.: Stanford University Press, 1971.

Upton, George P. *Musical Memories.* Chicago: A. C. McClurg and Company, 1908.

Van Doren, Carl. *Contemporary American Novelists: 1900–1920.* New York: Macmillan, 1922.

Van Vechten, Carl. *Excavations.* New York: Alfred A. Knopf, 1926.

———. "Henry Blake Fuller." *The Double Dealer* 3 (May 1922), 289–99.

Wallace, Elizabeth. *The Unending Journey.* Minneapolis: University of Minnesota Press, 1952.

Wendt, Lloyd, and Kogan, Herman. *Lords of the Levee.* New York: Bobbs-Merrill Company, 1943.

Williams, Kenny J. *In the City of Men: Another Story of Chicago.* Nashville: Townsend Press, 1974.

Wilson, Edmund. "Henry B. Fuller: The Art of Making It Flat." *New Yorker* 66 (23 May 1970), 112–16, 120–39.

Wright, Nathalia. *American Novelists in Italy.* Philadelphia: University of Pennsylvania Press, 1965.

Ziff, Larzer. *The American 1890s: Life and Times of a Lost Generation.* New York: Viking Press, 1966.

Index

Abbott, Reverend Layman, 49, 115
Adams, Henry, 6, 69, 82, 117
Addams, Jane, 6, 114, 159
Ade, George, 111
Adler, Dankmar, 114
Aguinaldo, Emilio, 113, 117
Aldis, Mary, 135
Aldrich, Thomas Bailey, 6
Alger, Russell, 115
Allen, James Lane, 135
Allison Classical Academy, 15–17, 19, 21, 33
"Allison Classical Academy," 8, 16, 20–25, 78, 107, 141, 152, 161
"America's Coming of Age," 157
"American School of Fiction, The," 62–63, 68, 86
Armour, Philip Danforth, 33, 77, 82, 115
"Art in America": essay, 118–20, 127, 129, 131; lecture, 117–19
Atlantic Monthly, 3–4, 53, 54, 57, 72, 104, 106
"At St. Judas's," 101–03, 150, 153

Bacheller, Irving, 137
"Ballade of the Bank-Teller, The," 49
"Ballade of the Tourist, The," 49
Banks, Nancy, 93, 94
Bayly, N. T., 17
Benedict, Mrs. Frank Lee, 50
Bertram Cope's Year, 9, 10, 30, 103, 138, 148–54, 160–61
"Between the Millstones," 57, 86

"Big Show at Canberra, The," 154
Bookman, 5, 93, 118, 121, 155
Boston, 3–4, 30, 49, 52–57, 58, 73, 74, 113
Boston Evening Transcript, 66, 67, 72, 74, 100
Boston Journal, 122
Bourne, Randolph, 147, 148
Boyesen, H. H., 5, 6, 84
Bradley, Mary Hastings, 157
Bromfield, Louis, 155
Browne, Charles Francis, 98, 128
Bryan, William Jennings, 140
Burnand, F. C., 14
Burnett, Frances Hodgson, 55
Burnham, Daniel, 84

Cabell, James Branch, 5, 155
Cable, George Washington, 54, 62
Capote, Truman, 10
Cather, Willa, 8
Catholicism, 37, 41–42, 44
Centennial Exposition (Philadelphia), 33–34
Century Club (New York), 137
Century Company, 100
Century Magazine, 3, 54, 72, 73, 74, 121, 122, 139, 144
Chap-Book, 102
Chaplin, Charlie, 8
Chatelaine of La Trinité, The, 4, 72–77, 83, 99, 122
Chatfield-Taylor, Hobart, 111, 135, 140, 144

Cheney, Bishop and Mrs., 38, 62
Chevalier of Pensieri-Vani, The, 4, 28,
    38, 40, 61, 62, 63, 65–71, 72, 73, 74,
    75, 83, 84, 90, 94
Chicago American, 139
Chicago Anti-Imperialist League, 6, 113–
    16, 126
Chicago Art Institute, 33, 126, 131–32,
    135
Chicago City Council, 12
Chicago Daily News, 71, 118, 129
Chicago Evening Post, 118, 122, 125, 127,
    134
Chicago High School, 14
Chicago Journal, 118
Chicago Record, 118, 144
Chicago's Old Settlers' Society, 12
Chicago Tribune, 9, 25–27, 35, 37, 57,
    74, 118, 144, 152
Christian Union: of Boston, 54, 56, 115;
    of Chicago, 49
Clarkson, Ralph, 4, 92, 98, 128, 144
Cliff-Dwellers, The, 4, 48, 82–91, 92, 93,
    96, 97, 99, 103, 105, 133, 147, 149, 160
Cliff-Dwellers Club, 129
Coleridge, Samuel Taylor, 27
"Color Line, The," 121
Commonweal, 7, 155
"Compliments of H.B.F. and Some
    More Allusions," 26
Contributor's Club, 126
Contributor's Magazine, 73
Coughlin, John, 32
Courier-Journal, 67
Crane, Stephen, 5, 90
Crawford, Francis Marion, 6, 54, 62, 63,
    112, 134
Critic, The, 5, 83, 93, 110
Cuba, 114–15
Current, 57
Curtis, Harold W., 106–08

Damrosch, Walter, 112, 116
D'Annunzio, Gabriele, 134–35
Dante, Alighieri, 77, 134

Darrow, Clarence, 6, 114
Darwin, Charles, 90
Dewey, Commodore George, 113
Dial, 7, 74, 146, 147
Dickens, Charles, 14, 17, 20, 51, 54
Donaldson, Frank, 21–25, 36
Dos Passos, John, 3, 148
"Downfall of Abner Joyce, The," 128–31
Dreiser, Theodore, 6, 8, 89, 90, 137,
    148, 153, 160–61
"Dr. Gowdy and the Squash," 126,
    131–32
Dumas, Alexandre, 89

Eagan, General Charles, 115
"Edmund Dalrymple," 23–24, 30, 141
Eliot, Charles W., 113
Elite, 100
"Eliza Hepburn's Deliverance," 121, 134,
    138
Ellsworth, W. W., 100
"Erroneous Ideas About Prospects for
    the Great American Novel," 134

Farina, Salvatore, 104
Farrell, James T., 148
Faulkner, William, 148
"Feast for the Gods, A," 27
Field, Eugene, 49, 71, 77, 92, 129, 131
Field, Marshall, 33, 82, 132
Field, Roswell, 92, 121
Fitzgerald, F. Scott, 3, 8, 155
Fogazzaro, Antonio, 134
Forum, 5
Frederic, Harold, 5
Freeman, 7, 155
Freeman, Mary Wilkins. *See* Wilkins,
    Mary
Friedman, I. K., 135
From the Other Side, 105, 108
Fuller, George, 11–12, 13, 17, 31–32, 33–
    34, 44, 57, 89
Fuller, Henry Blake: ancestors of, 11–13;
    childhood of, 13–14; education of, 13–
    17, 21, 27; employment of, 17, 25, 28,

Fuller, Henry Blake (*cont.*)
30, 33, 34, 48–49, 54, 56, 125, 134, 136, 144; and Chicago art studios, 4, 91–92, 93, 98, 100, 104, 111, 117, 133; homosexuality of, 8–10, 11, 18, 21–27, 30, 44, 46, 78–79, 82, 100–03, 106–08, 138, 141, 148–54, 161–62; literary realism of, 4–5, 58–60, 71, 76, 83, 89–91, 93–94, 97–98, 110, 129–30, 138; travels to Europe of, 11, 35–43, 49–52, 73–74, 92–93, 103–04, 156–57; travels in the United States of, 33–34, 105–08, 155. *See also* individual works
Fuller, Harriet, 30
Fuller, Judge Henry, 11–12, 44, 96
Fuller, Mary, 30
Fuller, Mary Josephine Sanford, 13, 31–32, 71, 77, 125

Gardens of This World, 4, 158, 160
Garland, Hamlin, 5, 9, 84–85, 90, 92, 94, 98, 100–01, 108, 110, 111, 112, 126, 127–31, 135, 136, 137, 139, 142, 154, 155, 156, 158
George, Henry, 129
Gibbon, Edward, 20
Gilbert, William Schwenck, 35, 63–64
Gilder, R. W., 72, 121, 138
Ginsberg, Allen, 10
Gissing, George, 135
Glasgow, Ellen, 108
Glasgow, Francis, 108
Goldoni, Carlo, 111
Grant, Frederick Dent, 128
Grant, Julia, 128
Grant, Ulysses S., 128
"Greatest of These, The," 108
Gregorovius, Ferdinand, 68
Griffith, D. W., 8
Gunsaulus, Reverend Frank, 49, 71, 131–32

Hanna, Mark, 115
Hare, Augustus, 37, 40
Harper, William Rainey, 132

Harper's Bazar, 84
Harper's Monthly, 3, 4, 5, 7, 68, 83, 127
Harper's Weekly, 93
Harte, Bret, 3, 55, 84, 130
Harvard Monthly, 75
Hatfield, James Taft, 112, 114, 135, 160
Haverly's Theater, 35
Hawthorne, Nathaniel, 70, 138
Head, Franklin, 71
Head, Mrs. Franklin, 126
Hearst, William Randolph, 139–40
Hecht, Ben, 153
Hemingway, Ernest, 3, 7
Hergesheimer, Joseph, 155
Herrick, Robert, 6, 112, 124
H.M.S. Pinafore, 35, 64
Hoffman, Frederick, 6
Hofstadter, Richard, 6
Hollywood, 8. See also *Not on the Screen*
"Holy Week in Seville," 77
Hopkins Theater (Chicago), 114
"Howells or James?" 58–60, 62–63, 69, 86
Howells, William Dean, 5, 6, 9, 15, 37, 43, 50–51, 53–54, 58–60, 62, 63, 68, 83, 84–85, 90, 92, 93, 94, 97, 99, 104, 108, 109–10, 111, 112–13, 134, 136, 137, 139, 141, 148, 157, 160; death of, 154–55
Hutchinson, Charles, 114, 118, 126, 127, 132–33, 135

Insull, Samuel, 128–29, 132
Isherwood, Christopher, 8
Italy, 28, 35, 38–42, 49–51, 57; in *The Chevalier*, 65–71; in *The Chatelaine*, 72–77, 83, 104, 106; in *The Last Refuge*, 121–23; in *Waldo Trench*, 138–41, 156; in *Gardens of This World*, 158

Jackson, Helen Hunt, 62
James, Henry, 3, 4, 5, 6, 15, 50–51, 54–55, 58–60, 62–63, 70, 84, 109, 135, 139, 152

James, William, 113
Jansen, McClurg, and Company, 49
Jeffrey, E. T., 82
Jenny, William Le Baron, 35
Jenson, Jens, 135
Jewett, Sarah Orne, 62, 84, 90, 130
Johnson, Robert, 141
Joyce, James, 148
Judson, Harry Pratt, 115

Kellogg, Clara Louise, 20
Kenna, Hinky Dink, 32
Kipling, Rudyard, 135

"Lady of Quality, A," 134
Last Refuge, The, 4, 121–23
"Legacy to Posterity, A," 17, 18, 20, 22, 25, 28, 29, 35, 78
Lewis, Sinclair, 155
Life, 3, 54, 55, 56, 109
Lindsay, Vachel, 155
Lines Long and Short, 7, 146, 162
Lippincott's Monthly, 86
Little Room, 4, 71, 92, 93, 98, 111, 116, 124, 126, 135, 144, 159
Lodge, Henry Cabot, 115
London, Jack, 6, 90, 135
"Long and the Short of It: A New England Idyl, The," 55
Lovett, Robert Morss, 10, 112, 160
Lowell, Amy, 144, 146
Lowell, James Russell, 65–66, 68
Luttichau, Max von, 144
Lytton, Edward George Earle Lytton Bulwer-, 14

Maeterlinck, Maurice, 102–03
"Mariquita: Opera in Three Acts," 63–64
Martin, Jay, 6
Masters, Edgar Lee, 7, 144–45
McClurg, General A. C., 114, 118
McCormack, Mrs. Cary, 108
McCormick, Cyrus H., 33, 132

McDonald, King Mike, 32
McGovern, John, 118
McKinley, President William, 6, 7, 114–16, 121, 125
McVicker's Theater, 20
Mead, Larkin G., 104
"Melting Pot Begins to Smell, The," 8, 157
Mencken, H. L., 9, 153
Millard, Everett, 135
Milton, John, 135
"Miranda Harlow's Mortgage," 134
Monroe, Harriet, 7, 14, 71, 83, 92, 98, 126, 144, 155
Monroe, Lucy, 98
Moody, William Vaughn, 7, 112, 116
Morgan, Anna, 92, 117, 124, 135, 144, 159
Morning News Record, 74
Moseley School, 13–14, 15
Murfree, Mary N., 62
"My Early Books," 61, 86–87, 88

Nabokov, Vladimir, 8
Nation, 7, 155
National Institute of Arts and Letters, 6, 112, 125, 136; Fuller's resignation from, 141
Neil, Paul, 25
Newberry Library, 71, 105
Newberry, Walter Loomis, 33
New Flag: Satires, The, 7, 114–17
"New Field for Free Verse, A," 146
New Republic, 7, 145
New York, 36, 112, 113, 125, 136–37, 155
New Yorker, 3
New York Herald Tribune, 155
New York Sun, 118
New York Times, 8, 122, 137, 155
New York Times Book Review, 7, 157
Nixon, Charles, 98
Norris, Charlie, 16, 22–25, 33–34
Norris, Frank, 6, 21, 90, 135
North American Review, 3
Northwestern University, 112, 149

Norton, Charles Eliot, 4, 5, 6, 65–66, 67, 68, 71, 72, 73, 76, 77, 78, 84, 85, 92, 94, 97, 102, 109, 113, 117, 121
"Not a Bit Scared," 26
Not on the Screen, 8, 48, 158–59

Ogden, William B., 132
"Oh, That Way Madness Lies," 102
On the Stairs, 7, 30, 31–32, 44, 147–48
Ovington's Crockery, 17, 33, 34

Palmer, Mrs. (Bertha) Potter, 77, 82, 95, 127, 128, 133–34
Palmer, Potter, 33, 77, 82, 128, 132
"Pasquale's Picture," 57, 61, 108–09
Payne, William M., 5, 111, 114, 121
"Pensieri Privati," 46, 48
Phelps, Elizabeth Stuart, 55
Pierce, President Franklin, 12
"Pilgrim Sons, The," 108–10
"Pipistrello: Opera in Three Acts," 63–64
Pirandello, Luigi, 8
Philippines, war in, 6, 113–17, 120, 123
"Plea for Shorter Novels, A," 146–47
Poetry: A Magazine of Verse, 7, 14, 145. *See also* Harriet Monroe
Pond, Allen, 92, 114, 159
Pond, Irving, 92, 114, 159
Poole, William F., 71
Pope, Alexander, 116
Potter, Bessie, 4, 91, 98, 104
Pound, Ezra, 3, 7, 144
"Private Diary," 14
Protestantism, 36, 41–42, 44
Puck, 49
Pullman, George, 33, 82, 132
Puppet Booth, The, 9, 100–04, 154

Radcliffe, Ann, 27
Ray, Clara, 33, 34, 35, 62
Reynolds, Myra, 112
Rhodes, Harrison, 98
Richardson, Frederick, 136, 147, 149, 154, 156, 157, 160

Rock River, Oregon, Illinois, 98, 110, 111, 144
Rockefeller, John D., 105
"Romance of a Middle-Aged Merchant and His Female Private Secretary, The," 57, 61
Roosevelt, Franklin Delano, 128
Roosevelt, Theodore, 115
Rostand, Edmond, 112
Ruskin, John, 34, 78
Ryerson, Martin, 126, 132, 133, 135

Sandburg, Carl, 3
Sanford, Thomas de, 13
Saroyan, William, 8
Saturday Evening Gazette, 67
Saturday Evening Herald, 100
Saturday Evening Post, 7, 113, 121
Savoy Theater, 50
Scott, Sir Walter, 15
Scribner's Magazine, 121–22, 139
Scudder, Horace, 72
Serao, Matilde, 134
Seymour, Ralph Fletcher, 135, 149
Shakespeare, William, 37, 134
Shepherd, William Emery, 156–57
Small, Albion, 115–16
Smart Set, 9
Smith, Minna, 72, 83, 100
"Society and the Arts," 127
"Some Day," 55
South Division High School, 15, 21
Spanish-American War, 113–17, 123, 140
Spencer, Allen, 121
Spencer, Herbert, 90
"Story of Naphtha: A Tale of Culture, Fashion and Duplicity, by Elizabeth Hodgson Phelps and Frances Stuart Burnett, The," 55
Stedman, Edmund Clarence, 6
Stevenson, Robert Louis, 135
Stone, Melville, 98, 116, 124
Strauss, Johann, 24
Streeter, Carrie, 16, 21
"Striking an Average," 134

Sullivan, Arthur Seymour, 35, 63–64
Sullivan, Louis, 5, 35, 92
Swift, Gustavus, 33, 115, 132

Taft, Lorado, 4, 91, 92, 98, 104, 110,
    126, 127, 128, 144, 146, 155, 160
Taft, William Howard, 140
Taft, Zulime, 111, 128
Taine, Hippolyte, 117–20
Tarkington, Booth, 134
Taylor, Mr. and Mrs. Bert L., 136
"This Young Man Needs Taking
    Down," 26
Thomas, Theodore, 33, 91
Thompson, Ernest, 16, 28
Times (of London), 83
Tincker, Mary Agnes, 50
"Toy Village Theatricals," 14
"Transcontinental Episode, or, Metamor-
    phoses at Muggins' Misery: A Co-
    Operative Novel by Bret James and
    Henry Harte, A," 55
"Troubles of the Short Story, The," 127
Twain, Mark, 6, 7, 37, 113, 157

Under the Skylights, 4, 98, 120, 124–34,
    140, 143, 159, 160–61
University of Chicago, 7, 78, 105, 112,
    115, 124, 126, 129
Upward Movement in Chicago, The, 104–
    05, 123

Van Nostrom, Flora, 21, 23
Van Vechten, Carl, 116, 153
Veblen, Thorstein, 78
Verdi, Giuseppe, 24
Vidal, Gore, 10
"Visit from His Majesty, The," 134

Waldo Trench and Others, 134, 138–41,
    143
Wallace, Elizabeth, 112, 121, 125

Washburn, Louise, 13, 19, 31, 33, 34, 35,
    37–38, 39, 41–42, 44, 46, 50, 51, 52,
    53, 54, 55, 56, 62, 63, 78–79, 84, 92–
    93, 99, 103–04, 111, 138
Webster, Henry Kitchell, 152
"We Girls," 35
Weiss, Paul, 23
Wentworth, John, 132
West, Nathanael, 8
Wescott, Glenway, 8, 155
"Westminster Abbey," 77
Wharton, Edith, 8, 135
"What Youth Can Do," 108–10
Wheaton, General Lloyd, 115
Whitman, Walt, 7, 157
"Why the Anglo-Saxon Is Disliked," 121
Wilde, Oscar, 9, 57, 78, 101, 103, 150,
    154
Wilder, Thornton, 7, 8, 155, 159, 161
Wilkins, Mary, 5, 130
Williams, Kenny J., 5
Williams, Tennessee, 10
Wilson, Edmund, 3, 4, 7, 9
Wisconsin, Oconomowoc (Coonie), 13,
    16, 20, 24, 28, 56–57, 62, 65, 74, 111
With the Procession, 4, 5, 92–97, 99, 100,
    105, 149, 160
Woolf, Virginia, 148
World Review, 134
World's Columbian Exposition, 4, 33,
    74, 76, 82, 84, 94, 99; photographs,
    80–81
Wynne, Madeline Yale, 92

"Year in Europe, A," 37–43, 49, 50, 68
Yerkes, Charles, 33, 82
"You'll Catch It For This," 26
Young, Mrs. J.W.A., 144

Zeisler, Sigmund, 114
Ziff, Larzer, 5
Zola, Emile, 5, 83, 84

3 5282 00115 9204